"Cornell and Hargaden are to be congratulated for editing a second and much revised edition of their original book on the emergence of a relational tradition in transactional analysis (TA). Taking account of the original material in the first volume as well as further developments over the past 15 years, the editors have selected articles that have been published in the international *Transactional Analysis Journal* which both honour the history of TA and question its emphasis on the therapist–client dyad and, more generally, its representation as a one-person psychology. Their choice of articles represents a two-person psychology and for this volume, specifically, the threads of relational TA that hold the centrality of transference and countertransference, and examine unconscious communication, enactments in contrast to games, and intersubjectivity.

The introduction alone is worth the price of the book as it weaves the editors' original introduction to the first edition together with narratives of their own relationships with the relational; offers various critiques of the 'relational turn' both within and outside TA; and, overall, accounts for the impact of and interplay of our internal (intrapsychic) and external (social/political) worlds. I highly recommend this book."

Keith Tudor, Professor of Psychotherapy (Auckland University of Technology, New Zealand), Teaching and Supervising Transactional Analyst (International Transactional Analysis Association)

"These selected papers illustrate a collective journey of an integration of transactional analysis's past into the present by reclaiming its psychoanalytic roots and then from that position evolving a contemporary, two-person relational psychology. The editors trace the development of a relational paradigm in transactional analysis with an emphasis on working with unconscious processes as they emerge within the transference/countertransference dynamics, enactments, eros and sexuality, and the therapist's imaginative capacities.

Cornell and Hargaden demonstrate passionate commitments to their very different ways of thinking about, developing, and revising an approach in transactional analysis that stands alongside the contemporary thinking and practices of other psychodynamic psychotherapies."

Elana Leigh, Certified Transactional Analyst (CTA), Training and Supervising Transactional Analyst (TSTA), and President of the ITAA

"What is the significance in TA psychotherapy of being deeply recognised and responded to by another human being? This important book confirms the emergence of a new paradigm in TA that focuses on the live encounter in the therapeutic relationship. Developing the conscious and unconscious means to find new levels in the deconfusion of the Child ego states and enable transformational change is the significant aim and method of Relational TA

Cornell and Hargaden have provided provocative and profound introductions to this collection of seminal articles, inviting us to integrate the vitality of experiential process into Berne's more cognitive TA theory and method.

As the Relational paradigm in TA continues to evolve they warn against the development of a new dogma, invite self-critique, and see the limitations of the reparative models that have arisen in TA. Challenge, not security, is necessary for growth and they robustly stimulate our capacity for exploration, reflection, uncertainty, struggle and differentiation to create a living process between the theory and ourselves where new possibilities can emerge."

Adrienne Lee, Director of The Berne Institute, UK, university teacher and transactional analysis psychotherapist, supervisor and trainer for more than 40 years

THE EVOLUTION OF RELATIONAL PARADIGMS IN TRANSACTIONAL ANALYSIS

In this fascinating and robust volume, the editors have compiled a collection of articles that provides an account of their individual theoretical journeys as they trace the evolution of relational transactional analysis. They re-examine the term "relational," offering the reader a multiplicity of ways in which to conceptualize the theory of transactional analysis from a truly pluralistic perspective.

This collection of 14 stunning articles from the *Transactional Analysis Journal*, written over a period of nearly three decades, traces the evolutionary process of a way of thinking that incorporates both theoretical innovations and advanced methodological ideas. Central to the themes of this book is a theoretical understanding of the bidirectionality of the relational unconscious, alongside a methodology that, not always but most often, demands a two-person methodology in which the therapist's subjectivity comes under scrutiny.

Uniquely useful as a research tool for psychotherapists interested in the most up-to-date psychological theories, this book offers a perspective on relational theory that is both respectful and critical. It will be enormously helpful to the trainee, the researcher, the clinician, and the supervisor and will help inform the development of a clinical dialectical mind.

William F. Cornell, MA, TSTA-P, has maintained an independent practice of psychotherapy, consultation, and training for more than 40 years. Author of five books, Cornell served for many years as an editor of the *Transactional Analysis Journal*, and has edited several volumes of books exploring both psychoanalysis and transactional analysis.

Helena Hargaden, MSc, DPsych, TSTA-P, works in a private practice in Sussex. She co-authored the award-winning *Transactional Analysis: A Relational Perspective* with Charlotte Sills. Her most recent book, *The Art of Relational Supervision*, was published in 2016. She has had papers published in various journals and books including *Psychotherapy and Politics International*, the *Transactional Analysis Journal*, and *Self & Society*.

THE EVOLUTION OF RELATIONAL PARADIGMS IN TRANSACTIONAL ANALYSIS

What's the Relationship Got to Do With It?

Edited by William F. Cornell and Helena Hargaden

LONDON AND NEW YORK

First published 2020
by Routledge
2 Park Square, Milton Park, Abingdon, Oxon OX14 4RN

and by Routledge
52 Vanderbilt Avenue, New York, NY 10017

Routledge is an imprint of the Taylor & Francis Group, an informa business

© 2020 selection and editorial matter, William F. Cornell and
Helena Hargaden; individual chapters, the contributors

The right of William F. Cornell and Helena Hargaden to be identified
as the authors of the editorial material, and of the authors for their
individual chapters, has been asserted in accordance with sections 77 and
78 of the Copyright, Designs and Patents Act 1988.

All rights reserved. No part of this book may be reprinted or reproduced
or utilised in any form or by any electronic, mechanical, or other means,
now known or hereafter invented, including photocopying and recording,
or in any information storage or retrieval system, without permission in
writing from the publishers.

Trademark notice: Product or corporate names may be trademarks or
registered trademarks, and are used only for identification and explanation
without intent to infringe.

British Library Cataloguing-in-Publication Data
A catalogue record for this book is available from the British Library

Library of Congress Cataloging-in-Publication Data
A catalog record has been requested for this book

ISBN: 978-0-367-25927-3 (hbk)
ISBN: 978-0-367-25928-0 (pbk)
ISBN: 978-0-429-29058-9 (ebk)

Typeset in Bembo
by Swales & Willis, Exeter, Devon, UK

Printed and bound by CPI Group (UK) Ltd, Croydon, CR0 4YY

CONTENTS

Contributors	*ix*
Acknowledgments	*xiii*

Introduction   1
William F. Cornell and Helena Hargaden

1 The bilateral and ongoing nature of games   23
Jenni Hine

2 Through the looking glass: explorations in transference and
countertransference   37
Petrŭska Clarkson

3 An overview of the psychodynamic school of transactional
analysis and its epistemological foundations   50
Carlo Moiso and Michele Novellino

4 Therapeutic relatedness in transactional analysis: the truth of love
or the love of truth   57
William F. Cornell and Frances Bonds-White

5 Reflections on transactional analysis in the context of
contemporary relational approaches   74
Diana Shmukler

viii Contents

6 There ain't no cure for love: the psychotherapy of an erotic
transference 85
Helena Hargaden

7 Psychological function, relational needs, and transferential
resolution: psychotherapy of an obsession 94
Richard G. Erskine

8 The man with no name: a response to Hargaden and Erskine 104
Charlotte Sills

9 There ain't no cure without sex: the provision of a "vital" base 113
William F. Cornell

10 The place of failure and rupture in psychotherapy 124
Carole Shadbolt

11 Traversing the fault lines: trauma and enactment 141
Jo Stuthridge

12 This edgy emotional landscape: a discussion of Stuthridge's
"Traversing the fault lines" 160
William F. Cornell

13 Are games, enactments, and reenactments similar? No, yes,
it depends 167
Edward T. Novak

14 The role of imagination in an analysis of unconscious
relatedness 181
Helena Hargaden

Index *194*

CONTRIBUTORS

Frances Bonds-White, EdD, is a Teaching and Supervising Transactional Analyst (psychotherapy), a Fellow of the American Group Psychotherapy Assocation, and a Certified Group Psychotherapist. Dr. Bonds has taught group psychotherapy around the world and is the author of numerous articles as well as a chapter in a book on men and group psychotherapy. She is a full member of the Group Analytic Society (London). She also conducts team building and strategic planning training in business, industry, and non-profit corporations. She is now the President of the International Association for Group Psychotherapy.

Petrūska Clarkson (deceased) was a Fellow of the British Association for Counselling and Fellow of the British Psychological Society, a consultant chartered clinical psychologist, chartered counselling psychologist, accredited research psychologist, and a qualified management consultant with 125 publications. She co-founded the Metanoia Institute in London. She later founded her own institute, Physis. In both institutes she designed training and supervision programs for psychologists, psychotherapists, and counsellors.

William F. Cornell, MA, TSTA-P, maintains an independent private practice of psychotherapy and consultation in Pittbsurgh, PA. Having studied behavioral psychology at Reed College in Portland, OR, and phenomenological psychology at Duquesne University in Pittsburgh, PA, he followed his graduate program with training in transactional analysis and body-centered psychotherapy and has studied with several mentors and consultants within diverse psychoanalytic perspectives. A co-editor of the *Transactional Analysis Journal*, Bill is the author of *Explorations in Transactional Analysis: The Meech Lake Papers, Somatic Experience in Psychoanalysis and Psychotherapy: In the Expressive Language of the Living* (Routledge), *Self-Examination in Psychoanalysis and Psychotherapy: Countertransference and Subjectivity in Clinical*

x Contributors

Practice (Routledge), *At the Interface of Transactional Analysis, Psychoanalysis, and Body Psychotherapy: Theoretical and Clinical Perspectives* (Routledge), *Une Vie pour Être Soi* (Payot), and a co-author and editor of *Into TA: A Comprehensive Textbook* (Karnac), as well as numerous articles and book chapters. With Helena Hargaden, he co-edited *From Transactions to Relations: The Emergence of a Relational Paradigm in Transactional Analysis.* Bill edited and introduced *The Healer's Bent: Solitude and Dialogue in the Clinical Encounter,* the collected papers of James T. McLaughlin, and *Intimacy and Separateness in Psychoanalysis,* the collected papers of Warren Poland. He is the editor of the Routledge book series, "Innovations in Transactional Analysis." Bill is a recipient of the Eric Berne Memorial Award and the European Association for Transactional Analysis Gold Medal, in recognition of his writing.

Richard G, Erskine, PhD, is a clinical psychologist, transactional analyst, and licensed psychoanalyst who lives in Vancouver, BC, Canada. He has written numerous articles on the centrality of the therapeutic relationship in transactional analysis. He has been the co-recipient of both the Eric Berne Scientific Award and the Eric Berne Memorial Award for the development of transactional analysis theory and methods. He is well known as the co-author (with Janet Moursund and Rebecca Trautmann) of *Beyond Empathy: A Therapy of Contact-in-Relationship.* His most recent book, *Relational Patterns, Therapeutic Presence,* was published by Karnac Books in 2016. Several of his articles are available for free on the website www.integrativepsychotherapy.com

Helena Hargaden, MSc, DPsych, TSTA-P, works in Sussex where she has her private practice. Her first degree was in English literature at Liverpool University. Alongside her clinical training with Petrūska Clarkson at the Metanoia Institute in London she undertook Jungian analysis and supervision over several decades and has also worked with various psychoanalytic consultants to support her development as a pluralistic clinician. Drawing on her experience as a feminist, clinician, and as a trainer working in institutes throughout the country, she co-authored *Transactional Analysis: A Relational Perspective* with Charlotte Sills. Their theory of the "domains of transference" was awarded the Eric Berne Memorial Award in 2007. She co-edited *Ego States* with Charlotte Sills and co-edited *From Transactions to Relations: The Emergence of a Relational Tradition in Transactional Analysis* with William F. Cornell. Her most recent book *The Art of Relational Supervision* was published in 2016. She edited the *European Journal of Psychotherapy* with Joe Schwartz and has papers published in various journals and books including *Psychotherapy and Politics International,* the *Transactional Analysis Journal,* and *Self & Society.*

Jenni Hine, Dip. Sci. Humaines, TSTA-P, was the founder and director of the Center for Transactional Analysis in Geneva, Switzerland. Before her retirement, Jenni trained candidates for certification in transactional analysis in the fields of psychotherapy, counselling, and education. She was a leader in the development of theory and methodology in applying transactional analysis in the counselling professions.

Contributors **xi**

Carlo Moiso, (deceased) MD and psychologist, was a former assistant at the psychiatric Viarnetto of Lugano, Switzerland, one of the initiators of transactional analysis in Italy, and one of the first clinical TA teachers and supervisors in Europe. Recipient of the Eric Berne Award in 1987, he has authored books, articles, and TV programs. The ITAA issued a DVD on his neo-Bernean TA approach carried out with real patients in a group and with a study group led by Isabelle Crespelle. He was an international trainer and a clinical transactional analyst in Rome.

Edward T. Novak, MA, is a graduate of the National Institute for the Psychotherapies' National Training Program in Contemporary Psychoanalysis. He maintains a private practice in Akron, Ohio. He is the book review editor for the *Transactional Analysis Journal* and is the author of numerous papers.

Michele Novellino, MD, is a psychiatrist and psychologist, Teaching and Supervising Transactional Analyst, Director of the Eric Berne Institute, recipient of the 2003 Eric Berne Memorial Award, and author of many TA books, among them: *The Clinical Approach to Transactional Psychoanalysis, The Pinnochio Syndrome*, and *The Phantom Syndrome.*

Carole Shadbolt, M.Sc., CQSW, Dip. Social Science, Certified Transactional Analyst and Teaching and Supervising Transactional Analyst (psychotherapy), lives and practices in the United Kingdom. In a career approaching 30 years, she originally trained as a social worker, becoming a psychiatric social worker at the Maudsley Hospital in South London. She went on to train as a transactional analyst and qualified as a UKCP-registered practitioner. A relational psychotherapist by instinct, Carole is a founding member of the International Association of Relational Transactional Analysis. She is the author of several articles in the *Transactional Analysis Journal.* as well as several book chapters.

Diana Shmukler, Ph.D., Teaching and Supervising Transactional Analyst (psychotherapy), is a visiting tutor at Metanoia in London; clinical and research psychologist with the South African Medical and Dental Council; an integrative psychotherapist; a supervisor and teacher member of the United Kingdom Council of Psychotherapy; a former associate professor of applied psychology at the University of Witwatersrand in Johannesburg; and visiting professor of psychotherapy at the University of Derby, United Kingdom.

Charlotte Sills, MA, MSc Integrative Psychotherapy (UKCP registered), Teaching and Supervising Transactional Analyst, Professor of Coaching at Ashridge Business School, is an independent psychotherapist, supervisor, trainer, and consultant, and a member of faculty at Metanoia Institute and at Ashridge Business School, UK. She is the author or co-author of a number of publications on counselling and psychotherapy, including *Transactional Analysis: A Relational Perspective* with Helena Hargaden (Routledge 2002), from which the model of transference and countertransference won the Eric Berne Memorial Award in 2007; and co-editor with Heather Fowlie of *Relational Transactional Analysis: Principles in Practice* (Karnac 2011) and with Erik de Haan of *Coaching Relationships* (Libri).

Jo Stuthridge, MSc, TSTA-P, is a member of the New Zealand Association for Transactional Analysis and a registered psychotherapist in New Zealand. She maintains a private psychotherapy practice in Dunedin and is director of the Physis Institute, which offers training in transactional analysis. She is a Teaching and Research Associate with the Department of Psychotherapy and Counselling at the Auckland University of Technology. She is a co-editor of the *Transactional Analysis Journal* and author of numerous papers.

ACKNOWLEDGMENTS

Permission has been granted to republish the following articles from the *Transactional Analysis Journal*, courtesy of the International Transactional Analysis Association and Taylor & Francis Publishers.

Chapter 1: The bilateral and ongoing nature of games. Jenni Hine, *Transactional Analysis Journal*, 1990, 20:1, 28–37.

Chapter 2: Through the looking glass: Explorations in transference and countertransference. Petrūska Clarkson, *Transactional Analysis Journal*, 1991, 21:2, 99–107.

Chapter 3: An overview of the psychodynamic school of transactional analysis and its epistemological foundations. Carlo Moiso & Michele Novellino, *Transactional Analysis Journal*, 2000, 30:1, 182–187.

Chapter 4: Therapeutic relatedness in transactional analysis: The truth of love or the love of truth. William F. Cornell & Frances Bonds-White, *Transactional Analysis Journal*, 2001, 31:1, 71–83.

Chapter 5: Reflections on transactional analysis in the context of contemporary relational approaches. Diana Shmukler, *Transactional Analysis Journal*, 2001, 31:1, 94–101.

Chapter 6: There ain't no cure for love: The psychotherapy of an erotic transference. Helena Hargaden, *Transactional Analysis Journal*, 2001, 31:4, 213–219.

Chapter 7: Psychological function, relational needs, and transferential resolution: Psychotherapy of an obsession. Richard. G. Erskine, *Transactional Analysis Journal*, 2001, 31:4, 220–226.

Chapter 8: The man with no name: A response to Hargaden and Erskine. Charlotte Sills, *Transactional Analysis Journal*, 2001, 31:4, 227–232.

Chapter 9: There ain't no cure without sex: The provision of a "vital" base. William F. Cornell, *Transactional Analysis Journal*, 2001, 31:4, 233–239.

xiv Acknowledgments

Chapter 10: The place of failure and rupture in psychotherapy. Carole Shadbolt, *Transactional Analysis Journal*, 2012, 42:1, 5–16.

Chapter 11: Traversing the fault lines: Trauma and enactment. Jo Stuthridge, *Transactional Analysis Journal*, 2012, 42:4, 238–251.

Chapter 12: This edgy emotional landscape: A discussion of Stuthridge's "Traversing the fault lines." William F. Cornell, *Transactional Analysis Journal*, 2012, 42:4, 252–256.

Chapter 13: Are games, enactments, and reenactments similar? No, yes, it depends. Edward T. Novak, *Transactional Analysis Journal*, 2015, 45:2, 117–127.

Chapter 14: The role of the imagination in an analysis of unconscious relatedness. Helena Hargaden, *Transactional Analysis Journal*, 2016, 46:4, 311–321.

All papers republished here with the kind permission of the *Transactional Analysis Journal* and the International Association of Transactional Analysis.

INTRODUCTION

William F. Cornell and Helena Hargaden

The publication in 2002 of Helena Hargaden and Charlotte Sill's *Transactional Analysis: A Relational Perspective* was a landmark in the evolution of TA theory and technique. In 2005 Helena and Charlotte were recognized by the International Transactional Analysis Association in being conferred the Eric Berne Memorial Award, the most prestigious recognition offered by the association for major contributions to the field. That same year, Helena and Bill Cornell edited a collection of papers, *From Transactions to Relations: The Emergence of a Relational Tradition in Transactional Analysis* (Cornell & Hargaden, 2005), drawn from 20 years of the *Transactional Analysis Journal*. We think it timely that we now offer a second compilation of papers from the *Transactional Analysis Journal* that illustrate the continuing development of relational paradigms within TA, beginning this new volume with several key papers that had also been included in the first.

We begin this new volume with portions of our introduction to the 2005 volume.

When the therapeutic relationship is at the heart of the work

Over the past two decades there has been a paradigm shift in the theoretical and technical emphases in many models of psychoanalysis, psychotherapy, and transactional analysis. There has been a shift away from a focus on the observing ego and cognitive insight as the primary means of psychological change, to the importance of unconscious, affective, and relational interactions as a primary means of growth. In the formation of transactional analysis, Eric Berne sought to create a new model for psychodynamic psychotherapy. He challenged the stance and style of the classical psychoanalyst and redefined the therapeutic relationship as a mutual, contractual working relationship to promote rapid change in the client's self-understanding and patterns of relating. He developed a theory of ego states and their patterns of interaction within the self and with others. Berne also

2   William F. Cornell and Helena Hargaden

challenged the classical analytic conceptualization of the unconscious, instead emphasizing the young child's capacity to make adaptive script decisions (which could be brought into conscious awareness) as a means of coping with pathological childhood environments. In his later writings, Berne seemed almost to abandon any conceptualization of unconscious processes, which we believe impoverished the potential richness and depth of his model of transactional analysis psychotherapy. Berne's was a creative, often rebellious challenge to the prevalent theories (the classical psychoanalytic paradigm) of his day. As so often happens in the history of ideas, what was once novel and rebellious has become institutionalized by many of Berne's followers, creating yet another theoretical dogma, a kind of secular canon law for what had come to be known as "classical" or "Bernean" transactional analysis. The papers collected in this book, all from the pages of the *Transactional Analysis Journal*, challenge dogma, extend theory, and begin to generate a new paradigm for transactional analysis.

There is increasing attention in the clinical literature now being paid to the interplay of intrapsychic and interpersonal worlds and of patterns of conscious and unconscious modes of communication within the therapeutic relationship. The terms applied to this change in emphasis vary considerably—object relational, relational, interpersonal, self psychological, Kleinian, transferential, co-constructive, intersubjective—but in spite of this plethora of labels, they all have more in common than they have differences. Each in its own way adds a consistent and persistent attention to the relational dynamics, conscious and unconscious, between the therapist and the client as a primary means of understanding and change. Emmanuel Ghent, a founder of the relational psychoanalytic program at New York University, has described this paradigm shift:

> In the early years of psychoanalysis, the prevailing view was that therapeusis was essentially informational—insight and awareness would bring about changes in the ways one would experience events and respond to them. Over time, there has been a subtle shift from the informational perspective to the transformational, where insight is often retrospective rather than the active agent. The growing awareness of the need to be deeply recognized and responded to by another human being is reflective of this shift and has loomed ever larger in the interactive arena known as psychoanalysis.
>
> *(1995, p. 479)*

The shift from a cognitive, informational psychotherapy toward an affective, transformational psychotherapy has become evident in the evolution of relational paradigms in transactional analysis as well as psychoanalysis.

Berne's interpersonal foundation

Berne's development of transactional analysis provided a model in which different theories and perspectives could co-exist. He intentionally sought to create a humanistic model of psychotherapy, evolving out of psychoanalysis, that drew upon

Introduction **3**

both cognitive/behavioral interventions through the Adult ego state, which he saw as establishing the patient's capacity for "social control" (1961, pp. 176–183), and methods aimed at internal, structural change within the Child ego state, which he referred to as script level "cure" or the "deconfusion of the Child" (1961, pp. 162–164). Berne recognized that while the establishment of social control was the goal of the analysis of transactions and games, deconfusion of the Child required different levels and styles of intervention in order to work within the more emotional and transferential dynamics of the Child ego state. The relational perspectives reflected in the pages ahead give witness to therapists, often moved by "difficult-to-reach clients" (Beebe & Lachmann, 2002, p. 218), to extend the therapeutic field to find new means of deconfusing and re-informing the Child ego state through new relational experiences. The goal was that of creating lasting structural change of the Child ego state that could not be accomplished through exclusively Adult ego state interventions.

Despite Berne's recognition of this situation, his writings do not manifest any elaboration of these ideas. From the beginning it was also Berne's intent to establish transactional analysis as a humanistic "social psychiatry" (1961, p. 12). Unfortunately, even as he sought to humanize the psychoanalysis of his day, Berne's work remained firmly anchored in the ego psychology of his mentors—Federn, Weiss, and Erikson among others—who dominate the references of his books. Berne's remained a model of internal, intrapsychic conflict with treatment aimed at establishing an observing ego and the mastery and control of infantile beliefs and feelings. We find it strange that, aside from brief references to Fromm-Reichman and Burrow, the work of such peers as Harry Stack Sullivan, Clara Thompson, and Erich Fromm, all deeply involved in the social and interpersonal aspects of psychiatry and psychoanalysis, are absent from Berne's writings. In spite of his enduring interests in group, organizational, and transcultural dynamics, something of the truly social and intersubjective seemed to elude Berne. The therapeutic model he created remained, at its heart, a psychotherapy of the individual psyche, what is now referred to as a one-person psychology, as in the classical Freudian model (Stark, 2000). However, in setting up an interpersonal, transactional therapy Berne inherently implies a two-/ multi-person psychology, where the therapist's and client's subjective experiences could be further explored. Thus the shift toward relational exploration was inherent in a humanistic theory which brought the intrapsychic world into the social one through an analysis of transactions and relations.

Berne was well aware of transference–countertransference dynamics in the therapeutic process. Seeing through the lens of game and script theory, Berne described a transferential enactment of the therapist's script:

> By remaining independent of the patient's manoeuvres, and sticking strictly to his job of analyzing her resistances, her instinctual vicissitudes, and when necessary, the transference, the analyst avoids the possibility of being seduced physically, mentally, or morally. Counter-transference means that not only does the analyst play a role in the patient's script, but she also plays a role in

4 William F. Cornell and Helena Hargaden

his. In that case, both of them are getting scripty responses from each other, and the result is the "chaotic situation."

(1972, p. 352)

We see here how, for Berne, the emergence of transference and countertransference within the therapeutic process meant that one or both parties were "hooked into script," i.e., personal psychopathology, a model that continues to strongly influence TA in practice, training, and supervision. In Berne's model, these dynamics derail or interfere with treatment rather than contain the possibility to inform or deepen it. From a relational perspective, these dynamics are at the heart of the work—informing rather than interfering.

There is also a recognition to be made here of Berne's ingrained cultural misogyny, and its antecedent in Freud who once said: "The great question that has never been answered, and which I have not yet been able to answer, despite my thirty years of research into the feminine soul, is 'What does a woman want?'" (Jones, 1953, p. 421). The question we will leave with you, the reader, is how the epigenetics of this source in cultural misogyny is perpetuated to this day in our organizations, theories, and practice.

Berne goes on in the passage quoted above to suggest, with rather incredible naiveté to our minds, "a simple way to avoid these difficulties is to ask the patient right at the beginning, when the contract has been set up, 'Are you going to let me cure you?'" (1972, pp. 352–353). Berne's question implies that the block to treatment is in the client's resistance to the doctor's cure. In asking this particular question, Berne falls rather short of questioning the efficacy of his treatment approach. As will become evident in the papers here, many transactional analysts found themselves working with clients for whom a question such as that which Berne suggests was not sufficient for treatment to progress. Berne left us with a template for understanding the unconscious but stopped at an operational aspect of the dynamic. Although Berne acknowledged the unconscious, he frustratingly gave little clue about how to proceed with a deeper analysis of the psyche. Berne identified several methodologies such as working with dreams in order to access the unconscious, analyzing the psychological level of transactions and games, analyzing the plot of the script in action as a dramatization of the protocol, and telling us—in an oblique reference to Freud's psycho-sexual stages—to "think sphincter" (Berne, 1972, p. 19), but is nowhere specific about how to develop this methodology.

We will now shift our attention away from the foundations laid by Berne and move on to our accounting of the ongoing evolution of the relational turn(s?) within transactional analysis.

Since the publication of our first volume, many articles have been published in the *Transactional Analysis Journal* placing themselves within the relational turn. We have chosen articles that we consider to bring together pivotal themes that each in its own way seeks to underscore the recognition and exploration of the therapist's subjectivity and unconscious experience as a contributing factor to the therapeutic process. While we do not dismiss the regressive and archaic aspects of the Child ego state as they emerge in treatment, the relational perspective represented here carries a forward intentionality, with careful attention to the emergent and generative aspects of the transference–countertransference forces. We see the therapeutic relationship (or field, as it may well be more accurately described) as itself the object of scrutiny and inquiry. To hold this field—especially the powerful unconscious forces, defensive and enlivening alike—the self-reflections of the therapist with regard to her or his own subjectivity and countertransference are essential. As readers will see in the articles contained here, how various authors then address and work within the field of relatedness will vary.

Naturally the relational paradigm within transactional analysis has continued to evolve. So, too, has the thinking of the editors. So we decided to frame this introduction with brief accounts of the evolution of our own thinking and styles of work since we published the original volume.

Bill's reflections

In a review I wrote of *Transactional Analysis: A Relational Perspective*, I (Cornell, 2002) saw this book as a major contribution to transactional analysis theory:

> What they offer is … the most systematic articulation of transference and countertransference in the contemporary transactional analysis literature, one which richly extends our understanding of the unconscious underpinnings of game, racket, and script processes.
>
> *(p. 194)*

My review offered an extended appreciation of the many innovations and clinical insights brought to bear in Hargaden and Sill's book. This book challenged many of the tenets and unexamined assumptions of transactional analysis as it was taught and practiced at that time. They placed the dynamics of unconscious motivations and communications squarely at the heart of therapeutic process and transformed the task of the psychotherapist. Classical TA at that time was a "one-person" model in which the therapist was an outside observer of the patient's dynamics. Hargaden and Sills repositioned TA within a two-person frame and brought systematic attention to the domains of unconscious communication to the practice of transactional analysis.

At the same time, I cautioned that there seemed to be an overemphasis "on the therapist's effort to think about and understand clients, one that can lead to underestimating *clients' desire to think for and about themselves*" (p. 195). I had a concern that placing the working relationship at the core of therapeutic change could overlook the therapeutic force of personal agency. I closed my reflections by referencing a speech given by Emmanuel Ghent (2002/2018) at the first conference sponsored by the International Association for Relational Psychoanalysis and Psychotherapy in which he challenged the reduction of the term "relational" to "signify something like human contact or connection," arguing instead that the term was meant to include other forms of relations, such as one's relationship to history, context, things, fantasy, perception, cognition, and the relations among relations. I was seeing many ways in which among some transactional analysts and most relational psychoanalysts the therapeutic relationship was being idealized and framed as the primary means of "cure."

I have no question of the value that the relational perspective has brought to transactional analysis (and psychoanalysis) (Cornell 2019a, 2019b). But I have been troubled by the tendency of its practitioners to cast themselves as yet another new model of practice, to the point of establishing its own professional association distinct from the other TA associations. Here I saw the roots of dogma rather than creativity and growth. In an earlier era, TA had seen the division of its theory into three highly competitive "schools"—classical, redecision, and reparenting—that demanded the loyalty of followers rather than fostering the development of clinicians whose competency was to draw on multiple models of treatment. As the term "relational" has become valorized, it has been appropriated by models that use the term in radically different ways to characterize treatment approaches that are often in contradiction to one another (Fowlie & Sills, 2011). There has been far too little critical assessment within the relational TA movement. It is incumbent upon theorists and authors to explicitly define the ways in which to conceptualize and utilize the relational elements of the therapeutic process.

I think it best to start this dialogue with some brief reflections on the principles of relational TA as described by Fowlie and Sills (2011) in *Relational Transactional Analysis: Principles in Practice*: the centrality of relationship; the importance of engagement; the significance of conscious and nonconscious patterns of relating; the importance of experience (in addition to cognition); the significance of subjectivity—and self-subjectivity; the importance of uncertainty; the importance of curiosity, criticism, and creativity; and the reality of functioning and changing adults (pp. xxx–xxxii). However, these principles are not the unique domain of relational TA. Such clinical attitudes—like uncertainty, creativity, curiosity, unconscious communication, subjectivity—that have long been part of the discussion in contemporary psychoanalysis outside of the relational tradition— Christopher Bollas, Thomas Ogden, Maurice Apprey, Danielle Quinodoz, Anne Alvarez, Muriel Dimen, Adrienne Harris, and Wilfred Bion to name a few.

I am grateful to the relational movement in TA for its return to systematic attention to the importance of unconscious experience the formation of the self and to the vitality of the experiential as well as cognitive aspects of the therapeutic process (Cornell, 2005, 2008). I value the emphasis on a move "away from the 'parental paradigm' where the practitioner may be seen as temporary provider of unmet relational needs" (Fowlie & Sills, 2011, p. xxxii), providing a vigorous alternative to the reparenting and parentally reparative models that have plagued transactional analysis. A closer look, to my mind, reveals significant therapeutic limits and distortions of unconscious forces when attention to the therapeutic dyad is held as central. There is too often an implicit or explicit return to the parent–infant pair as the protocol for all things relational. Some transactional analysts who describe

Introduction **7**

themselves as relational intentionally structure the therapeutic relationship so as to be reparative. With the invocation of the mother–infant dyad and attachment patterns, other developmental stages that support differentiation are then under-represented in theory and practice. There is far too little attending to the fact that we are not in constant contact with other people, that there are many forces of development that are not based in an interpersonal dyad. The relational paradigm within TA that Helena and I seek to demonstrate in our selection of the articles included here is centered on fostering capacities for exploration, reflection, and differentiation.

It is also important to me to point out that other than Helena and me, there is virtually no writing about sexuality, which I find most peculiar in a model grounded in relationships.

Turning to contemporary psychoanalysis

In the late 1980s I had begun to immerse myself in the writings of D. W. Winnicott, Christopher Bollas—the foremost contemporary voice of the British Independents— as well as a group of analysts known as the "American Independents," that included James McLaughlin, Theodore Jacobs (1991, 2013), and Warren Poland (1996, 2018). They comprised a small group of quietly rebellious analysts who were trained post-war in the rigid ego psychological traditions of American psychoanalysis, as had Eric Berne been. While these analysts clearly identified themselves as Freudian analysts, each wrote seminar papers that challenged and enriched the Freudian paradigm and classical technique. Their work has had a lasting influence on my way of positioning myself in relation to my clients.

At the same time that Helena and I were editing *From Transactions to Relations*, I was also editing *The Healer's Bent: Solitude and Dialogue in the Clinical Encounter*, a collection of papers by the psychoanalyst James McLaughlin (2005). I was first drawn to McLaughlin's work by his papers on countertransference, enactment, and self-analysis. Written in the 1980s and 1990s, they were not well received by many of his analytic colleagues, but they became cornerstone writings in the emerging literature of relational psychoanalysis in the USA.

In 2001 a group of Pittsburgh colleagues and I attended the inaugural conference of the International Association for Relational Psychoanalysis and Psychotherapy in New York. It was an extraordinary event, one that signaled a clear paradigm shift in American psychoanalysis. Inspired by the conference, I subscribed to *Psychoanalytic Dialogues*, which was also inaugurated that year. McLaughlin was not there, but his papers were repeatedly referenced. When I returned home, I talked with Jim about the experience at the IARPP conference and the referencing of his papers. He was more than a little surprised, as he knew nothing about relational psychoanalysis, in spite of the influence of his writing in this emerging analytic community. That conference was the inspiration for editing his book. The IARPP conference was also the inspiration for our Pittsburgh group to create the "Keeping Our Work Alive" seminar series, which has been meeting continuously since then, inviting contemporary analysts from around the world to work with us.

8 William F. Cornell and Helena Hargaden

McLaughlin wrote extensively about impasses and enactments in treatment, placing his emphasis on the therapist's responsibility for self-analysis to move treatment forward. He did not readily move toward self-disclosure. Rather, he saw it as the therapist's job to understand their contribution to the impasse so as to find again the psychic, unconscious capacities to hear the patient more clearly. As I write in my introduction to McLaughlin's book:

> Jim offers a model of self-analysis that is an effort to hold his mind distinct and differentiated from that of his patient. His mind, consciously and unconsciously, is to be influenced by the patient, but not conjoined with it. … Quite likely, his patients did not know the specifics of *what* had changed in Jim, but they would feel and respond to the *experience* that *something* had changed.
>
> *(2005, p. 15)*

McLaughlin argued that the shift in the analyst's internal state was likely to be sensed by the client consciously without having to know the actual content of the analyst's countertransference analysis and would register unconsciously so as to free up the analytic process. The implications of the place of self-analysis are woven through much of my own most recent writing (Cornell, 2019a).

Jacobs has explored the complexities of self-disclosure in thoughtful detail. He does not stake a claim for the classical posture of neutrality and anonymity, but neither does he dismiss it. Jacobs (2013) urges caution:

> It is also true, as we know, that certain revelations on the part of the analyst can limit or inhibit aspects of the patient's imagination and the free flow of fantasy. Since we are interested in the patient's creations, and since, in some instances, these are stimulated by nondisclosure and analytic anonymity, the use of self-revelation may work against our aims.
>
> *(pp. 147–148)*

Each of these analysts has written about their use of self-disclosure during periods of enactment and impasse when the therapeutic difficulties are coming from both sides. But for them self-disclosure does not serve the function of fostering mutuality or a narrative of co-creation but that of taking responsibility:

> At moments of pain as one deals forthrightly with personal responsibility for one's role in what had been painful to oneself and others, at those moments it matters that another know, that another understand, that another have some appreciation of the implications. Recognition, not exoneration, is what is then called for.
>
> *(Poland, 2018, p. 18)*

I don't think these three analysts would accept a definition of working from a "one-person" model. Their work does not fit the stereotypic, straw man presentation of "one-person" models, rather they are keenly aware of there being *two* people in the room. What to *do with* those two people was their clinical question. Each of these analysts was acutely aware of, and responsible for, their own subjectivity. McLaughlin says it this way: "Here I emphasize the working of two separate minds so I can make clear that the central focus on the patient's reality view does not mean seeking unbroken agreement and oneness in the dyad" (2005, p. 205). Poland (1996) and Chodorow (2018) articulate a perspective of "two-person separate." In Poland's eyes, "we are two distinct people, two alert and sensitive to each other but *two who are profoundly apart even while immediately mattering to one another*" (2018, p. 22, emphasis in original). It's important to note that Lew Aron (2019) makes a strong argument that "both Poland and Chodorow grossly mischaracterize relational theory by depicting it as a two-person psychology of merger that negates the patient and analyst's individuality" (p. 109). Aron states a strong case:

> Relational theorists view experience as enriched by the presence of two distinct subjectivities. I agree that there are differences in emphasis and that we need to consider the variant implications of diverse theoretical orientations. ... The lesson that Mitchell took from Leowald was that sameness and difference were both essential to subjectivity throughout life.
>
> *(p. 109)*

The transactional analytic papers gathered together here also reflect the diversity of positions as to how one addresses and works with the ongoing dynamics between individuality, subjectivity, and relatedness.

Object usage

The other key has been my years of reading Christopher Bollas and the many opportunities of working with him in person. While deeply influenced by Winnicott and others within the British Independent model, Bollas situates himself firmly within the Freudian tradition (2007). His theory of the evolution of the self and the potential contribution that the analytic process can have to that evolution is unique in contemporary psychoanalysis. Bollas' work links in many ways to Berne's original project in the creation of transactional analysis (Cornell & Landaiche, 2008/2019). His concepts of the dialectics of difference, object usage, personal idiom, and the destiny drive redefine that nature of the psychotherapeutic project.

Much like the American Independents, Bollas has written extensively about his use of countertransference and self-analysis, which he describes as "the maintenance of a receptive space for the arrival of news from within the self" (1987, p. 239). His emphasis on the analyst's receptive capacity is central from his first book to the present. He has described a rather unique form of self-disclosure—that of sharing with a patient his own thought and associative processes that underlie an interpretation, which he then invites his patient to disagree with. He fosters what he terms "the dialectics of difference" (1989, pp. 64–67) in which the analytic pair establish the freedom to disagree with one another, thereby fostering associative freedom within each as well as within the working dyad. Bollas offers his thoughts and perceptions to patients as "objects" to be used, tossed around, kicked about, considered, rejected, all in the service of the patient's gradual self-articulation. These concepts transformed my use of self-disclosure. I rarely share my personal feelings with my clients unless that information is part of moving through a period of impasse or enactment. I do not want to bring the interference of my personhood too strongly into the therapeutic process in ways that compromise my clients' rights to use me as an object. I seek to foster and deepen a therapeutic *process* more than a therapeutic *relationship*.

Bollas links his concept of the personal idiom to Freud's conceptualization of the id, which he describes as Freud's "bold attempt to conceptualize this inner complex that fashions being" and to Winnicott's accounts of the "True self." Bollas writes:

> I believe that each of us begins life as a peculiar unrealized idiom of being, and in a lifetime transforms that idiom into a sensibility and personal reality. Our idiom is an aesthetic of being driven by an urge to articulate its theory of form by selecting and using objects so as to give them form.
>
> *(1995, p. 151)*

This process is driven by the unconscious force of a life instinct that he names the "destiny drive," which he sees as "the urge within each person to articulate and elaborate his idiom through the selection and use of objects" (1989, p. 211). In Bollas' early writing, rooted in the work of Winnicott and other object relations theorists, his focus was on the *transformational* object, the term he applied to the mother's function as the processor of the infant's experience, a formative (transformative) relationship then recapitulated within the analytic relationship. Bollas' work at that time had much in common with the perspectives of the emerging relational models.

But for Bollas, objects are *used* over the course of a lifetime not so much in the service of forming corrective relationships with others as in the discovery and elaboration of the self. The objects which Bollas (2009) came to refer to as *evocative* objects (1992) are not limited to people but will include a broad sweep of lived experiences/encounters with places, ideas, sensations, music that bring that fundamental, emerging idiom— the nascent sense of self—into more and more lived reality:

> In the course of a day, a week, a year, or a lifetime we are engaged in successive selections of objects, each of which suits us at the moment, "provides" us with a certain kind of experience, and, as our choice, may serve to articulate our idiom, recall some earlier historical situation, or foreclose true self articulation.
>
> *(1989, p. 48)*

> All the time, as we amble about in our worlds, we come across objects, whether natural or man-made, material or mental. For the unconscious there is no difference between a material and a non-material evocative object; both are equally capable of putting the self through a complex inner experience.
>
> *(2009, p. 79)*

Introduction   **11**

Thought that evolves out of lived encounters in the real—juxtaposed to thoughts arising purely from the mind alone—bear the marks of life.

(2009, p. 84)

Bollas' statement that for the unconscious there is no difference between the material and nonmaterial object had a profound effect on me, accounting for something that I had felt many times over the course of my own life, namely, the fundamental transformative impact of encounters I have had with "the non-human environment" (Searles, 1960). Bollas radically extends the notion of object usage beyond the interpersonal field (as did Ghent) and in so doing places the analytic dyad as but one object relationship in an expanse of experiences in relation to objects—traumatic, transformative, or evocative.

For the articulation of one's self

I am as interested in the events and characters from outside the consulting room as inside with me. The emergent transference–countertransference relationship is but one means (albeit an important one) of facilitating self-understanding and psychic growth. I have come to see my function in my clients' gradual articulation of selfhood in a more impersonal way. In saying impersonal, I am not suggesting neutral, distant, or detached; quite the contrary, I am deeply engaged but with my own personhood and subjectivity quietly in the background.

De-idealizing Relational Theory: A Critique from Within (Aron, Grand, & Slochower, 2018) provides a rich and stimulating example of the kind of self-critique I find lacking in relational TA. Several of the authors in this book critique the rush to relatedness and dialogical engagement. To use but one example, relevant to the position I have been trying to describe in these few pages, Seligman cautions that the valorization of enlivening interpersonal contact, mutual influence, co-creation, and/or enactment risks the sidelining of other aspects of therapeutic involvement:

But there is something quite generative and even transformative in disciplined observation and quiet concentration, even when this may involve a kind of reserve and even self-withholding that would not seem to be encouraged by the relational orientation, at least at its face.

(2018, p. 135)

Over the years, I have written about the idea of the "vital base" (Cornell, Chapter 9, present volume, 2008), which is an effort to extend John Bowlby's idea of the "secure base". We talk a lot in our teaching and literature about the importance of a secure base. From my point of view, this is a nice idea and a bit of fantasy. I think it often helps us feel good in our work to imagine that we can provide a secure base for our clients, but I don't think we actually can—and I'm not sure we should. I don't think there is a lot of security in life. When we are growing and changing, we are constantly going through periods of insecurity. Insecurity is necessary for growth. I don't think there is

12   William F. Cornell and Helena Hargaden

significant growth without periods of destabilization and insecurity. And yet there is a delicate balance: too much insecurity freezes growth and fosters adaptation—just as too much security can freeze growth and foster adaptation.

To provide a vital base is to work in ways that are as often challenging as comforting. This is a challenge that goes in both directions. I challenge my clients, and my clients challenge me. Life challenges us both. Sometimes I disturb my clients, and sometimes they disturb me. But we keep engaged, we keep thinking, and we keep working. There are those wonderful moments when understanding, intimacy, psychic freedom, startling recognitions, new possibilities emerge. In the vital base is the capacity for challenge, uncertainty, and experimentation. Conflict, disappointment—each of these is an opportunity for growth and new understandings and the maturation of the relationship. Within a vital base, both parties have the opportunity and the responsibility for challenging one another's frames of reference. This must be true for our professional communities as well.

Helena's reflections

In San Francisco in 2007, Charlotte Sills and I stood proudly on the stage as the first British recipients of the Eric Berne Memorial Award for our theory of the domains of transference. We had provided a way of thinking about transferential phenomena from a relational perspective in response to the general confusion that arose for clinicians when moving into the deconfusion phase of therapy:

> A central premise of the model is that elements of an undeveloped or disturbed early self emerge in the transference within the client–therapist relationship and that the transferential relationship is the major vehicle for deconfusion.
>
> *(Hargaden & Sills, 2002, p. 10)*

From the beginning, we were both clear that although we were the authors of *Transactional Analysis: A Relational Perspective*, we were part of an evolutionary process coming out of the psychodynamic school of transactional analysis (Moiso, 1985; Moiso & Novellino, 2000). Our theory was developed from a complex dialectical process of collaborations initially inspired by our clients, supervises, trainees, and colleagues. For instance the case studies in the book were taken from real clinical experience. We had also observed, when teaching in institutes throughout the UK, how many trainees who were attuned, intuitive, and reflective transactional analysts felt themselves to be automatically in the wrong when they could not map their work theoretically. They turned themselves upside down in order to fit into circles and triangles that eclipsed the essence of the work they had done. The value attached to so-called "objectivity" and detachment pitted them against their intuitive life in a clinically unhelpful way. It seemed that TA required a new direction to work with regression and to accommodate the emergence of unconscious processes. A major but more implicit collaborative process involved Petrūska Clarkson, founder of the Metanoia Institute in London. This inspirational and gifted woman provided an intellectual environment in which theoretical plurality was both modeled and encouraged. This creative environment encouraged the authors to think outside of the proverbial box and to make *theoretical links* with self psychology (Kohut, 1971), Jungian analysis, and object relational theorists such as Winnicott (1949), Guntrip (1962), and other independent writers such as Bollas (1987). Perhaps then this theoretical shift belongs also to a generational movement as part of a zeitgeist (across the board) that within transactional analyses was then validated by the EBMA award. This is borne out by the synchronicity of the publication of our 2002 book (Hargaden & Sills) with the inaugural conference on relational psychoanalysis of the International Association of Relational Psychoanalysts (IARPP) that also occurred in 2002. I believe that this synchronicity can be understood in the context of the influence of feminism on relational thinking. Feminism challenged the patriarchal view of woman as an "object" and had an implicit influence on the development of a theoretical perspective which allowed for a subject–subject connection described by Stark (2000) as a two-person psychotherapy. It is my view that relational perspectives also have the potential to liberate the therapeutic dyad from objectification by supporting the use of the therapist's imagination to use theory to illuminate rather than theory to pathologize/objectify the client.

Charlotte and I collaborated over a period of five years in writing the book. Together we played with ideas, particularly focusing on real-life case histories to write the narrative of how relational therapy works in practice.

> It is through the connection of the person of the therapist and the person of the client in open empathic mutuality and through what they create together that change comes about. Thus, there are two subjectivities in the room, and for change to occur, there must be mutual change: It is a bidirectional approach— therapy is a two-way street. The client's relationship with himself or herself and with the figures of his or her past and present emerge in the consulting room— as do those of the therapist, and for this reason the therapist is required to have done an in depth exploration of his or her own internal world.
>
> *(Hargaden & Sills, 2008, p. 9)*

We described the ubiquity of unconscious process and how it makes itself known indirectly "and with peculiar effects!" (Meier, 1995). Our most vital contribution was a focus on the *bidirectionality* of the relational unconscious that was *unknown* to the parties involved and so brought into focus the challenge of unconscious relatedness in the therapeutic encounter. Our work moved transactional analysis into the next stage of the evolutionary process. Whilst making links with other modalities we proposed a different methodology which involved moving the relational connection between client and therapist from a one-/one-and-a-half-person process to a two-person psychotherapy (Stark, 2000).

Crossing theoretical bridges

Shortly after the publication of our book, Bill Cornell (personal communication, 2002) wrote to us: "Hey guys, do you realize that your work is very like the clinical perspective currently being developed by relational psychoanalysts in New York?"

At the same time I was invited by Andrew Samuels to join a relational psychoanalytic group in London with a number of diverse psychotherapists and psychoanalysts. These were exciting and pivotal moments in the development of not only my theoretical mind but also in relational TA becoming known across theoretical divides. I was delighted to find other colleagues in London, and across the pond, who were thinking, feeling, conceptualizing, and being curious along the same lines as we were. I joined the International Association of Relational Psychoanalysis and Psychotherapy (IARPP) and attended a conference in Rome in June 2005. There I met, among others, Dr. Anthony Bass, one of the founder members of IARPP. I found the American IARPP members friendly and inclusive, which was different from my experience in the United Kingdom at that time, where British psychoanalysts seemed to have a superior sense of their own theoretical perspective (as described in the introduction to *The Art of Relational Supervision*, Hargaden, 2016). I invited Dr. Bass to teach with me in my relational TA course in Kent and was delighted when he accepted. To prepare for the workshop, he read the book Charlotte and I had written and replied as follows:

> It is really surprising to me to see that transactional analysis is alive, well, and developing over there. Most analysts here, and I have checked, are completely oblivious to that fact. When I point out that it has been evolving, and indeed, was way ahead of the curve on multiplicity and self-state work in the framework of adult–parent–child [they were quite interested].
>
> *(Bass, 2006 personal communication)*

Well, Charlotte and I cannot take credit for the multiplicity of self-states manifest in the theory of ego states. We have Eric Berne to thank for the genius that he was in developing the theory of ego states. Dr. Bass' response was validating of our work and important because it was outside of our TA community, meeting us across the theoretical divides that previously had seemed impossible to traverse. Perhaps our work also symbolized our willingness to belong to a wider community and not stay in the arrogance of insularity that, according to English (2007), seems to be part of the script of TA. (Although in my experience, until the beginning of this century, an insular attitude was pretty common across the theoretical board.)

I have argued elsewhere (Hargaden, 2014b) that the term *relational* provided the impetus for the cross-fertilization of theory. The term relational was not just a theory but perhaps, even more, a *symbol of integration* because "ultimately the overarching relational principle is one of integration; that it continues to open up the doors for continuing dialogue between the modalities of psychology in a way which enhances our work with clients and patients" (Hargaden, 2014b).

As my own learning and involvement in all matters relational increased, I found myself to be on an ever-widening curve. For instance, when I co-edited with Joe Schwartz (2007) a special issue of the *European Journal of Psychotherapy and Counselling* I learned from him that the relational perspective has, in fact, deep European roots that began with Eugen Bleuler at the Rheinau Hospital for the Insane just outside

Strasbourg. Bleuler maintained the possibility of relating to and understanding the utterances of the deeply disturbed people that he called *schizophrenic*.

From a TA perspective, I proposed (Hargaden, 2005) that the relational concepts of mutuality and reciprocity, much discussed by relational psychoanalysts, have their *roots* in the work of humanistic authors such as Martin Buber and his theory of "I–Thou." Buber wrote that taking the dialogic path is risky because it involves working in the dark, in worlds of traumatic devastation, uncertainty, loneliness, and loss.

In the relational psychoanalytic group I had joined in London at the invitation of Andrew Samuels, there was genuine collegial delight from Jungian, psychoanalytic, and other colleagues on hearing about our EBMA award. "Mazel tov," texted Susie Orbach in 2007.

Why the founding of the International Association for Relational Transactional Analysis?

Feeling immensely encouraged and validated by all of the developments just described, I began an online internet discussion with a view to sharing, evolving, and working through the ideas that were now expanding and developing in all directions. This eventually led on to the founding of the International Association for Relational Transactional Analysis (IARTA). Initially, it was conceptualized as an interest group, but there was momentum for making a bigger statement, and before long the interest group grew into an organization.

Initially this was because the emergence of relational theory implied the need for a shift in treatment direction that challenged some of the traditional ideas of transactional analysis. For instance the relational turn introduced a way of thinking which turned the spotlight onto the interiority of the therapeutic couple, with a view to examining the mystery, uncertainty, and nonlinear process of the unconscious, and in particular the relational intersubjective unconscious (Hargaden, 2005).

Unfortunately, the founding of IARTA seemed to deepen divisions within the UK transactional analysis community. Was this unnecessarily tribal or was it just part of a crucial element of growth and diversification? Of course there will be many different narratives about why there was a split within the UK TA community. My tendency is to reflect upon the symbolism of events, and from this perspective I wondered if on an unconscious, more primitive level there was a deeply felt sense of the dangers inherent in the feminine (in the Jungian sense of the word) approach, that the relational approach, more concerned, as it was, with introversion and the focus on the internal worlds of both client and therapist, was too much of a contrast to the more external and predominantly cognitive focus of classical TA.

Founding IARTA was tremendously exciting, and we were supported hugely across the board in our efforts. One example of someone who grasped one of the underlying issues was Andrew Samuels, as reflected in the following comment:

> One thing I feel confident about now that IARTA is up and running is that we really have a TA fit for the twenty-first century, able to make its contribution,

not only to the understanding and easing of personal distress, but also to wider social and cultural problems. In terms of the politics of the profession of psychotherapy, the advent of your group is further proof that we all—not just you yourselves—have been held back in too many areas by hidebound thinking and by the influence of poorly comprehended power dynamics.

(personal communication, Samuels, 2009)

This was further proof that we were addressing the theoretical divide. Samuels, of course, has a history of encouraging, and sometimes aggressively demanding, theoretical plurality. (A description he would agree with!) He has been tremendously supportive of the development of relational TA, and now TA has become part of common parlance among diverse groups of clinicians.

Returning to the domains of transference

I have always proposed that our relational theory (Hargaden & Sills, 2002) was meant to be more akin to a Monet painting than a route map. This metaphor suggests evolution, movement, the effects of the passage of time, and the changing process of light (which in this context stands for *perspective*). Nevertheless, we need theories, and I think that those that provide a guiding light rather than a heavy-handed set of dogmas are most useful to the clinician—although one cannot, of course, prevent someone from creating dogma out of any theory.

As a reminder of the specific meaning of the domains of transference, I present here a brief reprise of the theory, which offers the clinician the opportunity to examine the transferential process through three coexisting lenses which include one-, one-and-a-half- and two-person psychotherapy.

The introjective transference involves clients' developmental needs that have never been met—such as mirroring, validation, and witnessing of internal feeling states— to support the development of a healthy narcissistic sense of self (Kohut, 1971). Since Fonagy's (2004) work, which I describe below, I have come to understand that the client's experience of being on the mind of the therapist is paramount in fostering an increase in mental functioning, health, and a sense of self. What is introjected is not the therapist, per se, but the *relational experience* of knowing and accepting one's vulnerability.

Projective transference involves splitting and projection (Klein, 1975/1988), which occurs when someone is overwhelmed by feelings and experiences that have never been expressed directly but rather indirectly by adopting a game position (Berne, 1964) in which defensive dynamics from past relationships are repeated. The therapist's ability to work with projection enables the client to make meaning with a reflective other by getting to the original sources of the pain through a process of metabolizing the previously unexamined experiences and feelings. This process is more consciously driven because it manifests in the interpersonal realm and is thus distinguished from the next domain, which is at the heart of bidirectional unconscious relatedness.

The transformational transference refers to primitive affective experiences that are encoded in the psyche but have never come into consciousness. They are linked to traumatic phenomena that can only find meaning through a process of projective identification. In this context, projective identification means that the client evokes feelings in the therapist as a way of conveying his or her unconscious, unmetabolized feelings and experience, requiring the therapist *to do* something about them. As Bollas (1987) put it, "In order to find the patient we must look for him within ourselves" (p. 202). Unlike the traditional psychoanalytic view of projective identification as a feeling projected by the client into the therapist, who experiences it as an alien feeling, Hargaden and Sills (2002) argued that if the therapist is experiencing a feeling, regardless of how odd it feels, it belongs to her or him and therefore requires that the therapist initially think about what the meaning is for her or him. In humanistic therapy, the therapist owned the feeling as hers or his. In psychoanalytic therapy the therapist used the feeling to make a transference interpretation. In relational therapy, we need to reflect on the meaning for us as the therapist and how that can be used to deepen our understanding of what might be happening in the bidirectional relational unconscious. This process requires the therapist to be changed in some way, to be willing to feel, think, reflect, and maybe take some risks in the therapy relationship.

Challenging the myth of an interpersonal methodology

The term relational is sometimes *reduced to the notion of relationship*, and misunderstood solely as an interpersonal connection. Care needs to be taken over this. Clarity can come with the following distinctions, which I made when analyzing the impact of our relational contribution for my 2009 doctoral dissertation entitled "The Bi-directionality of the Relational Unconscious":

- Mutuality does not mean either empathy or equality.
- Mutuality need not involve self-disclosure by the therapist.
- The unconscious cannot be accessed without the hard discipline of thinking, reflecting, and self-examination by the therapist outside of the therapy sessions.
- The term "interpersonal" refers to the conscious communication process whilst the term "relational" involves complex intersubjective and unconscious dynamics.
- "Countertransference" is different from "bidirectionality," and both are important.

The idolization of "the relationship" and a failure of understanding

Why is it that I have had several clients, who are also trainees, *accusing* me of not being relational? I have come to understand that the term "relational" is easily confused with being in "relationship"; that the idea of being in a relationship encourages the projection onto the therapist of a conflict-free connection involving harmony, and soothing encounters. When we (Hargaden & Sills, 2002) emphasized the use and significance of empathy by redefining Berne's original therapeutic operations as empathic transactions, there was a tendency to elevate empathy as the main vehicle of psychic change. In his inauguration speech for the IARPP (2002/2018) Emmanuel Ghent made a similar observation acknowledging that the term "relational" could raise expectations of the type described above that would neither be accurate nor particularly therapeutic. Empathic attunement is fundamental to a "working therapeutic relationship," but it has to be authentic and a state to which both therapist and client can return, after upheaval, with a deeper sense of truth about each other.

I make a vital distinction between empathy and attunement (Hargaden, 2014a) by describing empathy as a more cognitive and normal social response to suffering. In contrast, attunement takes us into the heart and source of the wounds in our clients and is more likely to feel, at times, uncomfortable for both therapist and client. It most often takes us into the domain of the projective transference whereby the original historic misattunement reveals itself through the relationship between therapist and client. For instance, a client might experience an intervention as harsh but then connect it with someone from his or her past. In this way, the person can integrate the "bad therapist" (father/mother) and the "good therapist" (empathic person) when we segue back into the introjective domain. To stay in empathic relatedness means no real psychic change will occur. "I miss my therapist's warmth," said a client who had been in therapy for five years previously. However, she had clearly not moved an inch from her original wounded Victim place and needed to become more familiar with what she projected outwards.

Along with others, I have also come to think of the relational approach more as a sensibility than just a set of theories (Hargaden, 2014b). The relational approach involves a living process between theory and ourselves as practitioners consistently reflecting on *what* we are doing and *how* we are doing it. But it should never involve us forcing relatedness into an *idée fixe*. It should, instead, involve us in a continuous search for new language that paves the way for more nuanced and in-depth ways to examine our subjective experiences. It involves us in the rights to our existential choices and acts of freedom in the therapeutic encounter.

New ways to think about relational transactional analysis

During the emergence of the relational turn both within psychoanalysis in the United Kingdom (Fonagy, Gergely, Jurist, & Target, 2004) and the International Association for Relational Psychoanalysis and Psychotherapy, as well as within the transactional analysis community as a whole (see our acknowledgments later and more recent articles in the *Transactional Analysis Journal*), new ideas and meanings have emerged. There will, of course, always be some who make any theory into a dogma, and in the case of the term relational, they miss the central idea that the therapist uses her or his self as a vehicle for change with the focus on in-depth reflective ideas as earlier suggested by the symbol of an impressionist Monet painting.

In the following section I identify some of those creative and clinically rich ideas that have developed over the last decade or so and suggest how they can be incorporated into the domains of transference for a relational transactional analyst.

Mentalization and the Anna Freud Centre

The chief executive of the Anna Freud Centre in London, Peter Fonagy, with others (Fonagy et al., 2004), helped to develop contemporary psychoanalytic theory by describing the rich and clinically sophisticated process of *mentalization*. This body of work has had an inspirational impact on many people's lives, particularly in the area of child development and adolescence at the Anna Freud Centre. What does this have to do with relational TA? A major development in Fonagy's work has been to bring the idea of *the developing mind* to the forefront of our consciousness. Mentalization involves the therapist in a sophisticated clinical process that enables her or him to offer her or his thoughts and to ask the "right" type of question so that clients can learn to think and reflect about themselves in different ways. This might appear to be a straightforward cognitive process, but this concept has its source in a great deal of knowledge based on a deep examination of the self in which the therapist is able to use her dialectical mind whilst engaging with the rich psychoanalytic, Jungian, and other psychotherapy literature so widely available.

For example, in the *introjective domain*, the therapist can use the therapeutic alliance to invoke deeper thought in the client by asking specific questions related to the process between client and therapist: "I can hear how much you suffered in that situation. Do you think there might be anything positive for you to take from it?" This type of question will emerge in the therapist from a sense of the client being steeped in the superiority of her Victimhood for example. Such a question might lead the client and therapist into the projective transference whereby the client feels angry because she feels misunderstood. In the *projective domain* the therapist will need to be vulnerable enough to both participate in an enactment and at the same time be able to detach from the projection by saying, for example,

> I understand how you have just experienced me in quite a harsh way, and that puts you back in touch with feelings you had with your father. Is there any way, though, that you can see how I am different from your father?

These are obviously shorthand versions of what is often a profound and complex process for both client and therapist. In the *transformational domain*, after therapists have worked hard to examine, reflect on, and think about themselves, they can use their mind by sharing their thoughts as a way of furthering the treatment direction. This idea is linked to the concept of *the third* as described below.

The "third" based on the Oedipus complex

The concept of the third, which I examined elsewhere in detail (Hargaden, 2014a, 2016), refers to the therapist using a thought, idea, or question, based on her or his transferential experience. The idea is to interject an Other between the therapist and the client, creating a space in which to reflect and think together. The source of the idea of the third is in the Oedipal complex, in which the father is a symbol for an interruption in the symbiosis between mother and child.

Using one's thoughts can be particularly powerful when offered in a neutral way by asking the client to *think* about her or his *thoughts*, thus using the therapist's mind as a tool for developing the client's mind. The third is also an effective way to bring in the cognitive teaching tools inherent in classical TA. For example, recently a supervisee of mine demonstrated how he used the egogram (Dusay, 1972) as a third to enable his client to think differently about his self-destructive behaviors. No amount of empathic responding or transferential interpretations based on the therapist's reflections or confrontations were working for him because he was stuck in a helpless, passive position projecting all his power onto the therapist, waiting for the therapist to cure him. By using the third in that way, the client had to think about how to heal himself. It is in this way we can understand too how classical TA can be integrated into the relational process.

In the final analysis, transactional analysts now have access to a significant amount of literature to support them through the deconfusion phase of psychotherapy where once there was just confusion about how to proceed. The domains of transference theory offer the creative clinician with an independent and imaginative mind the opportunity to work from a plurality of perspectives within the light touch of a clinical guiding plan.

The dialectics of meaning making

As will be evident from this introduction, Bill and I have different takes on the term relational. I find this encouraging and hopefully beneficial for clinicians. In my own journey as a relational transactional analyst and as a client of many years with a Jungian analyst who is also a rabbi, I have learned that uniformity of meaning is a type of spiritual weakness, that the ego seeks comfort, security, and satiety, but the soul demands meaning and struggle (Freeman, personal communication—over many years). I have come to recognize that not everything—indeed, if anything at all—can be understood; that the goal for us as therapists is to *engage* with the disillusionment, to stay with the frustration, and thereby to enable the client and the therapist to develop their reflective capacities to find and indeed to *search* for meaning that is inherent in our suffering (Frankl, 1984).

References

Aron, L. (2019). Discussion of "Bread and roses: Empathy and recognition." *Psychoanalytic Dialogues*, *29*, 92–102.

Aron, L, Grand, S. & Slochower, J. (Eds.). (2018). *De-idealizing Relational Theory: A Critique from Within*. London: Routledge.

Beebe, B. & Lachmann, F. (2002). *Infant Research and Adult Treatment: Co-constructing Interactions*. London: Analytic Press.

Berne, E. (1961). *Transactional Analysis in Psychotherapy: A Systematic Individual and Social Psychiatry*. New York: Grove Press.

Berne, E. (1964). *Games People Play*. New York: Grove Press.

Berne, E. (1966). *Principles of Group Treatment*. New York: Oxford University Press.

Berne, E. (1972). *What Do You Say after You Say Hello? The Psychology of Human Destiny*. New York: Grove Press.

Bollas, C. (1987). *The Shadow of the Object: Psychoanalysis of the Unthought Known*. New York: Columbia University Press.

Bollas, C. (1989). *Forces of Destiny: Psychoanalysis and Human Idiom*. Northvale, NJ: Jason Aronson.

Bollas, C. (1992). *Being a Character: Psychoanalysis and Self Experience*. New York: Hill & Wang.

Bollas, C. (1995), *Cracking Up: The Work of Unconscious Experience*, London: Routledge.

Bollas, C. (2007). *The Freudian Moment*. London: Karnac.

Bollas, C. (2009). *The Evocative Object World*. London: Routledge.

Chodorow, N. (2018). Warren Poland: Humanist, ethicist, friend. In Warren S. Poland, *Intimacy and Separateness in Psychoanalysis*, pp. ix–xiv. London: Routledge.

Cornell, W.F. (2002). Book review: Transactional Analysis: A Relational Perspective. *Transactional Analysis Journal*, *32*, 193–197.

Cornell, W.F. (2005). In the terrain of the unconscious: The evolution of a transactional analysis therapist. *Transactional Analysis Journal*, *35*, 119–131.

Cornell, W.F. (2008). What do you say if you don't say "unconscious"? Dilemmas created for transactional analysts by Berne's shift away from the language of unconscious experience. *Transactional Analysis Journal*, *38*, 93–100.

Cornell, W.F. (2019a). *Self-Examination in Psychoanalysis and Psychotherapy: Countertransference and Subjectivity in Clinical Practice*. London: Routledge.

Cornell, W.F. (2019b). *At the Interface of Transactional Analysis, Psychoanalysis, and Body Psychotherapy: Clinical and Theoretical Perspectives*. London: Routledge.

Cornell, W.F. & Hargaden, H. (Eds.). (2005). *From Transactions to Relations: The Emergence of a Relational Tradition in Transactional Analysis*. Chadlington: Haddon Press.

Cornell, W.F. & Landaiche, N.M. (2008/2019). Nonconscious processes and self-development: Key concepts from Eric Berne and Christopher Bollas. In William F. Cornell, *At the Interface of Transactional Analysis, Psychoanalysis, and Body Psychotherapy: Clinical and Theoretical Perspectives*, pp. 162–185. London: Routledge.

Dusay, J. (1972). Egograms and "the constancy hypothesis". *Transactional Analysis Journal*, *2*, 3, 37–41.

English, F. (2007). I'm now a cognitive analyst. Are you? *The Script*, *37*, 5, 1–7.

Fonagy, P., Gergely, G., Jurist, E., & Target, M. (2004). *Affect Regulation, Mentalization and the Development of the Self*. London: Karnac.

Fowlie, H. & Sills, C. (Eds.). (2011). *Relational Transactional Analysis: Principles in Practice*. London: Karnac.

Frankl, V.E. (1984). *Man's Search for Meaning: An Introduction to Logotherapy*. New York: Simon & Schuster.

Ghent, E. (1995). Interaction in the psychoanalytic situation. *Psychoanalytic Dialogues*, *5*, 3, 479–491.

Ghent, E. (2002/2018). Relations: Introduction to the first IARPP conference. In V. Demos & A. Harris (Eds.), *The Collected Papers of Emmanuel Ghent: Heart Melts Forward*, pp. 245–248. London: Routledge.

Guntrip, H. (1962). The schizoid compromise and psychotherapeutic stalemate. *British Journal of Medical Psychology, 35*, 273–287.

Hargaden, H. (2005). Routes to relational psychotherapy. Paper given at Routes to Relationality Teach-In. South Hampstead School for Girls Only.

Hargaden, H. (2014a). Building resilience: The role of firm boundaries and the third in relational group therapy. *Transactional Analysis Journal, 43*, 4, 284–290. DOI:10.1177/0362153713515178

Hargaden, H. (2014b). Relational as theory? Relational as a principle? Relational as symbol of integration? In D. Loewenthal & A. Samuels (Eds.), *Relational Psychotherapy, Psychoanalysis and Counselling*, pp. 176–183. Hove: Routledge.

Hargaden, H. (2016). *The Art of Relational Supervision*. Abingdon: Routledge.

Hargaden, H. & Schwartz, J. (Eds.). (2007). *Relational Psychology in Europe*. Special issue of *European Journal of Psychotherapy and Counselling, 9*, 1.

Hargaden, H. & Sills, C. (2002). *Transactional Analysis: A Relational Perspective*. Hove: Brunner-Routledge.

Hargaden, H. & Sills, C. (2008). Acceptance speech on receiving the 2007 Eric Berne Memorial Award. *Transactional Analysis Journal, 38*, 8–16.

Jacobs, T.J. (1991). *The Use of the Self: Countertransference and Communication in the Analytic Situation*. Madison, CT: International Universities Press.

Jacobs, T.J. (2013). *The Possible Profession: The Analytic Process of Change*. New York: Routledge.

Jones, E. (1953). *The Life and Work of Sigmund Freud*, Vol. 2. London: Hogarth Press.

Klein, M. (1975/1988). *Envy and Gratitude and Other Works 1946–1963*. London: Virago Books.

Kohut, H. (1971). *The Analysis of the Self*. New York: International Universities Press.

McLaughlin, J.T. (2005). *The Healer's Bent: Solitude and Dialogue in the Clinical Encounter*. Hillsdale, NJ: Analytic Press.

Meier, C.A. (1995). *Personality*. Einsiedeln, Switzerland: Daimon (original work published 1977).

Moiso, C. (1985). Ego states and transference. *Transactional Analysis Journal, 15*, 3, 194–201.

Moiso, C. & Novellino, M. (2000). An overview of the psychodynamic school of transactional analysis and its epistemological foundations. *Transactional Analysis Journal, 30*, 3, 182–191.

Poland, W.S. (1996). *Melting the Darkness: The Dyad and Principles of Clinical Practice*. Northvale, NJ: Jason Aronson.

Poland, W.S. (2018). *Intimacy and Separateness in Psychoanalysis*. London: Routledge.

Searles, H.F. (1960). *The Nonhuman Environment: In Normal Development and in Schizophrenia*. New York: International Universities Press.

Seligman, S. (2018). Inaction and puzzlement as interaction: Keeping attention in mind. In L. Aron, S. Grand, & J. Slochower (Eds.), *De-idealizing Relational Theory: A Critique from Within*, pp. 132–149. London: Routledge.

Stark, M. (2000). *Modes of Therapeutic Action*. Northvale, NJ: Jason Aronson.

Winnicott, D.W. (1949). Hate in the countertransference. *International Journal of Psycho-Analysis, 30*, 69–74.

1

THE BILATERAL AND ONGOING NATURE OF GAMES

Jenni Hine

For a number of years I have been dissatisfied with some aspects of the way game theory and game analysis are described in transactional analysis. These concerns were highlighted by the keynote speech on "Game analysis and racket analysis" given by Marilyn Zalcman at the July 1986 EATA conference in Holland (Zalcman, 1987). The most serious concerns about game theory relate to its use by the unwary. By inviting the use of perjorative labels for games, the theory actually furthers games while pretending to offer a solution to a painful process. This misuse is inherent in the one-sided analysis proposed by Berne in Formula G (Berne, 1972) and in his theoretical game analysis: "The analysis is undertaken from the point of view of the one who is 'it'," that is, the person seen as responsible for starting the game (Berne, 1964, p. 47). The bilateral nature of games was implied when Berne spoke of games as "an on-going series of complementary ulterior transactions" (Berne, 1964, p. 44), an idea we give lip service to when we say, "It takes two to play a game." However, as long as we continue to use this model to analyze only one of the participant's motivations, and we use such a plethora of names for games, game theory will continue to provoke "Not-OK" labeling and much controversy about what is actually going on.

In the view of games presented here, new definitions of the concepts in Formula G are proposed along with diagrams which provide visual clarity and emphasize the bilateral, transactional nature of games and the cumulative effects of game playing. Such a presentation is needed if the game concept is to remain useful theoretically and therapeutically.

The general dynamics of game mechanisms, including an analysis of the intrapsychic components and how they relate to other TA concepts, together with related theoretical examples using role analysis, discount analysis, and racket system analysis, are discussed in the latter part of this article. Also covered are some of the dysfunctions that lead to the switch and make for the ongoing nature of games. However, specific games are not discussed, nor are the transactional ways of moving out of a game.

Games and their relationship to other TA concepts

Games have been analyzed by various authors in terms of different TA concepts. Each view has added useful insight into the complex phenomenon defined by Berne as a game.

1. The concept of ego states is the basis of the analysis of games originally proposed by Berne (1964) using transactions: Games are viewed as a series of manipulative transactions between ego states which are designed to reach a predictable payoff. The intrapsychic dynamics described in Berne's theoretical, as opposed to transactional, game analysis are based on biological and libidinal needs as conceptualized in psychoanalytic theory, rather than on concepts specific to TA.
2. Role analysis is the basis for Karpman's (1968) analysis of games using the Drama Triangle, with the switching of the roles of Rescuer, Persecutor, and Victim being a major feature.
3. Discount analysis, based on identifying an individual's distortions of reality and his or her need to maintain a constant frame of reference, is highlighted in the Schiffian identification of games (Schiff et al., 1975). In this framework a game is initiated as each discount occurs, mostly in the form of a redefining transaction aimed at establishing one of the six specific roles on the Redefining Hexagon (Schiff et al., 1975, p. 67).
4. Rackets and the analysis of emotional experiences with their subsequent effects on behavior are the basis for the racketeering approach to games developed by English (1976). In this approach the payoffs and switches are a panic reaction to the possibility of losing the exchange of familiar racket strokes.
5. Script and the existential life position are the vehicle by which the Not-OK miniscript dynamic was developed by Kahler and Capers (1974). Driver behaviors stemming from counterscript messages, stoppers stemming from script injunctions, and payoffs are described as the elements of an ongoing process. Although not in itself a game, this nearly instantaneous sequence may describe what happens internally when a player is making a switch in the course of game playing.
6. Racket system analysis (Erskine & Zalcman, 1979) and interlocking racket systems, although not intended to be the analysis of game processes, describe well the intrapsychic processes which underlie the gimmick (a particular sensitivity) and which show the ongoing nature of the process due to the reinforcement factors and the cumulative effects they produce. Reinforcement is seen between past and present; between belief, behavior, and emotion; and between reality and fantasy.

The fact that so much thought has been put into the analysis of the intrapsychic and psychodynamic aspects of games reflects the importance of the phenomenon and its relevance for clinical work, whether acknowledged or not. In addition, the fact that there are so many aspects of games to consider has contributed to the difficulty in developing an overall conceptualization for this phenomenon.

Bilateral participation

It is important to keep the bilateral nature of games in mind at all times. Each party to a game is playing his or her own version, which is complementary to the version played by other participants.

Formula G gives a unilateral analysis of a game episode and is a fine tool for examining one player's part, even though the player may be labeled Not OK in the process. Berne (1972) explains the formula as follows:

$$C + G = R \rightarrow S \rightarrow X \rightarrow P$$

C + G means that the con hooks into a gimmick, so that the respondent responds (R). The player then pulls the switch (S) and that is followed by a moment of confusion or crossup (X), after which both players collect their payoffs (P). Whatever fits into this formula is a game, and whatever does not fit it is not a game (Berne, 1972, p. 443).

The fact that Formula G is neither completely one-handed nor a true bilateral picture with mutual responsibility should, in a sense, imply two Formula Gs superimposed. The bilateral nature of games is better shown in Karpman's Drama Triangle (1968), although even there showing each person's moves is complicated. Nevertheless, Formula G does indicate how the intrapsychic motivations (the gimmicks) give rise to the ulterior stimuli in the transactions (the cons).

The newly proposed diagram for Formula G (Figure 1.1) shows the two-handed nature of a game, the interlocking of each player's cons and gimmicks, and the buildup to the familiar climax of the switch, the crossup, and payoffs.

In this diagram players are represented separately, and their intrapsychic processes are highlighted with different patterns. The gimmicks are depicted as components of the intrapsychic experience of each player and so are the payoffs. Each stimulus is shown as a con whether labeled con, response, or switch. The darker inner line represents each person's current experience of the game in which they are involved.

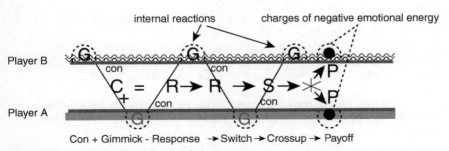

FIGURE 1.1 Formula G: game episode or segment

26 Jenni Hine

The important points to emphasize in relation to this diagram are:

- every stimulus in a game is a con in that each person's response to a con is not accidental, but another invitation to continue the game;
- each person is motivated by his or her own particular gimmick—depicted as buried in each player's intrapsychic internal experience—which forwards the game he or she is playing;
- the switch can be initiated by either player;
- the crossup is a moment of surprise and heightened awareness that the other person is disappointingly "other" in a symbiotic sense;
- each time a switch and a crossup occurs, each person takes an intrapsychic payoff in the form of charges of negative, unresolved emotional energy of a non-problem-solving nature.

This game process is illustrated in Table 1.1 by two examples of a game episode involving players A and B.

To demonstrate the bilateral responsibility in a game, Episode 2 shows player B with a "helpful, bossy" type racket (English, 1976, p. 184) generating the first *apparent* stimulus, whereas in Episode 1 it was generated by player A with a "helpless, bratty" type racket (English, 1976, p. 182).

The con

In this conceptualization every stimulus in the game is a con, whether it is labeled con, response, or switch in Formula G. That is, a con is a specific provocative stimulus which says one thing while intending or wanting something else. No response is "direct" or "accidental" in a game. The con, shown in Figure 1.1 as a line going from player to player, is overt transactional behavior with a covert message. One might say that it is one person's "act" in the transaction. Table 1.2 gives some examples.

TABLE 1.1 Case example: two game episodes by player A and B

Example Episode 1	Example Episode 2
Players	Players
A "I can't find my ruler"	B "Where did you put your bag?"
B "Where did you leave it?"	A "I'm not sure"
A "I don't know"	B "Maybe it's in the car"
B Jumps up to look for it	A Makes no reply and continues to read
Possible Switches when B comes back with ruler:	Possible Switches in Episode 2:
A "Who told you to go rummaging in my personal belongings?"	A Rattles his newspaper and says "Are you ready?"
or Switch by B	or Switch by B
B "You really are a hopeless case"	B "Hurry up you slow coach"

The bilateral and ongoing nature of games **27**

TABLE 1.2 Cons in example Episode 1

CON from A: "I can't find my ruler."
In a game process this really means "Go and get my ruler for me," which to player A is a forbidden thing to say or want.
CON from B: The player B jumping up to find the ruler and asking helpful questions.
His covert message is, "Don't forget to admire me for my kindness when saying thank you."

The gimmick

Figure 1.1 shows that each player's gimmick is embedded in his or her intrapsychic experiences. In fact, the gimmick can be viewed as an intrapsychic sensitivity to a particular type of provocative stimulus, and the subsequent response as a reaction stemming from that sensitivity. Berne (1972) defined a gimmick as "A special attitude or weakness which makes a person vulnerable to games or scripty behavior" (p. 443). As examples he gave "fear, greed, sentimentality, or irritability." The desire to be "helpful," "helpless," or "hurtful" described by English (1976, p. 176) as rackets which form the basis for games also clearly falls into the category of gimmicks. Script injunctions and early decisions determine the particular beliefs and sensitivities that make up the gimmick. Table 1.3 shows examples of gimmicks for players A and B.

The switch mechanism

The switch is an unexpected change of role or ego state which results in a crossed transaction leading to the crossup and payoff. This crossed transaction is also a con. The switch is initiated by the player whose intrapsychic tolerance is first

TABLE 1.3 Gimmicks in example Episode 1

GIMMICK for A: is likely to be a desire to be passive or helpless.
Comment: Other possibilities could be rebelliousness or fear of autonomy and responsibility.
GIMMICK for B: is likely to be a desire to be helpful and liked.
Comment: This may mask an underlying fear of failure and depression.

TABLE 1.4 Switches in game Episode 1

SWITCH by A:	(on receiving the ruler from B) "Who told you to go rummaging in my personal possessions?" —instead of the hoped for reply of, "Thank you, how kind of you."
Comment:	The underlying con or cover message in this stimulus might be, "Try again, I'll be grateful one day (maybe!)."
SWITCH by B:	(on giving the ruler to A) "You really are a hopeless case"—instead of saying "Here you are, dear"
Comment:	The con in the switch might be: "I'm not a sucker, ha ha!"

28 Jenni Hine

overstepped by the tension specific to the game, that is, the one whose gimmick is at that moment the most heavily charged and sensitive to the provocation.

Table 1.4 gives typical switches in first-degree game playing in the ruler example (Episode 1, Table 1.1).

The crossup

In all these cases the crossup might be a shocked "What went wrong?" or "What's the matter with him/her?" It is a moment of realizing the distance and difference between self and other. The other is really in a disappointingly Not-OK sense "other."

The payoffs

The payoff is an intrapsychic experience following the switch and crossup, composed of feelings accompanied by thoughts and behaviors which reconfirm a player's script, generating negative script-reinforcing energy. This is later referred to as a "negative charge." The payoff is a point at which the transference is played out, reinforcing the symbiosis that exists between the two players, which may be either of a dependent or of a competitive nature (Schiff, 1975). The payoffs in the first-degree game example about the ruler would vary according to who initiated the switch. Table 1.5 shows some possibilities as A switched to "Who told you to go rummaging in my personal belongings?"

The ongoing nature of games

The Game Formula does not show the ongoing, continuing nature of games, but implies instead that there is an initiator and a responder, with a clear beginning and an end.

However, pragmatic observation of the game phenomenon clearly demonstrates that even a switch and the mutual payoffs are not enough to stop the process, which can start up again at the very next transaction.

Whereas injunctions according to Kahler and Capers (1974) are "stoppers" (p. 33), games might be described as "unstoppables." This idea is not new.

TABLE 1.5 Payoff in game Episode 1

Payoff for A:	might be anger together with the thought "Nobody respects me"—leading perhaps to "What's the use of doing anything, it makes no difference in the end," accompanied by behavioral passivity.
Payoff for B:	Could be sadness, accompanied by the thought "What did I do wrong? I was only trying to help. When it comes right down to it I'm a failure"—leading perhaps to self-punishing behaviors.

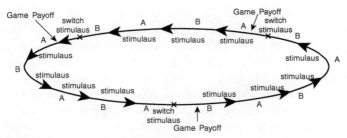

FIGURE 1.2 Ongoing game: simple diagram

Berne (1964) in *Games People Play* described games as "the most important aspect of social life all over the world" (p. 45), and Ernst (1971) wrote, "A game is a repetitively carried out series of transactions" (p. 257).

This repetitive, ongoing nature of games is illustrated by the circular diagram in Figure 1.2.

The genesis of this circular diagram was as a response to clients who said with great conviction, "S/he started it when s/he said or did x," together with my immediate reaction, "There is no beginning to a game, come and see on the board." With the help of this circle one could work backward around it, with the client asking each time, "So what did I do or say before s/he said/did that?" Often when the client had worked around the circle to where he or she had first written something, it would be noticeable that exactly the same remark or event had taken place, so that the whole sequence reproduced itself time after time. This work is very close to James's (1973) game plan worked in a visual way.

The recurrent and cumulative nature of games

Escalation

Often the first indicator that a game process is underway is the buildup of tension in one's body, a reflection of the rising stroke intensity. This reaches its maximum during the switch, crossup, and payoff. Although the result is mainly unpleasant or psychologically negative, the body is aware of excitement before any other racket or substitute feeling (English, 1976) takes over. "Negative charge" from successive payoffs builds up, despite some discharge at the switch. This might be called collecting successive trading stamps (Berne, 1972), that is, an accumulation of unexpressed feelings gets carried forward into future behavior.

Ongoing nature of games

After the switch, crossup, and payoffs, the players may (and usually do) continue playing the game with each other, as in a tennis match where the set and match are comprised of many games. This process is described as an ongoing game. For example, in Episode 2 in Table 1.1, the bag incident might well begin within minutes of the payoff from the ruler incident (Episode 1, Table 1.1). Player B may feel so sad at the crossup that he tries to be especially tactful when he wants his partner to get ready to go out. This leads him to say, "Where did you put your bag?" Player A, who is still angry at not being respected, says, "I'm not sure" and makes no other reply. They then may move into a new switch and payoff. Thus, a game can go on from one event to another without anyone really being aware of the repetition.

On the other hand, to continue the tennis metaphor, the players may move on to new partners, as in a tennis tournament. They may do this immediately or after a lapse of time, which can be a matter of minutes, hours, days, or months. Games can also be taken up again after an interval at the place where they were left off. Some people give up in a huff after each payoff and move on to new partners for each episode. This is, nevertheless, still a continuation of what they were doing with their last partner. (Some possible causes for this are suggested later in this article.)

The switch mechanism

It is important to look at the switch mechanism in detail and in relation to various factors such as tension, life position, and the miniscript sequence (Kahler & Capers, 1974).

Intrapsychic tension

As mentioned earlier, the switch mechanism is precipitated by intrapsychic tension. This is observable in the degree of agitation manifested by a player preceding his or her switch. The switch itself is initiated by the person whose tolerance for this type of tension is lowest.

Such intrapsychic tension may be created or maintained by any of the following dysfunctions:

- Disorder of the stroke economy (Steiner, 1974) leading to an exaggerated need for attention and stimulation.
- Permeable ego state boundaries (Berne, 1961) resulting in little resistance to incoming stimuli due to a tendency to introject and incorporate rather than to project. This incoming material is threatening to the way people see themselves— their frame of reference (Schiff, 1975)—and so creates internal stress.
- Low tolerance for frustration and stress, usually due to Child contamination of the Adult, where Child wants, desires, and fantasies are perceived as realities. When reality contradicts this view, frustration and stress can be high.
- Building up collections of trading stamps, or having poor ability to discharge feelings as they occur by means of effective action or self-expression.
- Symbiosis hunger—the internal pull toward regression or domination which marks the two poles of symbiosis.

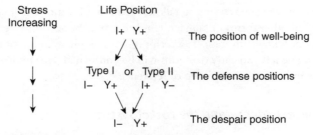

FIGURE 1.3 Effect of increasing stress on life position

Stress factors and life position

A person's frame of reference (Schiff, 1975), that is, the way he or she sees himself or herself, others, and the situation, is stongly influenced by the underlying life position. A person responds to stress from his or her life position with varying impact on the switch mechanism.

Two major personality types—Type 1, Helpless, and Type II, Bossy—were described in the articles on racketeering by English (1976) and further developed in my article on life position therapy (Hine, 1982).

Apart from the differences in character seen in these two types, they both display the same life position mobility under growing stress (Figure 1.3).

The greater the internal or external stress, the greater the probability of a shift, first from the position of "well-being" to the "defense position," and ultimately to the "despair position." Some people have stronger resistance to these shifts than do others, and thus the amount of stress required to provoke the shifts varies. A game is usually promoted by the person who is most entrenched in his or her defense position, and the switch is initiated by the person who most readily reaches the position of despair and thus gives up attempting to make contact.

Intrapsychic components

Script milestone—contact and distancing

English (1976) suggests—and I agree—that a game is an unsuccessful attempt to let down one's defenses and to reach for strokes and closeness of a familiar rackety nature which does not disturb script decisions and beliefs. This contradicts Berne's (1964) position that the payoff and switch are the premeditated goal of game players.

However, games visibly lead to distancing, and I suggest that the pain of successive payoffs (the cumulative negative charge) escalates in time into something like a climax for each partner. This may not be simultaneous, nor be lived out in the same way by each person. To continue the tennis metaphor, at this climax the player finishes the match with one person, causing a break in attempts to relate with that individual similar to the communication break which follows a crossed transaction. For example, this occurs when a couple or working partners start being merely

32   Jenni Hine

polite to each other, even refusing to talk to each other for months or years on end and avoiding all other forms of contact. This break may be accompanied by despair or triumph, but will, in any case, be a script milestone where injunctions and their accompanying beliefs and early decisions will be confirmed. This homeostasis helps maintain the individual's own frame of reference.

Intrapsychic experience and the racket system

The gimmick, the payoff, the script milestone, and the stacked-up game experiences all stem from intrapsychic dynamics. One of the best overall tools we have in TA for examining this material is the intrapsychic racket system analysis (Erskine & Zalcman, 1979). Table 1.6 shows a hypothetical analysis of the intrapsychic process of Player B, the helpful/bossy racketeer in Table 1.1, while Table 1.7 shows some of the existential causes of the gimmick, payoff, and script milestone.

Table 1.7 shows some of Player B's life experiences from which the intrapsychic game mechanisms have developed. Most have been drawn from the earlier racket analysis.

Frame of reference—cognitive factors

Games do much to reinforce constancy in frame of reference (Schiff, 1975), that is, the ability to hold over time to the same beliefs and feelings about oneself, other people, and one's life situation.

When considering the reasons for game playing it is necessary to understand the paradox in maintaining a constant frame of reference: One needs a constant frame of reference in order to maintain sanity, that is to say, stability, but a too-constant or rigid frame of reference can lead to decompensation and insanity. If an individual changes beliefs frequently, he or she may soon not know what to think, or may stop thinking, or may think wildly and out of touch with reality. Thus, people need a

TABLE 1.6 Case example of Player B's racket system

Beliefs	Observable behaviors	Reinforcing memories
self—I'm not lovable	—Unsolicited helpful	—Mother not noticing her
self—I'm not capable	—Forced cheefulness	—People being ungrateful and getting angry
other—Other's needs come first	—"Secret" crying	
life—I have to help people in order to be liked	*Reported internal experience*	—Standing beside father when he died and being unable to save him
	—Sleeps and eats poorly	
Repressed feelings	*Fantasies*	
—Anger	—One day s/he will	
—Hurt	change if only I can find the right way	

The bilateral and ongoing nature of games **33**

TABLE 1.7 Some existential causes for Player B's game mechanisms

Gimmick Material (Particular sensitivity; wants to be liked and to help someone get better)
A fear that people will not notice me, like it was with mother.
A desire to help and being powerless to do so, as it was with father.

Payoff Material (This is heavily charged intrapsychic experience that confirms script
emotionally, cognitively, and behaviorally.)
What did I do wrong, I was only trying to help. (Cognitive)
I'm not capable—confirming the script injunction Don't Succeed. (Cognitive and
behavioral)
People getting angry and being ungrateful—as result of switches made by B, out of
awareness.
"Secret" resentment (Emotional)
                    (Behavioral)
I couldn't save my father—I'm not OK. (Cognitive)
"Secret" crying—substituted for anger at powerlessness and frustration in relations with
significant others. (Emotional)

Script Milestone (At this point attempts to relate to the significant other are abandoned.)
I give up. It's no use trying anymore. S/he'll never change.
Becomes terribly busy and always away from home.
Maintains a critical silence about everything partner does.
Begins having migraines or other psychosomatic symptoms.

Cumulated Game Experiences
Brother who switched between asking for favors and being angry when I "helped
him out"
   – Memories of past game playing, recalled as incomprehensible negative experiences.
Mother now old, who won't listen to reason. Past game playing continued into the
present, still as out of awareness as when the behavior originated.
Colleagues who left all the boring jobs to me and then found fault with what I did.
   – Recalled social game-playing experiences played from an I−Y− "despair" position.

---

certain constancy and selectivity of belief over time in order to function effectively
and to stay sane.

On the other hand, apart from Adult reality testing, the psychological
mechanisms which help maintain a constant frame of reference discounting,
redefining, grandiosity, game playing, injunctions, and early decisions distort aspects
of reality. When adhered to blindly in spite of perceptual evidence, they can make
reality seem unbearable to such an extent that insanity or suicide appear as valid
alternatives.

For example, anyone who believes all she or he is told about God has a hard
time holding on to sanity: God is all powerful, God does not exist, God knows
everything you do or think, God punishes sinners, God is Love, God will answer
your prayers, God is above all earthly concerns, God condemns unbaptized babies
to damnation, God created the world, God didn't create the world.

Imagine if the same kind of conflicting messages invaded all of a person's
convictions and perceptions about self, others, and the world, with only perceptual
reality testing to help sort these messages out. It is easy to see why mechanisms such

34 Jenni Hine

as games that select and maintain a constant image of the world are so vital and entrenched in the human personality.

The need for a constant of frame of reference is as existentially important to human functioning as is the need for strokes. Some of the behavioral and social factors that impact an individual's intrapsychic frame of reference are considered in the following paragraphs.

Frame of reference—behavioral and social factors

Among the ways of structuring time, rituals, pastimes, games, activities, intimacy (Berne, 1964), and play (Boyd & Boyd, 1980) are all ways of being with and interacting with other people. One important way in which they differ from each other is the impact each has in terms of changing or defending a person's frame of reference:

Withdrawal—removing oneself from the company of others—tends to maintain one's frame of reference.

Pastimes and rituals allow a person to be with and interact with others without letting down his or her psychological defenses, thus keeping his or her frame of reference unchallenged. In *intimacy*, which is both strokeful and meaningful contact, each person lets the other through his or her defenses in such a way that their frames of reference about each other and self are modified, perhaps permanently.

In *games* there is a momentary breakthrough in a person's psychological defenses up to the switch point. Letting down one's defenses is exciting, so this moment is rich in strokes. However, the overall game process maintains homeostasis, and the switch ensures that distance will be reestablished. Thus the person stays defended and makes no changes to his or her frame of reference about self, other, or the situation.

Play, as described by Boyd and Boyd (1980), may be viewed as an innocent antithesis to games. It is a shared strokeful experience with defenses at a minimum, which can, but does not necessarily, open the door to intimacy and change in frames of reference.

Activity may be more neutral in its impact on frame of reference because the activity and being with other people can be equal objectives of this time structure.

Factors in the occurrence of games

The main thrusts of therapy are toward self-awareness, which implements decontamination; self-expression, which favors the discharge of emotions as they occur and consolidates the permission to exist; and successful closeness and intimacy leading to stroke satisfaction. These processes contribute to the treatment of stroke economy problems, permeable boundaries, symbiosis hunger, and other dysfunctions already mentioned, as well as to release from games.

These emphases, common to nearly all schools of therapy, diminish intrapsychic tension and render a player less likely to initiate a switch. Individuals who are new to therapy are more likely, then, to make the switch. Because games were first identified in a therapy setting where old-timers and the therapist had much more self-awareness than newcomers, it must have seemed natural to view one person— usually a newcomer—as the initiator, or "it" as Berne (1964) so often said, while the others merely responded.

This is not so clear in settings where self-awareness among players is about equal. In relationships such as marriages or professional hierarchies, the circular, ongoing, unstoppable nature of games is much more obvious. People who break off relationships and move on to a new partner between each game episode (as implied by the Game Formula) are probably:

- more entrenched in their $I-Y-$ despair position;
- playing at high, or second- and third-degree intensity;
- being distanced by other people who have already reached climax point with this person, so that the number of willing game-playing partners in his or her circle is reduced

Conclusion

Through this general discussion of the game phenomenon and the accompanying diagrams, it is hoped that readers will develop a more integrated understanding of the concept of games and a better feeling for its homeostatic strength, leading them to give more weight to its multiple psychological functions.

The validity of a concept and proof of the existence of the phenomenon itself lie in the consistency with which it can be demonstrated to and recognized by people with sufficient awareness. This is true of the game concept, just as it for the concepts of ego states, transactions, and other TA concepts. Most TA therapists and many of their clients are rarely in doubt as to when ongoing gaming is in progress. Even people new to the theory readily recognize the game process as something that they encounter in their daily lives.

Nevertheless, game terminology and game analysis are today viewed with disfavor by many TA therapists. However, the pragmatic validation presented here would indicate that game theory is, in fact, a valuable diagnostic tool, especially when emphasis is placed on the bilateral and ongoing nature of games, thus reducing harmful interventions and the resistance of clients to working on games.

Berne's view that game analysis and the search for the Little Professor's involvement in games can be sophisticated, fascinating, and enjoyable (Berne, 1964, p. 54) even to the players, seems to have been forgotten over time, with even the definition of games having become vague in the plethora of games that are discussed. The entire concept needs a searching new look along the lines suggested by Zalcman (1987).

References

Berne, E. (1961). *Transactional analysis in psychotherapy*. New York: Grove Press.

Berne, E. (1964). *Games people play*. New York: Grove Press.

Berne, E. (1972). *What do you say after you say hello?* New York: Grove Press.

Boyd, H. S., & Boyd, L. W. (1980). Play as a time structure. *Transactional Analysis Journal*, 10, 5–7.

English, F. (1976). Rackets as a basis for games. In F. English (ed.), *Selected Articles* (pp. 176–191). Philadelphia: Eastern Institute for TA and Gestalt.

Ernst, F. H., Jr. (1971). The OK Corral: The grid for get-on-with. *Transactional Analysis Journal*, 1(4), 33–41.

Erskine, R. G., & Zalcman, M. J. (1979). The racket system. *Transactional Analysis Journal*, 9, 51–59.

Hine, J. (1982). Life position therapy. *Transactional Analysis Journal*, 12, 190–194.

James, J. (1973). The game plan. *Transactional Analysis Journal*, 3(4), 14–17.

Kahler, T., with Capers, H. (1974). Miniscript. *Transactional Analysis Journal*, 4(1), 26–42.

Karpman, S. (1968). Fairy tales and script drama analysis. *Transactional Analysis Bulletin*, 7(26), 39–43.

Schiff, J. L., with Schiff, A. W., Mellor, K., Schiff, E., Schiff, S., Richman, D., Fishman, J., Wolz, L., Fishman, C., & Momb, D. (1975). *Cathexis reader: Transactional analysis treatment of psychosis*. New York: Harper & Row.

Steiner, C. M. (1974). *Scripts people live*. New York: Grove Press.

Zalcman, M. J. (1987). Game analysis and racket analysis. In *Keynote speeches: Delivered at the EATA Conference, July, 1986, Noorddwijkerhout, the Netherlands*. Geneva, Switzerland: European Association for Transactional Analysis.

2

THROUGH THE LOOKING GLASS

Explorations in transference and countertransference

Petrūska Clarkson

In Latin the word *transference* means "to carry across." The phenomenon of "carrying across" qualities from what is known (based on past experience) to what is analogous in the present has probably always been a feature of human psychology. Such processes occur between husband and wife, teacher and pupil, citizen and state functionary. Thus, it is important to recognize that transference and countertransference in this sense are ubiquitous and necessary components of any learning process. *They occur whenever emotions, perceptions, or reactions are based on past experiences rather than on the here-and-now.*

The subject of transference involves an astonishing variety of contradictions, ambiguities, and connotational disputes. The number of "types" of transference and related phenomena also decreases or increases depending on the author and the method of classification used. It is this author's view that apparent theoretical inconsistencies are often the result of confusion about definitions, which are herein reviewed. This article presents a practical map for use by transactional analysts and other psychotherapists. It is effective when used as a tool in supervision (from self or supervisor) and not as an analytic disturbance to the development of the transference modality in the psychotherapeutic relationship. Of course, the map is not the territory. However, it has been found effective for planning or anticipating directions in treatment or helping the psychotherapist understand the situation better when there are intractable difficulties or unrelenting plateaus.

Transference, of course, is only one of several therapeutic relationships potentially present between patient and therapist in psychotherapy. It is to be differentiated from the working alliance, the reparative/developmentally needed relationship, the real (I–You) relationship, and the transpersonal relationship (Clarkson, 1990).

38 Petrūska Clarkson

Transference phenomena—definitions and types

In Freudian psychoanalysis transference was originally regarded as an unfortunate phenomenon which interfered with psychoanalysis (Freud, 1958). Later, however, Freud (1955) saw it as an essential part of the psychotherapeutic process and indeed one of the cornerstones of psychoanalytic practice. Fairbairn (1952), Klein (1984), and Winnicott (1975) assumed that patients' responses in the transference relationship were valid evidence on which to base their theories about the origin of object relations in infancy.

Definitions of transference

Rycroft (1983) defined transference as:

> 1. The process by which a patient displaces on to his analyst feelings, ideas, etc., which derive from previous figures in his life; by which he relates to the analyst as though he were some former object in his life; by which he projects on to his analyst object-representations acquired by earlier introjections; by which he endows the analyst with the significance of another, usually prior, object. 2. The state of mind produced by 1 in the patient. 3. Loosely, the patient's emotional attitude towards his analyst.
>
> *(Rycroft, 1983, p. 168)*

According to Racker (1982), Freud denominated as transference all the patient's psychological phenomena and processes which referred to the analyst and were derived from other previous object relations. Therefore, in one usage transference refers to all feelings of the patient toward the psychotherapist which are transferred from past relationships. The *phenomenological time* of transference is thus the past replayed in the present as if it were the present. The *phenomenological shape* of transference is the fantasized externalization of an internal relationship between the individual and one or more others (Manor, 1992, relates this to intrapsychic and external transactional object relations). These others represent significant relationships in the individual's past (e.g., the mother–infant dyad, the child–parental couple triad, the child–family group, or the child–teacher–peer relationships).

Transference is thus that anticipatory pattern of relationship which the individual seeks to replicate with significant others, regardless of the other's individual, unique qualities experienced at that moment. Transference is that relational pattern people carry with them from situation to situation. The other person is not freely met for the first time, but more often through a screen on which the person is projecting his or her own particular movie.

This article concentrates on dyadic transferential relationship patterns, leaving the triadic and group transferential phenomena for later discussion. However, the same analytic map presented here can be easily extrapolated to fit triadic or group transferences.

Transference is one of the primary mechanisms by which human beings learn from their past relationships to anticipate how to behave in future relationships. For many people past object relationships have been traumatic or strained (Pine, 1985), and they carry the pattern of these learned relationships into their present lives and future as well as into the psychotherapeutic relationship. Therefore, until the transference is resolved, the *anticipated other* remains psychologically unchanged as the script process unfolds outside of Adult awareness.

> The decisive part of the work is achieved by creating in the patient's relation to the doctor—in the "transference"—new editions of the old conflicts; in these the patient would like to behave in the same way as he did in the past, while we, by summoning up every available mental force [in the patient], compel him to come to a fresh decision.
>
> *(Freud, cited in Racker, 1982, p. 46)*

Regardless of whether the psychotherapist intentionally attempts to present a blank screen or not, workable transference phenomena occur with sufficient duration and intensity in most therapeutic relationships for effective psychotherapy to take place.

Perspectives on transference

Although the terms complementary and concordant are used by Freud (1955) and Racker (1982) to describe forms of countertransference rather than transference, they are used here to describe several other kinds of transferential phenomena. In his discussion of countertransference, Novellino (1984) appeared to use the term "conforming identification countertransference" (p. 63) in the same way that Racker (1982) used "concordant countertransference," but he retained the use of "complementary identification countertransference" (p. 84). In addition, the terms "abnormal" and "normal" were used by Winnicott (1975) in relation to countertransference. This article suggests that the terms "facilitative" and "destructive" are better suited to these phenomena, and it extrapolates their use to other categories of transference phenomena found in psychotherapeutic and supervisory relationships.

Also introduced in this context are Lewin's (1963) terms *pro-active* and *reactive* to designate whether the subject of the discussion originates the stimulus (pro-acts) or responds to (reacts) a stimulus from the other. Because the psychotherapeutic space belongs essentially to the patient, the psychotherapist's pro-activity is usually, although not always, viewed as detracting from the primary task—enhancing the patient's autonomous pro-activity.

It is important to remember that transferential or countertransferential stimuli may be verbal or nonverbal. According to Berne's (1975) third rule of communication, the ulterior or psychological level will generally determine the outcome. The mechanism by which this occurs is probably a form of hypnotic induction (Conway & Clarkson, 1987). Under the circumstances described by Conway and Clarkson, ulterior messages (communications) can have the force

40   Petrūska Clarkson

of hypnotic inductions when an individual's Adult is decommissioned. Script decisions often influence or interfere with integrated Adult functioning (good contact with current reality). Therefore, whoever (analyst and/or patient) is not in Adult may be influenced *outside of awareness* to feel or act in ways consistent with the other's script expectations. This corresponds with and explains the idea of projective identification: "A complex clinical event of an interpersonal type: one person disowns his feelings and manipulatively *induces* [italics added] the other into experiencing them" (Hinshelwood, 1989, p. 200).

Watkins (1954) also speculated on the similarities between trance and transference, enumerating several ways in which psychoanalytic procedures *induce* changes of consciousness resembling trance induction. Unlike the intimates of patients, who have been *roled into* the patient's games, psychotherapists who have been through their own personal psychotherapy are trained to remain with Adult in the executive while doing psychotherapy. Thus they can notice the transferential projections and expectations in the ways they react to the patient, using such information to benefit the patient. Such *objectivity* necessitates considerable self-knowledge, regular supervision, and interpersonal satisfactions outside of psychotherapeutic work.

Categories of patient transference

Complementary transference

In this form of transference the patient seeks completion of the symbiotic relationship. In a complementary transference toward the projected Parent of the psychotherapist, the patient projects the actual or fantasized past historical parent onto the therapist. For example, a patient expects the therapist to humiliate him in the same way as his historical parent did. Alternatively, the patient may hope for an idealized fantasy parent based on childhood wishes.

In another variation of complementary transference, the patient projects the actual or fantasized past Child ego state/s of the parent onto the therapist. For example, the patient takes care of the psychotherapist's Child by protecting him or her from the patient's rage, or behaves in a way similar to the punitive parenting which the patient introjected from his or her own abusive parent/s.

Because of the nature of the psychotherapeutic relationship, projections onto the Child of the psychotherapist tend to be those of the second-order structural symbiotic kind. For example, because it is not the patient's function to take care of the therapist, but vice versa, the justification for such caretaking is usually based on a fantasy, for example, that the psychotherapist needs to be taken care of because he or she is frightened. Likewise, an impaired therapeutic relationship may arise, for example, when the therapist inappropriately shows vulnerability or makes demands on the patient for such caretaking. To avoid the despair of realizing and reliving the failure of the original parents, the patient may move into the complementary Child-to-Parent transference.

Concordant transference

This form of transference occurs when the patient projects his or her own past Child onto the psychotherapist in an attempt to find identification. For example, the patient imagines that the psychotherapist feels sad and lonely, whereas the patient's historic Child is grieving over an early parental abandonment. In this form of transference, the patient may experience both self and therapist as equally helpless. People with a narcissistic personality disorder often use this form of transference, particularly in the beginning of psychotherapy: "I see in you, my psychotherapist, the ways you are like me." So, in a sense, this kind of patient experience has similarities to the mirroring or twin transferences described by Kohut (1977).

Either complementary or concordant transference may contain potential for or elements of destructive or facilitative forces.

Destructive transference

This form of transference involves the patient's acted-out or fantasized destructive past as manifested in the psychotherapeutic relationship. Of course, this only refers to occasions when third-degree games are played to the payoff point and not to the therapeutic use of destructive feelings and fantasies. It specifically refers to behavior that exceeds the boundaries of the psychotherapeutic contract and that can no longer be dealt with in the psychotherapeutic arena. Such acting-out of second- or third-degree games—e.g., homicide, suicide, or transference psychosis—effectively destroys the psychotherapeutic contract and often represents a script payoff or conclusion. Such destructive acting-out makes management procedures (e.g., hospital admission or daily supervision) that are extraneous to the psychotherapeutic relationship necessary.

Facilitative transference

It is important to differentiate normal or healthy transference phenomena from other types of transference. The patient may transfer (carry over) onto the current psychotherapeutic relationship a temperamental preference or style on the basis of what has been effective for him or her in the past. An easy-going, phlegmatic patient who has a temperamentally slow pace (Eysenck & Rachman, 1965) may prefer a psychotherapist of a similar temperament. This is not necessarily pathological.

The facilitating form of transference does not fit the definition of script. In fact, it may represent productive learned patterns from the past which are transferred into the present with a successful outcome. Because these patterns are not self-limiting (as scripts are), but, rather, self-actualizing or aspirational (Clarkson, 1989), they should not be pathologized, but viewed as the possible basis for choosing a compatible partner for the psychotherapeutic journey. However, they are technically transferential in the sense that they are transferred from past affective relationships, not newly formed in the here-and-now.

Figure 2.1 summarizes the forms of transference and countertransference for the sake of comparison, clarity, and overview. It is most useful to look only at one segment of Figure 2.1 at a time after a particular topic has been discussed. Figure 2.1 also adds brief (because of space limitations) explanations in TA terms. Diagonal arrows are used in relation to complementary transferences to indicate the psychological inequality of the complementary relationships; horizontal arrows visually demonstrate concordance or identification; downward arrows allude to

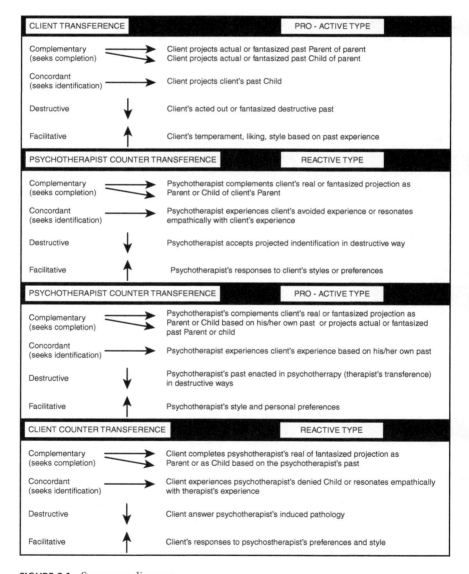

FIGURE 2.1 Summary diagram

Through the looking glass **43**

the destructiveness of unhealthy transference and its possible relationship to the force of *destrudo* (Berne, 1969; Weiss, 1950); upward-pointing arrows represent the aspirational arrow, possibly related to physis, the generalized creative urge that reaches upward out of the individual's past experiences toward the transformative potential inherent in human nature (Berne, 1969, p. 89).

Countertransference phenomena—definitions and types

Rycroft (1983) defined countertransference as:

> 1. The analyst's TRANSFERENCE on his patient. In this, correct, sense, counter-transference is a disturbing, distorting element in treatment. 2. By extension, the analyst's emotional attitude towards his patient, including his response to specific items of the patient's behaviour. According to Heimann (1950), Little (1951), Gitelson (1952), and others, the analyst can use this latter kind of countertransference as clinical evidence, i.e., he can assume that his own emotional response is based on a correct interpretation of the patient's true intentions or meaning.
>
> *(p. 25)*

As can be seen from Rycroft's standard definition, there are two major categories of countertransference: one constituting the analyst's transference onto the patient, and the other the analyst's responses to the patient. Winnicott (1975) defined as abnormal countertransference "those areas that arise from the analyst's past unresolved conflicts that intrude on the present patient" (p. 175). In a sense these are the psychotherapist's transferences—he or she is transferring material from his or her past onto the client. Winnicott (1975) also differentiated another type of countertransference which he described as normal—those reactions that describe the idiosyncratic style of an analyst's work and personality, which I view as facilitative. Winnicott (1975) also identified a category he called "objective countertransference. ... Those reactions evoked in an analyst by a patient's behaviour and personality ... [which] can provide the analyst with valuable internal clues about what is going on in the patient" (p. 195).

I also differentiate between two major kinds of countertransference depending on whether the psychotherapist is *reacting* to a patient or pro-actively *introducing his or her own transference* into the psychotherapeutic relationship. What Winnicott (1975) called "objective countertransference" (p. 195) is referred to here as *reactive countertransference* to emphasize that the psychotherapist is reacting accurately or objectively to the patient's projections, personality, and behavior in the therapeutic relationship. Winnicott's (1975) "abnormal countertransference" (p. 195) is referred to here as *pro-active countertransference* (psychotherapist transference) to emphasize the potential pitfalls that may result from the intrusion of the psychotherapist's unresolved conflicts into the psychotherapeutic relationship. As Novellino (1984) pointed out, the efficacy of

44 Petrūska Clarkson

this exploration depends on the ability of therapists to separate their issues from their reactions to their patient's issues.

As already discussed, patients project their script expectations onto their therapists, and this often forms the matrix from which script redecisions can evolve. Whether therapists use the emotional, symbolic, or associative impact on themselves of their patients' transferences to benefit the patients (reactive countertransference) or as a vehicle for enacting their own historically determined relationship patterns (pro-active countertransference) is largely determined, not by psychological perfection, but by integrated Adult awareness of self and the impact of the other.

Understanding and feeling the impact and nature of the transferences or projective identifications that patients attempt to elicit from the psychotherapist provides useful information if the therapist's Adult is unimpaired. With a fully functioning Adult, therapists can avoid being pulled into their patients' script dramas and can remain available to experience these dramas (not being a mirrorlike projective screen) while at the same time acting as an "integrated personality" (Federn, 1977, p. 218) who maintains conscious awareness and control.

Categories of reactive psychotherapist countertransference

Complementary reactive countertransference

The psychotherapist complements the patient's real or fantasized projection (as Parent or Child of the patient's parent) by responding with the feeling probably experienced by the original parent. For example, the therapist responds to the patient's projection of his or her over-nurturing mother by feeling the urge to rescue.

Concordant reactive countertransference

The therapist experiences the patient's avoided experience or resonates empathically with the patient's experience. For example, after a session the therapist feels unaccountably and uncharacteristically despairing; although the patient talked about her brother's death, she did not let herself experience her corresponding emotions, and the therapist is left with the weight of the unexpressed feeling.

Destructive countertransference

The therapist accepts the projected identification out of awareness and acts on it in an unhealthy way. For example, the patient sees the therapist as her neglectful mother: The therapist responds by forgetting appointments and going on holiday without giving the patient due notice. The patient's expectation acts as a subliminal, hypnotic induction to the therapist, who responds outside of his or her awareness. It is the therapist's responsibility to be aware of such indicators and to use them therapeutically, not destructively.

Facilitative countertransference

It is again important, as Winnicott (1975) indicated, to differentiate countertransference that is normal, healthy, and even possibly facilitative for the patient. It is natural to feel affection for a lovable patient, appreciation for a creative one, and respect for a humble one. Such feelings may be based on one's past experiences of patients. Withholding emotional responses to the healthy self-expressions of one's patients can make the process of psychotherapy quite barren and may lead us to neglect important opportunities for enhancing creative capacities and reinforcing healthy behavior patterns.

Categories of pro-active psychotherapist countertransference

Complementary pro-active countertransference

This describes the process whereby the therapist brings into the therapeutic relationship his or her script transferences, projections, and expectations based on past experiences. This is usually considered to be unhelpful and is frequently destructive to the therapeutic process. Of course therapists are not perfect, and are on their own personal journeys of self-discovery and self-development. That personal script issues, suppressed feelings, or avoided sensitivities may be present in psychotherapists at work cannot be denied. Whether or not these are in awareness, acknowledged, owned, worked through, supervised, humbly accepted, or truly transformed is what makes the difference between unconscious exploitation and helpful empathy for the human struggle.

Complementary pro-active countertransference occurs when the psychotherapist complements (or completes the gestalt of) the patient's real or fantasized projection as Parent or Child based on the therapist's own past, or projects the actual or fantasized past Parent or Child. For example, the therapist may behave in a withholding, passive, and coldly analytical way in response to the patient's neediness, not because this is therapeutically appropriate, but because this is the way the therapist was treated by his or her parents.

Concordant countertransference

The psychotherapist experiences the patient's experience based on the therapist's own past. For example, the therapist assumes that the patient feels guilty about injuring a school friend in the same way that he or she did when younger. The patient may or may not have a similar experience, and such identification needs from the therapist may be unhelpful or actively hindering to the therapy process.

Destructive pro-active countertransference

The psychotherapist enacts (or acts out) his or her own past in the psychotherapy in ways that are destructive or limiting to the patient's welfare. This, of course, is identical to what would be understood by Rycroft (1983) as the psychotherapist's transference in the broad sense (i.e., of transferring relationship patterns from the past into current relationships) or in the narrow sense (i.e., the feelings engendered toward the analyst based on transferring relationship patterns or expectations from the patient's [or in this case the psychotherapist's] past). For example, a young psychotherapist may expect that an older patient will find fault with him in the same way as the therapist's father did; he may then reject the patient at the first sign of negativity. Alternatively, the therapist may transfer his or her own suicidal tendencies on to the patient; if the patient is obliging and, for example, needs a parent for whom sacrifice is necessary, the patient may commit suicide, in a sense, for the psychotherapist/parent. English (1969) referred to the hot potato (or episcript) passed from parents to children. In addition, I believe that it can be passed from psychotherapist to patient.

Facilitative pro-active countertransference

This form of countertransference is based on the unavoidable and probably necessary existence of the psychotherapist's individual style and personal preferences. For example, a therapist may enjoy working with people with creativity problems rather than control issues. What makes this transferential, and not based on a newly created Adult discovery in the here-and-now, is the fact that the therapist assumes this on the basis of his or her past experiences. Thus he or she may disallow himself or herself the potential delights of working with patients who are controlling.

Categories of reactive patient countertransference

Every psychotherapist occasionally introduces pro-active countertransference elements–that is, the therapist's self-generated issues–into the therapeutic relationship. For example, a therapist may come to a session late as result of a car accident and the resulting traffic snarl-up. Naturally, patients respond to such events and to the therapist's demeanor, possibly in archaically determined ways via transference or in ways that are more reactive to the therapist's past than to their own.

I also identify another form of countertransference: the patient's reactive countertransference to the therapist's introduction of his or her own material. Technically this is not the patient's transference because it is not based on his or her past material, but is elicited by the therapist's abnormal or pro-active countertransferences. Just as patients can induce therapists to respond/react in ways that are script-reinforcing by means of the hypnotic induction of ulterior communications, so too, can therapists project onto their patients or even affect them by means of projective identification.

Langs (1985) and Casement (1985) have repeatedly addressed the many ways in which the patient provides the psychotherapist with feedback, supervision, and active attempts to "heal" the therapist. However, when neither is aware of this collusion, therapeutic progress may be undermined or destroyed. Searles (1975)

Through the looking glass **47**

also suggested the idea that the patient needs to heal his or her psychotherapist. Alternatively, the patient may try hard to be a good patient because the therapist needs children who work hard but never achieve success.

Complementary patient countertransference

The patient may react complementarily by completing the psychotherapist's real or fantasized projection as Parent or as Child based on the therapist's history or recent past. For example, a patient who does not have issues about taking care of his or her parents may find that he or she is invited or induced to take care of the psychotherapist when the therapist is experienced as tired, burned out, or fragile. The important factor differentiating this from psychotherapist-induced reaction lies in *not* attributing projection to the patient. He or she is *correctly* perceiving the therapist's emotional states as they impinge upon the therapy.

Good therapeutic management of this form of patient countertransference involves identifying what both the psychotherapist and the patient bring into the therapy room, without blaming or attributing causality to the pathology or projection of the patient. The therapist is responsible for separating out such elements from the psychotherapeutic relationship and taking preventive or corrective action through, for example, further analysis and/or additional supervision.

Concordant patient countertransference

Concordant patient countertransference occurs when, for example, the patient identifies with the therapist's denied Child or resonates empathically with the therapist's experience, whether or not those feelings or experiences are valid for the patient. A patient may sense the therapist's fear of violence based on the therapist's unresolved issues about a violent childhood home; in resonating with these feelings, the patient avoids sharing his or her feelings of violence or murderous rage toward the therapist, fearing that the therapist could not cope with it. This process is frequently at work with patients who with a second or third psychotherapist begin to talk about issues that they could not share with the first. According to Miller (1985), such avoidance may also be based on the patient protecting the parent/therapist from dealing with his or her own feelings of abandonment or abuse.

Destructive patient countertransference

This refers to particularly damaging acted-out patterns between psychotherapist and patient that are primarily based on the therapist's pathology. In such cases the therapist's transference may induce pathological responses of an extreme nature, such as "going mad for the psychotherapist," which allows the therapist to avoid dealing with his or her own madness while dealing with the patient's madness.

Facilitative patient countertransference

This form of patient countertransference involves the patient's natural responses to the therapist's style and way of being. After a long and intimate therapeutic relationship which leads to productive changes in a patient's life, he or she may feel fondness and affection for certain qualities of the therapist. An example would be a particularly apt use of metaphor or a clarity of thinking and expression which is not counter-therapeutic but which is based on an appreciation of the particular attributes of the helper.

Conclusion

The meanings of transference and countertransference have been explored and refined in this article by means of comparison, contrast, and clarification. The understanding and application of these various forms of transference and countertransference in psychotherapeutic and supervisory settings using transactional analysis will be developed in an article to be presented in an upcoming issue of this journal (Clarkson, 1991).

References

Berne, E. (1969). *A layman's guide to psychiatry and psychoanalysis.* London: Andre Deutsch.

Berne, E. (1975). *Transactional analysis in psychotherapy.* London: Souvenir Press. (Original work published 1961.)

Casement, P. (1985). *On learning from the patient.* London: Tavistock.

Clarkson, P. (1989). Metanoia: A process of transformation. *Institute of Transactional Analysis News, 23*, 5–14.

Clarkson, P. (1990). A multiplicity of psychotherapeutic relationships. *British Journal of Psychotherapy, 7*, 148–163.

Clarkson, P. (1991). Further through the looking glass: Transference, countertransference, and parallel process in transactional analysis psychotherapy and supervision. *Transactional Analysis Journal, 21*, 3, 174–183.

Conway, A., & Clarkson, P. (1987). Everyday hypnotic inductions. *Transactional Analysis Journal, 17*, 17–23.

English, F. (1969). Episcript and the "hot potato" game. *Transactional Analysis Bulletin, 8*(32), 77–82.

Eysenck, H. J., & Rachman, S. (1965). *The causes and cures of neurosis.* London: Routledge & Kegan Paul.

Fairbairn, W. R. D. (1952). *Psychoanalytic studies of the personality.* London: Tavistock.

Federn, P. (1977). Ego psychological aspect of schizophrenia. In P. Federn (Ed.), *Ego psychology and the psychoses* (pp. 210–226). London: Maresfield Reprints. (Original work published 1949.)

Freud, S. (1955). Beyond the pleasure principle. In J. Strachey (Ed. and Trans.), *The standard edition of the complete psychological works of Sigmund Freud* (Vol. 18, pp. 1–64). London: Hogarth Press. (Original work published 1920.)

Freud, S. (1958). The dynamics of the transference. In J. Strachey (Ed. and Trans.), *The standard edition of the complete psychological works of Sigmund Freud* (Vol. 12, pp. 97–108). London: Hogarth Press. (Original work published 1912.)

Gitelson, M. (1952). The emotional position of the analyst in the psychoanalytic situation. *International Journal of Psychoanalysis, 33*, 1–10.

Heimann, P. (1950). On countertransference. *International Journal of Psychoanalysis, 31*, 81–84.

Hinshelwood, R. D. (Ed.) (1989). *A dictionary of Kleinian thought.* London: Free Association Books.

Klein, M. (1984). *Envy, gratitude and other works.* London: Hogarth Press and Institute for Psychoanalysis.

Kohut, H. (1977). *The restoration of the self.* New York: International Universities Press.

Langs, R. (1985). *Workbooks for psychotherapists* (Vols. 1–3). Emerson, NJ: Newconcept.

Lewin, K. (1963). *Field theory in social science: Selected theoretical papers.* London: Tavistock.

Little, M. (1951). Countertransference and the patient's response to it. *International Journal of Psychoanalysis, 32*, 32–40.

Manor, O. (1992). Transactional analysis, object relations, and the systems approach: Finding the counterparts. *Transactional Analysis Journal, 22*(1), 4–15.

Miller, A. (1985). *Thou shalt not be aware: Society's betrayal of the child* (H. & H. Hannum, Trans.). London: Pluto Books. (Original work published 1981.)

Novellino, M. (1984). Self-analysis of countertransference in integrative transactional analysis. *Transactional Analysis Journal, 14*, 63–67.

Pine, F. (1985). *Developmental theory and clinical process.* New Haven, NJ: Yale University Press.

Racker, H. (1982). *Transference and countertransference.* London: Maresfield Reprints. (Original work published 1968.)

Rycroft, C. (1983). *A critical dictionary of psychoanalysis.* Harmondsworth: Penguin.

Searles, H. F. (1975). The patient as therapist to his analyst. In P. L. Giovacchini (Ed.), *Tactics and techniques in psychoanalytic therapy* (Vol. 2, pp. 94–151). New York: Aronson.

Watkins, J. G. (1954). Trance and transference. *Journal of Clinical and Experimental Hypnosis, 2*, 284–290.

Weiss, E. (1950). *Principles of psychodynamics.* New York: Grune & Stratton.

Winnicott, D. W. (1975). Hate in the countertransference. In D. W. Winnicott, *Through paediatrics to psychoanalysis* (pp. 194–203). London: Hogarth Press.

3

AN OVERVIEW OF THE PSYCHODYNAMIC SCHOOL OF TRANSACTIONAL ANALYSIS AND ITS EPISTEMOLOGICAL FOUNDATIONS

Carlo Moiso and Michele Novellino

One of the things that motivated us to choose transactional analysis as the form of psychotherapy we would use was that its interventions are based on patients' actual behaviors. This made it necessary to train ourselves to be good observers of what is actually occurring. Observation being the key point for the transactional analyst, we begin this article with some observations about transactional analysis itself.

1. *At the level of the general public:* Many people have a distorted view of transactional analysis as a short-term psychotherapy, as a behavioral therapy applied in groups, or as merely a form of intervention that focuses on resocialization. We might consider all of these to be prejudices, but to those who hold such views, they usually represent fact.

2. *At the academic level:* Stewart (1992), quoting Kovel (1976) and Yalom (1970), pointed out that transactional analysis is often viewed in academia as a sort of Freudian theory made simple in which the dominant philosophy invites conformism and the only methodological value is linguistic. However, even the language used in transactional analysis is considered a weak point because it is often colloquial and sometimes esoteric. We have also observed that in the present scientific culture there is generally a lack of bibliographical referencing to transactional analysis. The fact is, in the academic world transactional analysis is rather isolated with respect to the study of psychotherapy, leading to the minimization of the influence of Bernean thinking.

3. *At the level of the transactional analysis world:* First, we have observed an epistemological uncertainty as manifested by many inconsistencies both within transactional analysis theory itself and between the theoretical model and clinical methodology. Second, theoretical debates in the transactional analysis community are used less as a vehicle for intellectual challenge and more as a pretext for political fights between factions and trends.

We think that all of these problems stem from the fact that the original analytic roots of Berne's work have been almost completely abandoned instead of becoming the object of in-depth studies, research, and updating. The continuous use of clinical techniques borrowed from other approaches, rather than furthering a coherent clinical methodology for the analysis of actual transactions, games, and scripts, has resulted in "identity diffusion" (Novellino, 1998) for transactional analysis and transactional analysts.

The birth of transactional analysis can be traced back to 1949 when psychiatrist Eric Berne wrote the first in a series of six articles on intuition. In these initial writings we find some of the epistemological concerns of transactional analysis, such as, on one hand, its psychoanalytic matrix and, on the other, attention to cybernetics, nonverbal communication, and neurophysiology. These latter areas of study led Berne to conceptualize ego states as phenomenological developments with clinical relevance. In 1957 he published "Ego states in psychotherapy," in which for the first time the concepts of Parent, Adult, and Child along with contamination and structural analysis were presented. In 1958, "Transactional analysis: A new and effective method of group psychotherapy" was published, and transactional analysis was officially born for the broader academic world.

It is worthwhile noting that Berne's personal and professional positions were similar to those of some other founders of new approaches (such as Perls and Reich) who, although originally trained in orthodox psychoanalysis, "rebelled" against Freudian theory and its analytical setting. Considering the different historical phases in the development of transactional analysis, it is clear that stressing only this rebellious aspect has blurred the position of transactional analysis in the panorama of psychotherapies. Transactional analysts themselves often do not agree on where to place the approach (is it humanistic? Or psychoanalytic? Or eclectic-integrative?). While some colleagues view this as evidence of the great flexibility of transactional analysis, we see it as the manifestation of severe epistemological uncertainty.

In his chapter on the evolution of transactional analysis, Dusay (1977) outlined the development of Berne's theory in terms of phases. The first three phases—ego states, rules of communication and games, and script theory—referred to theory development while Berne was alive. We think that an analytical review is needed to study the evolution of transactional analysis since Berne's death. First, we need to take into consideration two approaches that, even before Berne's death, were considered to be recognized "schools" of transactional analysis: the Schiffs' (Schiff et al., 1975) reparenting approach and the Gouldings' (1979) redecision therapy. The Schiffs applied the frames of reference of transactional analysis to the treatment of schizophrenic disorders to develop an analytic-transactional system based on a clinical perspective. The Gouldings, colleagues of both Perls and Berne, laid the foundation for the integration of transactional analysis and other therapies (in their case, gestalt therapy) that has dominated post-Bernean transactional analysis.

The Gouldings' influence on the worldwide growth of transactional analysis in the late 1970s led to two opposing phenomena:

1. An enormous process of professional affiliation that resulted in the ITAA acquiring thousands of members all over the world.
2. A progressive detachment from early Bernean analytic roots that we believe left transactional analysis not only with the identity diffusion already mentioned, but also with an unfortunate lack of recognition of the Bernean approach by the other classical schools of psychotherapy, including psychoanalysis, systemic therapy, cognitive-behavioral therapy, and constructivism. This is even more disconcerting when we realize that many of Berne's original concepts are now fully integrated into these other approaches.

In our view, one of the main factors contributing to the difficult position transactional analysis finds itself in today is the existence of epistemological problems inherent in Berne's work. Many transactional analysis scholars have pointed out such inconsistencies, such as differing definitions of ego states (e.g., metaphors, biological structures with specific functions, manifestations of historical persons) and vagueness in clinical methodology, especially regarding the treatment of script. Reading the transactional analysis literature and participating in international conferences, we can clearly see that it is still difficult to articulate a unitary version of Bernean theory. We suggest that the unavoidable conclusion to be drawn from all of this is that the origin of the problem lies in a lack of scientific method with regard to Bernean theory. If we in the transactional analysis community were to accept this view instead of defending Berne at all costs, the effects could be revolutionary.

Let us return to some observations. Berne often gave different versions of his own ideas without explaining the reasons for these changes in his thinking. In relation to psychoanalysis, for example, Berne seemed to oscillate between frequent references to it and an apparent compulsion to differentiate transactional analysis from it absolutely. Even the post-Bernean history of transactional analysis has been marked by this ambivalence. As evidence of this situation we recall the resistance that the clinical use of the concept of transference (which is currently so fashionable) in transactional analysis met in the early 1980s, when transactional analysis coincided primarily with redecision therapy.

Today, in 2000, the importance of the psychoanalytic roots of transactional analysis is muddled by integrating the concept of transference as one element among many others, thus setting up a process that neutralizes the enormous methodological and clinical consequences of accepting and working with the transferential and countertransferential dimensions of transactions that occur within the psychotherapeutic relationship.

In our opinion, the best of Berne can be found in his pioneering criticism (now largely shared by the psychoanalytic world) that Freud, anchored as he was to the medical-mechanistic view of his time, was detached from problems of a phenomenological nature. Berne (1961) proposed transactional analysis as an advancement of psychoanalysis: It originated as an attempt to build a systematic phenomenology aimed at filling the void in social theory that limited psychoanalysis. In these terms, the concept of psychological games is an excellent example of the attempt to move away from a closed, genetic epistemology (e.g., defense mechanisms) to a motivational epistemology that is open and interpersonally based. This was Berne's primary teaching, one that the scientific transactional analysis community could have, or should have, followed. Instead, often this teaching has been lost in attempts to blend transactional analysis with a multitude of other approaches in a sort of eclecticism that has led transactional analysis to intellectual and professional isolation (see Stewart, 1992). Thus we see that an essential theme for transactional analysis at this point in time is to clarify its place within the world of psychotherapy. Fortunately, work aimed at realigning transactional analysis with a more scientifically sound perspective is already underway. We would like here to draw attention to some of the works that, in our opinion, can enhance the credibility of transactional analysis.

Zerin (1989), writing on the application of epistemology to psychotherapy, pointed out that modern developments in the philosophy of science emphasize a movement during the 20th century away from an epistemology of certainty toward an epistemology of uncertainty. That is, movement has been away from the "search for truth" to the search for models of knowledge that can inform our search for truth and thus our understanding of the universe. The conflict between the Platonic (deductive) model and the Aristotelian (inductive) model has given way to an interdependency between deductive and inductive models. Zerin stressed the profound influence that non-psychological models (e.g., Heisenberg, Tarsky, Godel) have had on psychotherapy. By so doing, he highlighted the risk of reifying Bernean theory and thus confusing theory with reality and maps with territory. Similar concepts were brilliantly outlined by Loria (1990, 1995). He described how Berne used metaphors to explain mental abstractions, forgetting to keep their figurative use in the foreground. In time, such metaphors assumed a meaning of their own, that is, theory became reality (e.g., Parent, Adult, and Child became synonymous with values, thinking, and feeling). In this process, Berne was following psychoanalytic tradition.

Another author worthy of mention is Rath (1993), who made a fundamental proposal: to revisit the theory of ego states in light of the principle of self-organization. This principle states that the mind can be considered as a self-organizing system, in equilibrium with the environment through transactions.

There is, in our view, one major misunderstanding that needs to be cleared up before it is possible to resume the thread of Bernean research. That is the idea that transactional analysis is a humanistic theory and practice and therefore different from the psychoanalytic and behavioral approaches (Clarkson, 1992). This classification of transactional analysis involves a confusion of logical levels. The humanistic psychology movement (Rogers, May, Maslow, etc.) is, from an ontological perspective, a movement of opinions and ideological positions about the nature of human beings and the role of the therapist in counseling and psychotherapy. This does not have much to do with establishing methodological or meta-psychological grounds!

By viewing transactional analysis as a humanistic theory and practice, the psychoanalytic roots of Berne's work have been repressed (probably not totally unconsciously), thus diminishing the depth of its theory. If we want to stop the impoverishment of Berne's approach, we must acknowledge that its revolutionary nature must be found in terms of psychoanalysis, in relation to which Berne offered both continuity and antithesis. It is relevant to note that external sources, such as Freedman, Kaplan, and Sadock (1976), put transactional analysis in the psychoanalytic-interpersonal school. Likewise, Brown and Pedder (1979) considered transactional analysis to be a "valid psychodynamic school" (p. 44).

The last, but by no means the least, issue we want to address here is the clinical methodology of transactional analysis. Keeping in mind the criteria set by Barnes (1977, pp. 3–13), we think that today there are five schools within transactional analysis: classical, redecision, reparenting, integrative-eclectic, and psychodynamic (or neo-Bernean). The last of these, articulated in our earlier work (Moiso, 1985; Novellino, 1985, 1987, 1998; Novellino & Moiso, 1990), finds its origins in the work of Haykin (1980) and Woods and Woods (1981, 1982). It sets precedents for two styles of working: within the group setting (Moiso) or in individual work that involves the clinical use of the psychoanalytic roots of transactional analysis (Novellino). In both cases, our epistemological aim is to reconstruct that form of internal congruence that will return transactional analysis to its rightful position within the modern psychoanalytical movement.

One direct consequence of reviving the psychoanalytic roots of transactional analysis is that in the psychodynamic approach the therapeutic operation of interpretation once again plays a central role in the psychotherapeutic process. This has fundamental clinical consequences, especially for the treatment setting. For example, an essential tool in the psychodynamic approach is the analysis of transference and countertransference (Moiso, 1985; Novellino, 1985, 1987; Woods, 1995). We take care to differentiate our approach, which is based on actual transactions (especially as manifestations of transferential phenomena such as, for example, the ongoing differentiation of the group imago) between a patient and the transactional analyst or the other patients in a group, from other approaches in which the transferential phenomena are theoretically integrated but do not form part of a planned, analytical clinical process and instead are handled with gestalt redecision or reparenting techniques.

Thus, the clinical methodology we use is based on the constant analysis of actual transactions and games, considered as behavioral and social manifestations of internal narratives. We agree with Allen and Allen (1997) that the script is a story that is cocreated in an ongoing process and that transference is cocreated in the present. Our point is that transactional analysis is absolutely based on the analysis of transactions and games as they occur in therapy. There are many other excellent, effective forms of psychotherapy based on transactional analysis concepts, but in our opinion, blending non-transactional analysis methodologies with almost abstract versions of Bernean concepts has been detrimental to the internal congruence and epistemological validity of transactional analysis.

We think that there are a few points that cannot be relinquished or set aside. A therapy contract must be developed that indicates the desired outcome of therapy, although a routine session contract is often contraindicated in ongoing weekly therapy based on Bernean operations. The analysis of the patient's mental constructs (ego states being the Bernean metaphor to describe them) at any specific time is done through the analysis of actual transactions between the patient and the therapist or the patient and other group members. Special emphasis is placed on duplex (ulterior) transactions based on transference and countertransference. Transactions are analyzed conversationally and are viewed as an expression of the ongoing creation, re-creation, and cocreation of the script. In fact, we find that the constructionistic approach is the best bridge between the Bernean theories of ego states and script and the phenomena of transferential and countertransferential transaction.

The analysis of games is based on their function as a means of binding people together to recocreate past dramas and the fact that they represent the reenactment of a basic impulse-frustration internal narration loop.

The analysis of scripts is not confined to an induced emotional reexperiencing of protocol scenes; rather, scripts are seen as lived-out stories that are cocreated in an ongoing process.

The trend in psychoanalysis today (often referred to as interpersonal or intersubjective) is clearly Bernean in that interpretation consists of supplying the patient with a decoded, detoxified narration about the coded narration offered by the patient through the use of ulterior transactions or games. Note that "narration" is the only word added here to how Berne (1966) presented interpretation in *Principles of Group Treatment*.

When people think of a psychoanalytic approach to transactional analysis, they often remember how Berne made frequent links to classical Freudian theory. We should instead consider the most recent evolution of psychoanalysis, such as (but not limited to) object relations theory. We consider that therapy is a cocreated conversation between people, and we think that the new conversationalist approach to psychoanalysis shows how Berne was a great innovator of psychoanalysis and how Bernean (and, if we might be allowed, neo-Bernean) transactional analysis is perhaps the most promising form of a neo-psychoanalytic psychotherapy.

References

Allen, J. R., & Allen, B. A. (1997). A new type of transactional analysis and one version of script work with a constructionist sensibility. *Transactional Analysis Journal, 27*, 89–98.

Barnes, G. (1977). Introduction. In G. Barnes (Ed.), *Transactional analysis after Eric Berne: Teaching and practices of three TA schools* (pp. 3–13). New York: Harper's College Press.

Berne, E. (1949). The nature of intuition. *Psychiatric Quarterly, 23*, 203–226.

Berne, E. (1957). Ego states in psychotherapy. *American Journal of Psychotherapy, 11*, 293–309.

Berne, E. (1958). Transactional analysis: A new and effective method of group psychotherapy. *American Journal of Psychotherapy, 12*, 735–743.

Berne, E. (1961). *Transactional analysis in psychotherapy: A systematic individual and social psychiatry*. New York: Grove Press.

Berne, E. (1966). *Group treatment*. New York: Grove Press.

Brown, D., & Pedder. J. (1979). *Introduction to psychotherapy*. London: Tavistock.

Clarkson, P. (1992). *Transactional analysis psychotherapy: An integrated approach*. London and New York: Tavistock/Routledge.

Dusay, J. M. (1977). The evolution of transactional analysis. In G. Barnes (Ed.), *Transactional analysis after Eric Berne: Teaching and practices of three TA schools* (pp. 33–52). New York: Harper's College Press.

Freedman, A. M., Kaplan, H. I., & Sadock, B. J. (1976). *Modern synopsis of comprehensive textbook of psychiatry*. Baltimore: Williams & Wilkins.

Goulding, M. M., & Goulding, R. L. (1979). *Changing lives through redecision therapy*. New York: Brunner/Mazel.

Haykin, M. D. (1980). Type casting: The influence of early childhood experience upon the structure of the child ego state. *Transactional Analysis Journal, 10*, 354–364.

Kovel, J. (1976). *A complete guide to therapy*. Harmondsworth: Pelican.

Loria, B. R. (1990). Epistemology and reification of metaphor in transactional analysis. *Transactional Analysis Journal, 20*, 152–162.

Loria, B. R. (1995). Structure determinism and script analysis: A bringing forth of alternative realities. *Transactional Analysis Journal, 25*, 156–168.

Moiso, C. (1985). Ego states and transference. *Transactional Analysis Journal, 15*, 194–201.

Novellino, M. (1985). Redecision analysis of transference: A TA approach to transference neurosis. *Transactional Analysis Journal, 15*, 202–206.

Novellino, M. (1987). Redecision analysis of transference: The unconscious dimension. *Transactional Analysis Journal, 17*, 271–276.

Novellino, M. (Ed.) (1998). *L'approccio clinico dell analisi transazionale [The transactional analysis clinical approach]*. Milan: F. Angeli.

Novellino, M., & Moiso, C. (1990). The psychodynamic approach to transactional analysis. *Transactional Analysis Journal, 20*, 187–192.

Rath, I. (1993). Developing a coherent map of transactional analysis theories. *Transactional Analysis Journal, 23*, 201–215.

Schiff, J. L., with Schiff, A. W., Mellor, K., Schiff, E., Schiff, S., Richman, D., Fishman, J., Wolz, L., Fishman, C., & Momb, D. (1975). *Cathexis reader: Transactional analysis treatment of psychosis*. New York: Harper & Row.

Stewart, I. (1992). *Eric Berne*. London: Sage.

Woods, K. (1995). The indirect analysis of manifestations of transference and countertransference. *Transactional Analysis Journal, 25*, 245–249.

Woods, M., & Woods, K. (1981). Ego splitting and the TA diagram. *Transactional Analysis Journal, 11*, 130–133.

Woods, M., & Woods, K. (1982). Treatment of borderline conditions. *Transactional Analysis Journal, 12*, 188–300.

Yalom, I. (1970). *The theory and practice of group psychotherapy*. New York: Basic Books.

Zerin, E. (1989). Epistemology and psychotherapy. *Transactional Analysis Journal, 19*, 80–85.

4

THERAPEUTIC RELATEDNESS IN TRANSACTIONAL ANALYSIS

The truth of love or the love of truth

William F. Cornell and Frances Bonds-White

The past decade has seen a shift in clinical theorizing among ego-oriented psychodynamic theories, transactional analysis among them. Interpretation and insight are no longer viewed as the primary means of therapeutic change. Therapists of many theoretical orientations now focus on the relational, transferential, and countertransferential components of the therapeutic process. The clinical literature is overflowing with relational models and language: mutuality, empathy, attunement, attachment, the holding environment, object relations, implicit relational knowing, intersubjectivity, reciprocity, emotional synchronicity, connectedness, the moment of meeting, and resonance. The relational zeitgeist has been further fueled by the popularity of such feminist-centered models as the relational model being developed at the Stone Center of Wellesley College and trauma-centered perspectives, both of which emphasize the active, maternal/corrective/relational role of the therapist. While the maternal/relational perspectives have done much to correct the unidirectional, paternalistic, authoritarian styles that dominated classical psychoanalytic and cognitive/behavioral orientations, we now see unquestioning applications of various relational models in contemporary transactional analysis that we think merit serious critique.

In "Analysis terminable and interminable," a deeply reflective clinical essay written by Freud (1964) shortly before his death, he was still struggling with the nature of the therapeutic process. For Freud it was the love of the truth—the willingness to acknowledge psychic realities, to face oneself as honestly as possible—that was at the heart of the therapeutic process. We also see the commitment to therapy as a commitment to ruthless honesty on the part of both client and therapist. However, it seems that in many contemporary therapies, the relational field between therapist and client has been reversed from the love of truth to the truth of love, where the experience of being cared for and mirrored supersedes the experience of facing and understanding emotional and characterological realities. We suggest that in the long, often hard process of psychotherapy, it is ultimately the love (a facing) of the truth that is curative.

There has always been a tendency within transactional analysis psychotherapy to focus on personal change and management of emotions, rather than to struggle for a deeper understanding of the ambivalences of love and hate that motivate all human relationships. The central premise of this article is that if transactional analysis does not face and treat the darker, more conflictual aspects of people's functioning, we will be limited in what we offer clients and equally limited as to which clients we can effectively treat.

This article examines applications within transactional analysis of theories that emphasize empathy, attunement, and attachment as the primary tools in the therapeutic repertoire. We suggest that such an orientation can lead to enacting a subtle form of reparenting, which represents a considerable deviation from Berne's emphasis on personal responsibility, intrapsychic conflict, interpersonal manipulation, and the construction of one's life script. We find that the overuse of relational concepts in contemporary transactional analysis can result in an oversimplification of the therapeutic process, an overemphasis on the activity of the therapist, and a turning away from intrapsychic and interpersonal conflicts as crucial elements of psychotherapy.

The Parent ego state and the role of the therapist

Since its origin, transactional analysis has placed great emphasis on the therapist's use, in one form or another, of his or her Parent ego states. Berne's delineation of the Parent ego state, both in structure and function, was an important correction for the classical psychoanalytic position of the neutral observer and the mechanistic operations of the behavioral models that Berne challenged during his lifetime. However, there has been a long-standing and problematic tendency in transactional analysis theory and technique to project the "bad stuff" out onto parental failure, environmental failure, and the larger social structure. This projective stance has been imbedded in transactional analysis language and theory from the beginning, as exemplified by Berne's (1972) notions of the "ogre father" and the "witch mother," Steiner's (1974) use of the term "Pig Parent," and the entire reparenting model of treatment (Schiff, 1977; Schiff et al., 1975). All too often the transactional analysis therapist is cast as a provider of the "good stuff" rather than as a clarifier of how the client maintains ineffective, other-destructive, and self-destructive patterns of defense. This bias in transactional analysis theory creates a consequent pressure on the therapist to move into a good parent/good object position vis-à-vis the client. When we help a client to "experience enough," to draw on a frequently advertised transactional analysis parenting slogan as an example, frequently all that we have accomplished is a temporary, mutually gratifying, narcissistic merger. When we envelope a client in empathic and attuned mirroring, we suggest that little is actually repaired and that nothing is changed in the client's psychological structure. By calming distress—the therapist's as well as the client's—we merely eliminate or postpone the struggles that are necessary for characterological change and psychological mastery. More problematically, we are in danger of promoting a nostalgically idealized infantile/maternal fantasy split off from the ongoing difficulties of actual life, not to mention the meaner side of human nature.

Berne's departure from the psychoanalysis of his day represented an effort at a radical critique of the traditional analysis of the individual psyche through free association, dream interpretation, and other classical techniques. He clearly created a transactional analysis, not a relational psychotherapy. Nowhere in his writings did he suggest that it was the internalization of the therapeutic relationship itself that cured the client. Rather, the task of the transactional analysis therapist is to facilitate the client's reflection on the ways, reasons, and beliefs in his or her style of relating so that the client has the choice to change how he or she relates. The therapist is a careful, honest observer of relationship patterns and beliefs, as we see in Berne's conceptualizations of games, rackets, and scripts. Berne (1967) watched, listened, thought about, described, interpreted, analyzed, and disrupted how people transacted with one another.

Ultimately, Berne maintained a one-person psychotherapy in that these interactions were analyzed in light of the social and psychological advantages the individual believed could be gained from the interactions. He offered an opportunity to see, think about, and alter how one thinks and behaves. His transactional analysis was intended to unsettle a client's familiar, defensive frame of reference through description, confrontation, interpretation, and humor. It seems quite clear that Berne's intent, consistent with a classical psychoanalytic position, was to alter the intrapsychic structure and function of the client through clarifying interventions, not through offering a corrective relationship.

Introspection, on the other hand, takes the cover off the black box, and lets the Adult of the person peer into his own mind to see how it works: how he puts sentences together, which directions his images come from, and what voices direct his behavior (Berne, 1972, p. 273).

Thus we see that Berne's treatment group was not an empathic holding environment but an interpersonal study matrix. For example, in *Principles of Group Treatment*, he outlined eight therapeutic operations that "form the technique of transactional analysis" (Berne, 1966, p. 233). These included interrogation, specification, confrontation, explanation, illustration (humor and simile), confirmation, interpretation, and crystallization (pp. 233–247). These therapeutic operations are carefully described, illustrated, and clarified with warnings about how and when to use and not to use them. Note that empathy, holding, and attachment are not on this list. Rather, Berne's therapeutic interventions were designed to elicit self-observation and curiosity, to decontaminate and stabilize Adult ego state functioning.

Berne (1966) went on to describe "other types of interventions" (pp. 248–249) in which "the therapist may have to function deliberately as a Parent rather than as an Adult for a shorter or longer period, sometimes extending into years" (p. 248).

These Parental interventions are support, reassurance, persuasion, and exhortation, which Berne suggested are most appropriate and necessary in the treatment of active schizophrenics.

Unfortunately, we see here a vagueness and confusion in Berne's use of terms, a confusion repeated over and over again in his writing and transactional analysis practice. His capitalization of Parent and Adult in this section suggests that he was describing a shift from the therapist having the Adult ego state in executive to having the Parent ego state in executive. We doubt that Berne intended that the therapist become a parental figure, but that, in fact, has become common transactional analysis practice.

For Berne (1972), the therapist sometimes made explicit use of his or her Parent ego state, as is clear in his description of the Parental functions of the transactional analyst in the use of permission, protection, and potency:

> Now we can speak with some assurance of the "three P's" of therapy, which determine the therapist's effectiveness. These are potency, permission, and protection. The therapist must give the Child permission to disobey Parental injunctions and provocations. In order to do that effectively, he must be and feel potent: not omnipotent, but potent enough to deal with the patient's Parent. Afterward he must feel potent enough, and the patient's Child must believe he is potent enough, to offer protection from Parental wrath. Here the transactions are: (1) Hook the Adult, or wait until it is active. (2) Form an alliance with the Adult. (3) State your plan and see if the Adult agrees with it. (4) If everything is clear, give the Child permission to disobey the Parent. This must be done clearly and in simple imperatives, with no ifs, ands, or buts. (5) Offer the Child protection from the consequences. (6) Reinforce this by telling the Adult that this is all right.
>
> *(pp. 374–375)*

Berne clearly focused on the identification and management of intrapsychic conflict. He described the therapist's use of the Adult ego state to enhance the client's Adult functioning on behalf of the conflicts within the Child ego state. He was not offering an empathic, corrective parenting experience. Berne was, in essence, saying to the client, "I am strong enough to stand up to and outside of the psychic forces operating inside of you. You can see that it is possible to tolerate the internal conflict that attends change. You can make choices of your own." Berne modeled containment, offering not so much a holding environment as a facilitating environment, to draw on the language of Bion and Winnicott. He offered a model of challenge, alignment with the Adult, and thoughtfully timed interventions to free the client to think and feel autonomously. He did not close the "as if" space of the therapeutic process by becoming a parental figure, but he did draw on the force of the parental attitudes of permission, protection, and potency to create a psychological space within which the client has the opportunity to develop autonomous functioning.

Mother–infant research: clinical implications

Even as we appreciate Berne and his therapeutic stance, we do not wish to ignore his limitations. It is clear that cognitive insight, interpretation, the analysis of transactions, blackboard diagrams, and wittily phrased observations are not always sufficient to reach those deeper levels of the psyche that sometimes fear and oppose psychological awareness and change. Along with other psychodynamic therapies, transactional analysis has begun looking at research on early human development in order to develop deeper understandings of pre-Oedipal disorders. In fact, one of the strengths of approaches that emphasize empathy and attachment is the attention paid to preverbal formative experiences, since difficulties in the earliest months of life may underlie aspects of later script decisions.

Berne had little sense of the preverbal mother–infant relationship. In *What Do You Say after You Say Hello?* (1972), his discussion of prenatal and infant influences on script development consists of little more than clever lists of "breast-fed titles" and "bathroom scenes." He seems to have given little or no attention to Winnicott's (1958d, 1965) infant–mother observations, even though these were published during the time in which Berne was writing.

The mother–infant research that has taken place since Berne's death—including that of Mahler (1968), D. N. Stern (1985), Tronick (1998a), Lachmann and Beebe (1996), Emde (1988), Ainsworth (1969), and Main (1995), among others—has added rich dimensions to our understanding of the somatic and relational elements of script. This research has demonstrated the complexity of the infant's unfolding psyche, with its gradual and relentless integration of limbic, sensorimotor, and cognitive functioning (Bucci, 1997; Downing, 1996; Lichtenberg, 1989). Recent years have also seen the gradual application of infant research to adult psychotherapy. These clinical speculations are important, but it is equally important to understand that the adult therapeutic relationship is not a mirror or re-creation of the mother–infant relationship. Certainly aspects of the mother–infant experience will emerge in the therapeutic process with many clients, but so too will many other aspects and periods of psychic development. Green (2000) has written a compelling critique of the clinical applications of mother–infant research and offers a powerful reminder about the complexity of forces operating in adult psychotherapy.

An entire recent volume of the *Infant Mental Health Journal* (Tronick, 1998b) was devoted to a series of articles generated by the Change Process Study Group of Boston on the application of infant research to adult psychotherapy. These initial efforts are exciting, fascinating, and seriously flawed. In a critical discussion of the articles in that journal, Modell (1998) cautions:

> The analogy between adult and infant dyads breaks down at several points. One is that the adult therapeutic dyad, unlike the mother-infant dyad, is not a biologically determined process; second, in the adult therapeutic dyad both participants are encumbered with the weight of their affective memories of the past, whereas in the infant-mother dyad, the infant's past is just beginning.

> Therapeutic change in the adult entails a retranscription of affective memory; there is, especially in the cases of trauma, an implicit agenda—a transcendence and transformation of the past. This is not the infant's agenda.
>
> *(pp. 342–343)*

Overemphasis on the mother–infant relationship as the model for psychotherapy forces a regression in the therapeutic relationship and discounts the lived experience of the adult. Concerns over attunement, mirroring, or mutual regulation that have emerged from attention to the mother–infant relationship are one aspect of psychic development, but so are the infant's and child's capacities for motoric and cognitive competence, self-understanding, and individuation. Lichtenberg (1983, 1989; Lichtenberg, Lachmann, & Fosshage, 1992) presented a comprehensive application of infant research to developmental forces that span the human life and to adult psychotherapy. In a theory of motivation that is remarkably similar to Berne's conceptualization of human hungers, Lichtenberg (1989) described five motivational systems present at birth and operational throughout life. These include: (1) the psychic regulation of physiological requirements, (2) the attachment-affiliation system, (3) the exploratory-assertive system, (4) the withdrawal-aversive system, and (5) the sensual-sexual system.

Lichtenberg's motivational system involves, first, the infant/child's evolving capacities to use psychological capacities to respond to physiological needs and pressures. The attachment/affiliation system refers to the formation and maintenance of infant–parent bonds, extending the work of Bowlby and his followers, work now well known to most transactional analysis practitioners. The exploratory/assertive system refers to the capacity for aggression and moving out into the world, be it for self-protection or self-enhancing desires, while the withdrawal/aversive system describes the capacity to move away from the world for rest, privacy, or self-protection. Finally, the sensual/sexual system reflects the central, enduring importance of the body in relation to itself and others. Relational hungers are but one element in this motivational system, which emphasizes the infant's and young child's capacity for differentiation and competence as much as the need for relational attachment and contact.

We strongly suggest that any comprehensive model of psychotherapy must involve each of these motivational systems, being careful not to idealize one over another.

Bowlby and Winnicott: achieving a therapeutic stance

The understanding of infant psychic processes came as a new awareness to ego psychologists and enabled them to work more systematically and effectively with early developmental disorders. However, the psychic life of infants has been explored by the Kleinians and the British Independent/Middle school for decades. Analysands of Ferenzci—namely Melanie Klein, who began lecturing in England in 1925, and Michael Balint, who migrated from Hungary to England in 1939—addressed the

Therapeutic relatedness in TA **63**

manner in which infants apprehend, perceive, and experience relationships with objects, both internal and external. Fairbairn (1952), Guntrip (1961), (Winnicott, 1958c, 1965), Balint (1969), Bion (1977), and Bollas (1987, 1989) have built on this work. Decades before direct infant observation research in the United States, these theorists saw the foundations of psychic structure and unconscious processes as rooted in the earliest months of life. They emphasized the crucible of the mother–infant relationship and posited curiosity as a basic drive and phantasy as a basic mechanism of all mental activity. Parallel with the work of these object relations theorists, Bowlby (1969) conducted research with infants and children which led to his theories on separation, attachment, loss, and the secure base.

In current transactional analysis practice, versions of Bowlby's emphasis on attachment patterns, Winnicott's holding environment, and Kohut's empathic attunement are replacing the original conceptualization of the Nurturing Parent. There is much to be appreciated about this addition to transactional analysis practice. However, in our reading of recent transactional analysis literature and through our participation in examination preparations and processes, we have grown concerned about the misunderstanding and fusion of disparate theories and techniques. Mixing the ideas of Bowlby (an ethnological model based on instinctual drives) with those of Kohut (a relational model developed to address American ego psychologists' disinclination to work with pre-Oedipal conditions) and Winnicott (an observer of mother–child interactions) has occurred without also noting critical differences among these theoretical models. This theoretical "hash" creates an illusion of the convergence of ideas and clinical techniques. To those outside the transactional analysis community, this hash of ideas undermines the conceptual soundness of various efforts to deepen transactional analytic theory. To contribute to that deepening, and to the need for clarification, we concentrate here on the concepts and techniques that, in current discussions, are most frequently referenced: those of Bowlby, Winnicott, and Kohut.

As we examine the applications of Bowlby's work and attachment theory to adult psychotherapy (Bowlby, 1979; Gaines, 1997; Holmes, 1996; Karen, 1998), we find descriptions of a therapeutic relationship and process that are remarkably similar to Berne's. Attachment therapists use a concept of "internal working models" (Bowlby, 1979, pp. 117–118) that is virtually indistinguishable from the essence of Berne's script theory. In Bowlby's (1979, pp. 145–149) description of the tasks of the therapist, he sounds quite like Berne. The "secure base" (pp. 145–146), a fundamental concept in Bowlby's model, is not an empathic immersion but a solid ground from which the client can explore himself or herself and the world. Bowlby invited the client to observe relational patterns and their underlying beliefs to help him consider how the situations into which he typically gets himself and his typical reactions to them, including what may be happening between himself and the therapist, may be understood in terms of real-life experiences he had with attachment figures during his childhood and adolescence (and perhaps may still be having) and of what his responses to them then were (and may still be) (p. 146). In addition, attachment-based therapists now stress the client's development of the "reflexive self function" (Fonagy, Steele, Steele, Moran, & Higgitt, 1991; Holmes, 1996), which is again remarkably consistent with Berne's emphasis on capacities of the Adult ego state to observe the total person.

In Winnicott's object relations model, there is a progressive and ever-differentiating development that moves from absolute dependence to relative dependence to relative independence and finally to interdependence. This is paralleled by the development of interaction with the primary caretaker, which moves from merger with the object to relating to the object, to destroying the object, to the ability to use the object. In Winnicott's understanding of the role of the primary caretaker there is first a phase of "primary maternal preoccupation" (Winnicott, 1958b, pp. 300–305), which begins during pregnancy and lasts for the first few weeks of the baby's life. Winnicott described the mother as being in a special state of consciousness, with her self- and bodily experience centered almost exclusively on the baby's somatic life. In his description of the holding function in the parenting of an infant, Winnicott presented a protective and provisional phase of parenting that is deeply anchored in the body. He described the function of the holding environment as bringing the world of reality to the infant in manageable doses. He saw the need for the holding function reemerging throughout life at transitional phases of childhood and adolescence and during times of severe loss, stress, and disorganization in adult life.

The holding function is, however, more complicated than the simple provision of safety and empathic responsiveness to the infant. Winnicott stressed that during infancy there are times when the parent not only holds on to the infant but also holds against the baby by surviving aggressive urges and ruthless demands. Central to Winnicott's thinking was the importance of the parent surviving the infant's aggression and hatred without undue punishment and retaliation. While parental failure is inevitable and a healthy force in development, retaliation is not. The security that develops through the parent's survival of the infant's aggression gradually enables the infant to be alone with well-being in the presence of another. Winnicott postulated that only in this secure aloneness could the true self emerge.

Winnicott (1971) saw parallels with these ideas in the treatment of difficult, regressive clients:

> The analyst, the analytic technique, and the analytic setting all come in as surviving or not surviving the patient's destructive attacks. ... In psychoanalytic practice the positive changes that come about in this area can be profound. They do not depend on interpretive work. They depend on the analyst's survival of the attacks, which involves and includes the idea of the absence of a quality change to retaliation.
>
> *(p. 91)*

Slochower (1992) offered an excellent case discussion of this aspect of Winnicott's conceptualization of holding, which has far less to do with an attuned understanding of the client than it does with the containment of the therapist's own affect and her survival of her client's behavior.

The Winnicottian infant, rather like the Winnicottian client, is a complex creature, not simply the passive recipient of parental (or therapeutic) largesse. Aggression was defined by Winnicott as movement in the world, beginning with the infant's first kick. The Winnicottian infant, one remarkably similar to those we see in direct infant observation and research, is an active, ambivalent, and aggressive creature, moving away from as well as toward the parent. Winnicott's mother–infant observations and clinical writings are full of exquisite paradoxes. In an article on "Primitive emotional development," for example, he observed:

> I will just mention another reason why an infant is not satisfied with satisfaction. He feels fobbed off. He intended, one might say, to make a cannibalistic attack and he has been put off by an opiate, the feed. At best he can postpone the attack.
>
> *(Winnicott, 1958c, p. 154)*

How often does a therapist offer, wittingly or unwittingly, empathy and comfort—the opiate, the feed—to ward off the ambivalence or aggressiveness of a client?

The Winnicottian infant becomes impatient with holding or feeding. There is a powerful developmental pressure for conflict and differentiation. The primary parental activities shift—often at the infant's initiative—from providing comfort and responses to physiological and affective states to facilitating and enjoying the baby's motor activity, independence, and competence. According to Winnicott, the infant's psyche then begins to dwell within his or her body, and the baby begins to differentiate self from other. The infant, in its developing motoric and ego capacity, presses on:

> The ego *initiates object-relating.* With good-enough mothering at the beginning the baby is not subjected to instinctual gratification except in so far as there is ego-participation. In this respect it is not so much a question of giving the baby satisfaction as of letting the baby find and come to terms with the object (breast, bottle, milk, etc.).
>
> *(Winnicott, 1965, pp. 59–60, italics in the original)*

The Winnicottian infant (and client) is a restless, impatient, and demanding individual, much more interested in competence and differentiation than in perpetual contact and feeding. As clearly delineated in his classic article "Hate in the counter-transference" (Winnicott, 1958a), the Winnicottian mother and therapist are not perpetually attuned and contactful creatures either. Winnicott stressed that unless the mother can tolerate her hate of the baby, she cannot tolerate the baby's hatred of her, and no true affect and no true self can emerge. Instead, the false self will exhibit sentimentality, and the true self will remain hidden.

Therapeutic empathy: a critique

The centrality of an empathic stance in psychotherapy has emerged largely from the work of Kohut (1971) and other self psychologists. In Moses' (1988) detailed examination of the role of empathy in psychotherapy, he pointed out that Kohut was cautious, if not downright skeptical, of the use of empathy early in his work, warning against a "sentimentalizing regression to subjectivity" (Kohut, cited in Moses, 1988, p. 301) and empathy "when it is surrounded by an attitude of wanting to cure directly through the giving of loving understanding" (p. 307). By the end of his life, however, Kohut had come to see empathy and mirroring as curative agents, now warning against the consequences of empathic failure and arguing for a prolonged period of validating the client's reality. During this period it is the therapist's responsibility to demonstrate his or her understanding of how the client feels. This attitude casts the therapist/analyst into the role of the good selfobject, as presented in *The Theory and Practice of Self Psychology* (White & Weiner, 1986):

> The therapist ultimately has the task of trying to become the good self-object. ... [The therapist] will have to empathically try to understand where the adult patient failed to receive the emotional oxygen he or she needed to develop a healthy self and ... begin to fulfil this void.
>
> *(p. 36)*

This model views psychopathology as rooted in developmental deficits and deficiencies, which the therapist/analyst is then positioned to redress by filling voids and providing emotional nutrients.

Erskine and Trautmann are probably the most articulate representatives of this perspective within the contemporary transactional analysis literature:

> With my understanding that *life script and ego states are compensating attempts to manage relationship hunger and a loss of internal contact, the therapeutic focus can be placed on the relationship itself* (Erskine, 1980, 1988). From this perspective the purpose of analyzing ego states or a life script is not to erect a new, more useful structure, but rather to gather information about which relational needs were not met, how the individual coped, and even more importantly, how the satisfaction of today's relational needs can be achieved (Erskine & Trautmann, 1996). These therapeutic tasks are accomplished through contact-oriented, relationship-focused methods:
>
> * *inquiry* into the client's phenomenological experience, transferential process, system of coping, and vulnerability;
> * *attunement* to the client's affect, rhythm, developmental level of functioning, and relational needs; and
> * *involvement* that acknowledges and values the client's uniqueness.
>
> *(Erskine, 1997, p. 15)*

This description of the central therapeutic task is now common in the practice of transactional analysis, whether it carries a reparenting, parenting, corrective parenting, empathic, or attachment label. If psychopathology is environmental in origin, the argument goes, then psychotherapy must be environmentally compensatory in its essential tasks. Storr (1988) reminded us that when Freud was asked what constituted health, he replied that it was the ability to love and work. Storr pointed out that human relationships are "a hub around which a person's life revolves, not necessarily the hub" (p. 15).

D. N. Stern (1985) wrote about empathy in the context of the parent–infant research:

> Seen in this light [intersubjectivist and self psychology], the parent-infant "system" and the therapist-patient "system" appear to have parallels. ... I wish to inject some caution in drawing these analogies too closely, however. What is meant by the therapeutic use of empathy is enormously complex from our point of view. It involves an integration of features that include what we are calling core-, intersubjective, and verbal relatedness as well as what Schafer (1968) has called "generative empathy" and what Basch (1983) has called "mature Empathy." ... Attunement between mother and infant and empathy between therapist and patient are operating at different levels of complexity, in different realms, and ultimately for different purposes.
>
> *(pp. 219–220)*

Moses (1988) argued that "current theory and applications of empathic techniques, however, have become filled with illusions, fallacies and misapplications to the point that the concept is so overextended that it lacks any special meaning and its use has become quite unconstrained" (p. 578). He worried that empathy "has unconsciously and universally slipped into our clinical vocabulary with little scrutiny" (p. 579). Among the therapeutic liabilities that Moses discussed in connection with empathy is the risk that the treatment process and the therapist will be held hostage to the client's or the therapist's narcissistic wounds and vulnerabilities. The therapist may become preoccupied with the fear of being perceived as an uncaring or persecuting object. Perhaps there is also the fear of being perceived, by client or self, as a stupid object, an uncomprehending object, one that does not or will not understand. With the illusion of sufficient empathy, "The therapist does not have to confront the fear of not understanding the patient, or worse yet, let the patient know [that] he doesn't understand [that] certain experiences are beyond comprehension" (p. 590). The mutual wish and subsequent pressure for therapeutic empathy and attunement may create a process in which the therapeutic understanding takes place more in the effort and mind of the therapist than in those of the client, something that we imagine would trouble Berne and that certainly troubles us.

Not knowing or understanding the other can create a rich, if somewhat anxious, space. Bollas (1989) challenged the American demand for knowing and understanding:

> In the United States of America, where many people sue at the drop of a hat, psychoanalysts might live in dread of a patient bringing a court action on the basis that his psychoanalyst doesn't know what he is doing.

After all, other mental health professionals, armed with their diagnostic manual—the DSM III—can practice with certainty. To me this not knowing is an accomplishment.

(p. 62)

For Bollas, as for Winnicott, empathic failure, rather than inevitably creating or recreating a narcissistic wound, can offer creative space and opportunity. Bollas is far more invested in the creation of differentiated and imaginative space than of confluent contact and attuned relatedness.

Stark's work (1999) entered the contemporary debate about relational processes in psychotherapy by delineating three central and enduring modes of therapeutic action and interaction. She did not privilege one mode over another or valorize one at the expense of others. She defined the therapeutic purposes of different aspects of therapeutic relatedness, suggesting that a comprehensive psychotherapy requires differing modes of relatedness over the course of treatment. Stark defined the first mode as providing knowledge through insight and interpretation, a model based on intrapsychic, structural conflict as in the classical psychoanalysis in which Berne had his beginnings. The second therapeutic mode is rooted in the models of developmental/structural deprivation and deficit. In this mode the primary therapeutic action is the therapist's provision of a corrective relational experience, which is what we see emphasized in current transactional analysis approaches centered on attunement and attachment. As summarized by Stark, the second mode stresses: "(1) the therapist's actual participation as a new good object, (2) the therapist's actual gratification of need, and, more generally, (3) the therapist's provision of a corrective (emotional) experience for the patient" (p. 28). The third mode of therapeutic action is one of authenticity and intersubjectivity—therapeutic encounters between two real people in the here and now that manifest and alter archaic beliefs and behaviors.

In Stark's delineation of these modes, the deficit model (mode 2) emphasizes the absence of good in the client's life, while the object relations/intersubjectivist perspective of mode 3 examines the presence of bad in the client's motivations and functioning. In the third mode, the therapist participates authentically in a real relationship with the patient—the intention being both to enhance the patient's understanding of her relational dynamics and to deepen the level of their engagement. Accordingly, in the third mode, the intersubjectivist therapist might choose to focus the patient's attention on (1) the patient's impact on the therapist, (2) the therapist's impact on the patient, or (3) the here-and-now engagement (or lack thereof) between them (p. 126). Within this perspective, the therapist pays close attention to how the client—through actual interactions, projections, and fantasized distortions—creates and maintains bad objects and ineffective or destructive relationships.

Berne's own style, and that typified by classical transactional analysis practitioners, was certainly rooted in the model Stark characterized as mode 1. We suggest that the transactional analysis models based in reparenting, attachment, and attunement models are examples of mode 2. We are not arguing for a distant, neutral therapeutic stance or for one that is constantly interpretive and confrontive (Cornell, 1994, 1997, 2000); rather, we are saying that while empathy, attunement, or attachment are perhaps necessary conditions for therapeutic change, they are not sufficient for enduring psychological change. Our concern is that when empathy and/ or attachment are conceptualized as curative agents, a serious disequilibrium is introduced into the therapeutic process. Transactional analysis clinical theory has grown significantly past Berne's original style, but we strongly suggest that there was much in Berne's original model that continues to be of value. We further suggest that for transactional analysis to be an effective and comprehensive psychotherapy, it must include a process of mutually achieved relatedness in addition to the therapist's provisory relationship. We are arguing for the articulation within the transactional analysis literature of an understanding of the importance of a more complex and conflictual therapeutic space.

Inquiry, disturbance, and creativity

Bollas (1989) sees the therapist and a balanced therapeutic process serving the dual functions of soothing and disturbing the client. He delineates two fundamental, ongoing tasks in working within the transference relationship: elaborating and deconstructing. Elaboration has to do with states of mutual reverie in which the therapist enters the client's field of transferential desire so as to open the unconscious communication between therapist and client to new possibilities of self-expression and relational wishes. The therapist's quiet receptivity, inactivity, and frequent silence are crucial here. The therapist's silence allows the client an intrapsychic, associative freedom for self-discovery and a constructive solitude in the presence of the other. With the deconstructive function, the therapist serves as a disturbing force within the client's interpersonal field, presenting interpretations, queries, and disruptions in much the same way that Berne worked. Renick (1996) offers a similar perspective:

> What the patient wants—and, best case, gets—from the analyst is a perspective different from the patient's own. It is to be hoped that the analyst's perspective is a particularly wise one, but that cannot, and need not, be assumed. Ultimately, an analyst's expertise and appropriate authority do not rest on the premise that the analyst's view of the patient's conflicts is necessarily *more valid* than the patient's own, but rather on the fact that the analyst can provide an *alternative* perspective, a new way of constructing reality, that the patient can put to use—or not—according to the merit the patient finds in it.
>
> *(p. 508, italics in original)*

D. B. Stern (1998) contrasts empathy with the therapeutic function of "inquiry" as described by Sullivan:

> Tolerance of uncertainty and ambiguity are built into the clinical practice of detailed inquiry (Sullivan, 1954). The aim of psychoanalysis carried out

according to these precepts is not necessarily to know what the patient does not know, but rather to specify *that* the patient does not know, and where and when this not knowing takes place. The psychoanalyst who depends on inquiry is not responsible for knowing the patient before the patient does.

(pp. 602–603, italics in original)

Stern's thinking is similar to ours and to the model we want to offer as an alternative to or expansion of concepts of attunement and attachment. He acknowledges that the therapist's questions may well emerge at times from the therapist's empathic imaginings of the client's experience, but he argues that the therapist's task is to identify the client's gaps in experience, not to fill them. Filling the gaps in experience is the client's responsibility and choice. Stern's perspective is one in which the therapist "wishes to stimulate the patient's curiosity about experiences the patient never formulated" (1998, p. 601). The formulation becomes the client's, not the therapist's, much as Berne would say that the decisions are the client's, not the therapist's.

In *The Empathic Imagination*, Margulies (1989) cast the therapeutic uses of wonder and empathy in terms not of relationship and attunement but of self-discovery. He wrote:

I am interested here in the challenges of perceiving freshly and in particular of opportunities for the self to conceive of the self anew; in other words, the therapeutic activity of creativity to the image of self, the opening of new possibilities of self-perception.

(p. 10)

In Margulies's use of empathy, he sought to engage in a creative rather than compensatory process with clients. Empathy, in Margulies's model, is a means of wonder, challenge, questioning, enlivening—at times a clash of worldviews, rather different from a goal of matching and entering the client's lived perspective. The therapist's curiosity about the meaning the client has made of his or her lived experience can awaken the client's curiosity and lead to an examination of and reflection on underlying basic assumptions.

Conclusion

We have drawn here on the work of Margulies, D. B. Stern, Stark, and Bollas, among others, to offer transactional analysis therapists an expanded framework for considering the therapeutic relationship and the central tasks and activity of the therapist. We find that these perspectives are consistent with the stance originally proposed by Berne, although with a depth of affective understanding and involvement that Berne did not accomplish in his lifetime.

It seems crucial to us that transactional analysts draw on original sources to gain a thorough understanding of human development. The writings of Winnicott, Bowlby, Kohut, and others are often significantly more complex than is reflected in transactional analysis training and practices. The work of Winnicott and Bowlby—supplemented by the newer research of D. N. Stern, Emde, and others who are observing real children interacting with parents—is beginning to teach us the norms of human development. This knowledge can help therapists identify deviations from those norms when they are exhibited by clients. This is crucial to understanding childhood decisions and script formations and provides a reference point for the therapist's curiosity about what leads to these deprivations and deviations in a particular individual and how they are defensively maintained in adult life. We further suggest that it is the therapist's and client's mutual curiosity and exploration of an individual's experience that is ultimately curative rather than the alleviation of the psychic pain that developed because of these experiences.

Pain, ambiguity, paradox, and conflict are inevitable in life. They are necessary in a deeply searching psychotherapy and, most importantly, can become vitalizing resources in living one's life. After a half-century of writing about psychoanalysis and the nature of human beings, Freud was still wondering about the heart of the therapeutic process. For him, ultimately, it was the love of truth—the willingness and capacity to acknowledge reality about the self—that was essential in the therapeutic endeavor. Berne offered us a model of precise self-scrutiny, transaction by transaction. The parenting, attunement, and attachment models in transactional analysis suggest that it is the truth of love that is at the heart of psychotherapy. These theorists suggest it is the client's internalization of the therapist's love, understanding, and corrective provision that allows the client to leave the office and create a different life. While we would not disparage the experience of therapeutic empathy and attachment as an important element in the facilitation of the therapeutic process, we are warning against romanticizing and idealizing its curative power. We suggest that it is the gradual development of the client's capacities for curiosity, self-scrutiny, differentiation, and relational conflict within the therapeutic relationship that is carried outside the office as the basis for structural and interpersonal change.

References

Ainsworth, M. D. S. (1969). Object relations, dependency and attachment: A theoretical review of the infant-mother relationship. *Child Development, 40,* 969–1025.

Balint, M. (1969). *The basic fault: Therapeutic aspects of regression.* London: Tavistock.

Basch, M. F. (1983). Empathic understanding: A review of the concept and some theoretical considerations. *Journal of the American Psychoanalytical Association, 31*(1), 101–126.

Berne, E. (1966). *Principles of group treatment.* New York: Oxford University Press.

Berne, E. (1967). *Games people play: The psychology of human relationships.* New York: Grove Press.

Berne, E. (1972). *What do you say after you say hello? The psychology of human destiny.* New York: Grove Press.

Bion, W. R. (1977). *Seven servants.* New York: Jason Aronson.

Bollas, C. (1987). *The shadow of the object: Psychoanalysis of the unthought known.* New York: Columbia University Press.

Bollas, C. (1989). *Forces of destiny.* Northvale, NJ: Jason Aronson.

Bowlby, J. (1969). *Attachment. Vol. 1 of Attachment and loss*. New York: Basic Books.

Bowlby, J. (1979). *The making and breaking of affectional bonds*. London: Tavistock.

Bucci, W. (1997). *Psychoanalysis and cognitive science*. New York: Guilford Press.

Cornell, W. F. (1994). Shame: Binding affect, ego state contamination, and relational repair. *Transactional Analysis Journal, 24*, 139–146.

Cornell, W. F. (1997). If Reich had met Winnicott: Body and gesture. *Energy & Character, 28*(2), 50–60.

Cornell, W. F. (2000). Transference, desire and vulnerability in body-centered psychotherapy. *Energy & Character, 30*(2), 29–37.

Downing, G. (1996). *Körper und Wort in der Psychotherapie [The body and the word in psychotherapy]*. Munich: Koselverlag.

Emde, R. (1988). Development terminable and interminable I: Innate and motivational factors in infancy. *International Journal of Psycho-Analysis, 69*, 23–42.

Erskine, R. G. (1980). Script cure: Behavioral, intrapsychic and physiological. *Transactional Analysis Journal, 10*, 102–106.

Erskine, R. G. (1988). Ego structure, intrapsychic function, and defense mechanisms: A commentary on Eric Berne's original theoretical concepts. *Transactional Analysis Journal, 18*, 15–19.

Erskine, R. G. (1997). The therapeutic relationship: Integrating motivation and personality theories. In R. G. Erskine (Ed.), *Theories and methods of an integrative transactional analysis: A volume of selected articles* (pp. 7–19). San Francisco, CA: TA Press.

Erskine, R. G., & Trautmann, R. L. (1996). Methods of an integrative psychotherapy. *Transactional Analysis Journal, 26*, 316–328.

Fairbairn, W. R. D. (1952). *Psychoanalytic studies of the personality*. London: Routledge & Kegan Paul.

Fonagy, P., Steele, M., Steele, H., Moran, G. S., & Higgitt, A. C. (1991). The capacity for understanding mental states: The reflective self in parent and child and its significance for security of attachment. *Infant Mental Health Journal, 12*, 201–218.

Freud, S. (1964). Analysis terminable and interminable. In J. Strachey (Ed. and Trans.), *The standard edition of the complete psychological works of Sigmund Freud* (Vol. 23, pp. 209–253). London: Hogarth Press. (Original work published 1937.)

Gaines, R. (1997). Detachment and continuity: The two tasks of mourning. *Contemporary Psychoanalysis, 33*, 549–570.

Green, A. (2000). Science and science fiction in infant research. In J. Sandler, A.-M. Sandler, & R. Davies (Eds.), *Clinical and observational research in psychoanalysis: Roots of a controversy* (pp. 41–72). Madison, CT: International Universities Press.

Guntrip, H. (1961). *Personality structure and human interaction*. New York: International Universities Press.

Holmes, J. (1996). *Attachment, intimacy, autonomy: Using attachment theory in adult psychotherapy*. Northvale, NJ: Jason Aronson.

Karen, R. (1998). *Becoming attached: First relationships and how they shape our capacity to love*. New York: Oxford University Press.

Kohut, H. (1971). *The analysis of the self: A systematic approach to the psychoanalytic treatment of narcissistic personality disorders*. New York: International Universities Press.

Lachmann, F., & Beebe, B. (1996). Three principles of salience in the organization of the patient-analyst interaction. *Psychoanalytic Psychology, 13*(1), 1–22.

Lichtenberg, J. D. (1983). *Psychoanalysis and infant research*. Hillsdale, NJ: Analytic Press.

Lichtenberg, J. D. (1989). *Psychoanalysis and motivation*. Hillsdale, NJ: Analytic Press.

Lichtenberg, J., Lachmann, F., & Fosshage, J. (1992). *Self and motivational systems*. Hillsdale, NJ: Analytic Press.

Mahler, M. (1968). *On symbiosis and the vicissitudes of individuation.* New York: International Universities Press.

Main, M. (1995). Recent studies in attachment: Overview, with selected implications for clinical work. In S. Goldberg, R. Muir, & J. Kerr (Eds.), *Attachment theory: Social, developmental, and clinical perspectives* (pp. 407–474). Hillsdale, NJ: Analytic Press.

Margulies, A. (1989). *The empathic imagination.* New York: Norton.

Modell, A. H. (1998). Review of infant mental health papers. *Infant Mental Health Journal, 19,* 341–345.

Moses, I. (1988). The misuse of empathy in psychoanalysis. *Contemporary Psychoanalysis, 24*(4), 577–594.

Renick, O. (1996). The perils of neutrality. *Psychoanalytic Quarterly, 65,* 495–517.

Schafer, R. (1968). Generative empathy in the treatment situation. *Psychoanalytic Quarterly, 28,* 342–373.

Schiff, J. (1977). One hundred children generate a lot of TA: History, development, and activities of the Schiff family. In G. Barnes (Ed.), *Transactional analysis after Eric Berne: Teachings and practices of three TA schools* (pp. 53–76). New York: Harper's College Press.

Schiff, J. L., with Schiff, A. W., Mellor, K., Schiff, E., Schiff, S., Richman, D., Fishman, J., Wolz, L., Fishman, C., & Momb, D. (1975). *Cathexis reader: Transactional analysis treatment of psychosis.* New York: Harper & Row.

Slochower, J. (1992). A hateful borderline patient and the holding environment. *Contemporary Psychoanalysis, 28*(1), 72–88.

Stark, M. (1999). *Modes of therapeutic interaction.* Northvale, NJ: Jason Aronson.

Steiner, C. (1974). *Scripts people live: Transactional analysis of life scripts.* New York: Grove Press.

Stern, D. B. (1998). Not misusing empathy. *Contemporary Psychoanalysis, 24*(4), 598–611.

Stern, D. N. (1985). *The interpersonal world of the infant: A view from psychoanalysis and developmental psychology.* New York: Basic Books.

Storr, A. (1988). *Solitude: A return to the self.* New York: Free Press.

Sullivan, H. S. (1954). *The Psychiatric Interview.* New York: W. W. Norton.

Tronick, E. (1998a). Dyadically expanded states of consciousness and the process of therapeutic change. *Infant Mental Health Journal,* 19(3), 290–299.

Tronick, E. (Ed.). (1998b). Special issue. *Infant Mental Health Journal,* 19.

White, M., & Weiner, M. (1986). *The theory and practice of self psychology.* New York: Brunner/Mazel.

Winnicott, D. W. (1958a). Hate in the countertransference. In D. W. Winnicott (Ed.), *Through paediatrics to psycho-analysis* (pp. 194–203). London: Tavistock. (Original work published 1947.)

Winnicott, D. W. (1958b). Primary material preoccupation. In D. W. Winnicott (Ed.), *Through paediatrics to psycho-analysis* (pp. 300–305). London: Tavistock. (Original work published 1956.)

Winnicott, D. W. (1958c). Primitive emotional development. In D. W. Winnicott (Ed.), *Through paediatrics to psycho-analysis* (pp. 145–156). London: Tavistock. (Original work published 1945.)

Winnicott, D. W. (1958d). *Through paediatrics to psycho-analysis.* London: Tavistock.

Winnicott, D. W. (1965). *The maturational processes and the facilitating environment: Studies in the theory of emotional development.* New York: International Universities Press.

Winnicott, D. W. (1971). *Playing and reality.* London: Tavistock.

5

REFLECTIONS ON TRANSACTIONAL ANALYSIS IN THE CONTEXT OF CONTEMPORARY RELATIONAL APPROACHES

Diana Shmukler

In responding to some of the issues raised by *TAJ* editor Tony Tilney (2000) about transactional analysis in the new millennium, I find myself evaluating and contextualizing transactional analysis in terms of the development of its own theory and practice as well as in relation to its place within the broader fields of psychotherapy, counseling, and other psychologically based interventions. In doing so I position transactional analysis within what I call "contemporary relational approaches to psychotherapy," a phrase used by Maria Gilbert and me at a United Kingdom Association for Psychotherapy Integration meeting in London in July 2000. There we identified what we see as current debates in the field, which I will refer to as I consider questions about the current status of transactional analysis. I develop these ideas first from a clinical base, which is where they began, and then expand them to other areas of application. As with all important contributions to understanding human nature, such concepts have wider relevance. My understanding is, of course, connected to my personal and professional experience, and it is from this base, after all, that we test whether theoretical notions make sense to us or not.

Theoretical position in the field of depth psychotherapy

The originality and power of Berne's ideas have stood the test of time well. In many ways they are as relevant now as they were when transactional analysis first attracted people's attention in the early 1960s. People learning about transactional analysis for the first time today find its core concepts as compelling and impactful as ever. I think this reflects one of the most obvious strengths of transactional analysis: the clarity and accessibility of its ideas. Ironically, however, the clear language with which its concepts are communicated has also proved to be a drawback to the development and strengthening of the discipline, often leading it to be viewed as a pop psychology. As a result, transactional analysis tends not to be taken seriously in academic circles, thus undermining its future intellectual growth.

I see the concept of ego states as the key and most original contribution of transactional analysis to general psychological theory. Its second most important contribution is the notion of script. Many of the other ideas in transactional analysis are elaborations or extensions of these two central, core concepts. For the purposes of this article, I consider ego states to be descriptions of how our internal states of mind are constructed and developed through our experiences growing up, and script is the way in which we organize our experience into a narrative. As I will discuss later, the concepts of ego states and scripts also speak to core aspects of human experience (e.g., parents and children are universal in human experience). Our capacity and need to search for meaning and to construct narrative as a way to symbolize personal as well as shared history are reflected in the notion of script and cultural script as the way that society transmits its past and shapes its members.

From its conception then, transactional analysis has offered intrapsychic, interpersonal, and systemic models for understanding the structure and function of the human personality. The notion of ego states provides the basis for these models by incorporating family structure and developmental processes within the basic model. In fact, Berne's contribution, which was rooted in psychoanalytic thinking, was powerfully influenced by an understanding of child development. His own analyst, Erik Erikson, laid the foundation for an understanding of childhood and its broader significance in society, and his work still dominates the field of developmental psychology. Berne's ideas could be viewed as preempting today's movement toward relational theory, a revolution that took psychoanalysis away from drive theory into the arena of relationship. In this sense, all relational-developmental approaches to psychotherapy can be seen as highly compatible with transactional analysis. Furthermore, Berne's criticisms of classic psychoanalysis, which he answered by originating transactional analysis (1961), are still answered in part by an ego psychology that stresses social and interactional factors, as does current transactional analysis theory.

Thus transactional analysis as an approach to psychotherapy and human functioning is both compatible with other humanistic approaches (e.g., gestalt therapy) and a more active challenge to psychoanalysis. Current alternatives to classic psychoanalytic thinking also marry well with transactional analysis. For example, although object relations theory and self psychology (the latter of which is the most humanistically based form of psychoanalysis) have theoretical disagreements with each other, transactional analysis has successfully incorporated the emphasis that both place on our fundamental need for relationship and on the crucial role of early experience in structuring our subsequent capacities and ways of relating.

Current debates in contemporary relational approaches to psychotherapy

I started this article with a consideration of the therapeutic relationship because this is how transactional analysis itself began and its most useful theoretical notions developed. A relational approach to transactional analysis also places it well within other contemporary relational approaches. The central debates summarized here offer a frame for discussion, although the list is neither complete nor comprehensive. Rather, it is eclectic and reflects some of what we are hearing at international conferences both within and beyond transactional analysis, particularly from self psychologists, integrative psychotherapists, and other relationally oriented clinicians. Although many of these debates originally derive from clinical questions about technique and methodology, they also have theoretical implications.

For example, one wide-ranging debate concerns the use and usefulness of the notion of transference. How do you use it? When do you use it? When do you choose to ignore transferential implications? Falling under transferential phenomena but also requiring specific consideration are issues related to self-disclosure and touch. Another topic that generates a great deal of passion is whether and to what extent the therapeutic work is done to provide the developmentally needed relationship and how this relationship is worked with and conceptualized.

In terms of clinical methodology, some of the debated issues include where the emphasis is placed in clinical work in terms of past, present, or future. Another question concerns which view is primarily privileged: the therapist's, the patient's, or the intersubjective view. These are, or course, questions of emphasis rather than choice since in each case all views are relevant.

Self psychology can be regarded as a humanistic challenge to classical psychoanalysis, but one that is firmly rooted in psychoanalytic approaches. It emphasizes developmental processes and empathic attunement rather than clinically interpretative methodologies. Transactional analysis therapists have happily gravitated toward self psychology; they find the notions of empathic attunement and contributions such as the empathic transaction comfortable and validating. It is a style of working that feels congruent with the humanistic thrust and philosophical frame of transactional analysis. Transactional analysis can also be conceptualized as an object relations psychology, although the use of internal objects by Kleinians and other members of the British object relations school speaks more to the notion of unconscious processes rather than to an ego psychology. Nonetheless, Fairbairn's and Guntrip's ideas as they are being introduced into the broader field of psychotherapy, and particularly their contributions to concepts related to schizoid processes, have recently been usefully connected to transactional analysis. Although there are many theoretical contradictions and incompatibilities between self psychology and object relations theory, the integration of ideas from both schools of thought points to attempts by transactional analysis therapists to find ways of working in depth and long term with patients. Certainly the conceptualization and insight offered by this integration leads to useful clinical understanding.

If we regard any theory of therapy as a container for anxiety, then we see how theories are useful to practitioners in the face of ongoing clinical stresses. There is a continual search for theoretical models and ideas that will explain the complex process that occurs between therapist and patient. There is also a need to address the complicated psychological problems and difficulties that we see clinically in our rapidly changing world. Traditional institutions are giving way to social contexts for which there are no established rules (Parent ego state messages). For example, rapid globalization and the emergence of cyberspace are having profound effects on human relationships.

Working with specific ego states can be seen as dealing with the past, that is, the developmental and historical situations that led up to and shaped the current structure and function of the adult personality. This is similar to most analytic approaches. Further, from this perspective, the work would be seen as focused primarily on the developmentally needed relationship. Thus, when working with the past to understand deficits and provide some of the missing parental aspects, transactional analysis can be regarded as firmly rooted in the tradition of meeting missing developmental needs. It is valuable, however, to examine the rationale for working in this way in terms of transference and countertransference. The question is, whose needs are being met: the therapist's or the patient's?

A powerful and central aspect of transactional analysis psychotherapy is the value and emphasis it places on the past in an effort to change and free up the present. Personally, in whatever context I work, I place great importance on working in the here and now. Where past ego states or states of the mind are phenomenologically present, as Berne described, we are working with the past in the present with a view to changing the future. From this perspective transactional analysis provides an interesting integrated position on the time issue in psychotherapy.

Working with the child ego state

Many therapeutic methods of working long term and in depth have identified and described ways of working with the "inner child," that is, with patients' childhood histories and how their formative years shaped their adult personalities (e.g., Bollas, 1987; Klein, 1959; McDougall, 1986; Miller, 1980). The writings of these authors offer some of the best-known examples of post-Bernean psychoanalytic understandings that emphasize the internal dynamics resulting from child–drawn scripts or experience that shape and determine adult functioning. All of this work could be read as if written by a good transactional analysis therapist interested in treating the Child ego states in adult individuals.

These approaches were developed after Berne described a state of the ego that was really an early version of and based on the person's real childhood, a state that continues to exist in the adult personality. Berne's way of treating the Child ego state was, in the first place, transactional analysis. It was a cognitive approach based on insight. And if the patient needed further treatment, Berne then recommended psychoanalysis. In contrast, many transactional analysis therapists who were influenced by gestalt therapy and other forms of cathartic and enacting schools developed methodologies that could be conceptualized as focused regressions and other ways of directly intervening while people were phenomenologically in their Child ego state.

An important insight regarding regressive work is that sometimes people do not regress or use regression as a defense; rather, they are already regressed (i.e., their internal states of being, their inner worlds, are more or less permanently spent in a Child ego state). In such cases, the implications for treatment and the long-term nature of the work need to be considered seriously. These cases raise questions about the developmentally needed relationship since they clearly require work of this nature while posing all the dilemmas associated with reparenting and the pitfalls that such notions introduce into treatment.

I feel that these methodologies (i.e., those that work with regression and use experience-near language), which have been developed to access and work with Child ego states in adult patients, are powerful and effective. They work best when used with patients who have good ego resources (i.e., can access their Adult readily), can use insight, and are also to some extent psychologically minded. Patients with fragile, vulnerable personality structures who are nearer the personality disorder end of the narcissistic–borderline continuum and whose states of mind are regressed a good deal of the time need relational therapy. Such work takes place in the transference–countertransference interface as indicated for some of the reasons described later.

Therapy with the parent ego state

Another important, unique contribution of transactional analysis is Berne's identification of separate Parent ego states (see Ernst, 1971) and the development of Parent ego state therapy in which patients cathect Parent ego states and work as if they were their parents (i.e., working with the introjects). This innovative approach to psychotherapy enhances people's awareness and understanding of how their past influences their present, provides insight, and frees people to be more fully themselves and more fully in the here and now.

An integrated approach

Sometimes this approach provides a potent way forward in individual sessions in the same way that psychodrama and family constellation work can in a larger group: by leading to an understanding of transgenerational transmission and how parents' unresolved issues are picked up and carried by their children. These children then experience pressure to find solutions or ways of coping with traumas and deprivations that parents could not deal with themselves. Working directly with Parent ego states rather than in the complicated crucible of transference–countertransference and projection can be effective and enlightening. However, I restrict this work to brief or focused situations or to contexts in which I choose not to or cannot work strongly in the transference for reasons that I will elaborate later.

Thus far I have described the development of transactional analysis and its use as an individual in-depth therapy. As a clinical method, transactional analysis has a strong foundation because of its roots in psychoanalysis and developmental psychology. It forms a good base from which to develop an integrative approach that integrates humanistic and psychoanalytic understandings in a developmental

TA and contemporary relational approaches **79**

relational stance. In fact, currently many European integrative trainers and therapists are also transactional analysis therapists (many of them Teaching and Supervising Transactional Analysts). This also reflects the trend and the need, certainly in the United Kingdom and Europe, for people trained initially in humanistic methods to add to their work important clinical approaches from psychoanalysis. This is particularly true with regard to identifying and working with transference, countertransference, and projective processes. In contrast, other integrative therapists who came originally from a psychoanalytic base discover that they need to find more active, direct methods of working and so look to the humanistically based approaches for a methodology.

Of course, for clinicians, an integrative approach poses many problems and challenges. It demands that the therapist be aware of what happens to the transference when the work becomes more active or something is "acted out" or enacted with the patient rather than analyzed. It means asking what such shifts in technique mean or how they might reflect the therapist's countertransference. In-depth psychotherapy is difficult, and it demands that the therapist constantly work to make sense of what is going on, not only within the patient but also between patient and therapist. Most of all, it requires a high degree of self-awareness on the part of the therapist. In view of all of this, it is clear that integrative, developmental transactional analysis is no easy, simple, or quick "fix." At the risk of sounding prescriptive, I feel that it is incumbent on practitioners to constantly reflect on the meaning of their interventions with self-awareness and honesty.

Limitations of transactional analysis as an in-depth therapy

Although transactional analysis has much to offer as an in-depth individual psychotherapy, it also has limitations. The major one has to do with unconscious processes: Transactional analysis does not take them seriously enough, nor does it have enough understanding of them or a clear theoretical framework within which to work with them. Many transactional analysis therapists are not trained initially to work with transference. Although Berne took such training for granted because of his psychoanalytic background, it has not been a feature of much subsequent transactional analysis training.

Working "in the transference" is demanding and complex. It stresses the need to deal with conscious and unconscious processes. That which is unconscious is, by definition, out of awareness. This can be true with countertransference as well as transference. The strain of working with material that is out of awareness makes transference and countertransference work very demanding; close supervision is required if the therapist is to become aware of what he or she may unconsciously be communicating to patients (Casement, 1985).

In this regard, much enacting therapy unconsciously positions the therapist in a particular relationship to the patient, which poses certain dilemmas for the therapist. The major one is whether to intervene on a conscious or unconscious level. Many times therapists opt for conscious interventions, which is what Berne

80   Diana Shmukler

did when he formulated transactional analysis with an emphasis on social control and "cure" rather than on a lengthy process of "making progress." However, in the end these complex decisions are made by experienced therapists in relation to the nature of the work, the stage of therapy, the presenting issues, and a number of less easily accessible factors.

Having said all this, the challenge for transactional analysts is to retain the efficiency and effectiveness of Berne's challenge to psychoanalysis while simultaneously recognizing the impoverishment that can occur when important unconscious dynamics created by the therapy situation are not taken into account. How can we as integrative developmental-relational transactional analysts work with unconscious and conscious processes without reinventing the wheel, becoming psychoanalysts ourselves, or losing the power and efficacy of Berne's contributions?

This challenge requires transactional analysts who have done a good deal of personal exploration (including perhaps some psychoanalytic work themselves) as well as those who have the creativity and self-confidence to experiment and take risks. As long as we stay close to the patient's experience and remain empathically attuned, regardless of what we call the process, we will be doing sound clinical work. If we make a mistake, it is in recognizing and being willing to correct it that, as we learned from self psychology, can become a transmuting intervention. Setting ourselves up as "magicians" or the ones with the power can feed our own narcissistic and grandiose needs to be helpful and/or right and to make an impact. A counter to these tendencies is the capacity to self-reflect, to be open to feedback, and to seek to understand one's own unconscious interaction in the therapy relationship. In other words, we need to be aware of our own countertransference needs and wants and the countertransference relationships we create as well as the sorts of transferences that we attract or from which we defend ourselves.

Ultimately, every clinician needs to address issues related to transference and resolve or work out a position for himself or herself. I would make a strong plea for self-reflection, self-awareness, and an understanding of the transferences we attract by the nature of our personalities and styles. In addition, we need to be open to understanding how certain transferential positions are extremely gratifying while others are uncomfortable and difficult for us to experience.

Another topic that warrants careful reflection is self-disclosure: what we disclose, to whom, for whose benefit, and to what effect on the transference. While a detailed discussion of this subject would merit a separate article, I will make a few brief points here. The firmest ground we can be on with regard to self-disclosure is to disclose our own process in the here and now in the session. Often sharing our internal process can facilitate the therapeutic relationship. From a transactional analysis perspective, the patient's Child and Adult usually feel regarded, valued, and strengthened by such disclosure. It serves the developmentally needed relationship as well as facilitating the dialogue and is, in this sense, a powerful therapeutic tool. I am much more reluctant, reflective, and cautious about disclosing real facts about my life, and yet at times this too can serve therapeutic goals such as twinship needs and normalizing life circumstances. In so doing, this also can serve the developmentally needed relationship.

Issues related to touch and intersubjectivity, mentioned briefly in earlier sections of this article, form part of the broader debates about long-term work, although they demand a fuller debate than can be offered here.

Short-term brief or solution-focused therapy

As an approach to short-term or brief-solution focused work, transactional analysis is particularly effective. Many of its techniques and methods are especially useful for this kind of work, such as redecision therapy or helping people understand their rackets or script systems. These methods can form the basis of interventions that lead patients to more effective styles of relating and interacting. In fact, most of the broad, well-developed theory in transactional analysis is useful in short-term, solution-focused work, including, for example, the discount matrix and the drama triangle. People feel helped and relieved by the kind of insights they can gain from the clarity and succinct insight of good transactional analysis. Since there is an ever-increasing demand and pressure for short-term work, this is an important area of influence for transactional analysis.

Couples work is another area where transactional analysis can be particularly useful and effective. It can be used to analyze interaction patterns, look at interlocking scripts, point out how unmet child needs are projected into the relationship, and facilitate developing contracts around behavioral change. It can also invite Adult responses and meet playful Child or appropriate Parent needs (see Gilbert & Shmukler, 1996). The transactional analysis emphasis on clear, straightforward verbal contracts is an important strength in this kind of work.

Cross-cultural and social applications

Within the broader arena of social interventions transactional analysis has much to offer. In my experience of working cross-culturally in South Africa, transactional analysis formed a particularly useful way to teach and work with powerful psychological processes and ideas. Many people in developing countries have little formal education let alone any knowledge about psychology, yet they are excited and readily engaged with psychological concepts. Transactional analysis also provides a language by which people from different cultural backgrounds can share common experience and understanding; there is a universality of meaning inherent in parents and children, family histories, direct and indirect messages communicated between people, and so on.

In trauma debriefing and understanding the impact of traumatic events, the idea of trauma either forming or reinforcing script decisions is an important understanding. Working with people soon after traumatic experiences and knowing how trauma and the loss of control results in regression allows for the planning of suitable interventions as well as provides a language with which victims and interveners can verbalize and make sense of their experiences. The central therapeutic task is to prevent trauma from becoming script forming or script reinforcing.

Organizational applications

In organizational and management development fields, script as a key concept is both effective and useful. People in organizations want to make sense of their own irrational and emotional responses as well as those of others, but unlike some academics or intellectuals, they do not want lengthy, complex notions such as would be provided by object relations theory. Their needs are pragmatic and have to do with the here and now of the external world. However, it is the power of ideas such as working with the inner and outer worlds that speaks to the complexity of a modem business environment, one in which the major resource is human capital and intellectual property. In such arenas, marrying scripts and ego states with an understanding of organizations and systems is powerful and innovative.

I have described the range and flexibility of transactional analysis in various settings in which I have seen it used not only usefully but also to provide something that other systems of understanding do not by virtue of its clarity and power and the accessibility of its concepts. There is something about its broad-based applicability and wide-ranging use as a tool for thinking that makes it particularly relevant as a psychological approach for transferring understanding from clinical situations into the wider social and political arenas.

Future needs

There is a vital need for research in transactional analysis, a need that TA organizations (e.g., the ITAA, ITA, EATA, etc.) have recognized for many years. There is also some recognition of some of the problems associated with doing this research. For example, most practitioners who are not academics have neither the time nor the inclination to do research. One solution to this problem is to build into transactional analysis training from early on a genuine interest in questions that arise as well as an understanding of how to go about answering them. This is a major challenge for trainers, organizations, and practitioners committed to the development of transactional analysis.

Hand in hand with this is the need for theory development. On this score I was encouraged by the roundtable forum at the April 2000 Institute for Transactional Analysis conference in Canterbury, England. Presenters were invited to discuss questions that they were interested in and to really talk with each other rather than each person presenting a paper as is done on most conference panels. It was a moment when it seemed that theory was both being debated and formed. I see a real role for transactional analysis organizations to play in bringing together theoreticians and practitioners for this kind of debate, exchange, and discussion to develop ideas as well as training events for the next generation.

I also value the Training and Certification Council exam system. The Training Endorsement Workshops and other such events are a particular strength of transactional analysis organizations. The competency-based exams and the training of trainers have both provided models for others in humanistic fields. Many trained transactional analysis practitioners know through their own training experiences how to run good training events themselves, do good presentations, and run effective groups, whether they be for therapy or other forms of teaching.

In terms of the challenges facing us, although I think we have alive and vibrant transactional analysis organizations, we must equip ourselves to deal with an unpredictable future. One thing we can say about the future is that it is going to include rapid change, and we must be prepared to face many issues related to such change, including an ever-shrinking world as a result of globalization, instant access to information, e-commerce, and other aspects of the Internet: These are having profound effects on all of us.

We also know that both the speed and the scope of these changes imply ever-escalating stress on human beings. How do we equip ourselves to respond to this stress? It is clear that these trends will lead to a further breakdown in traditional ways of coping with our own and wider human issues. There is going to be an increasing need for spaces in our lives for reflection and recuperation. This brings to mind Winnicott's (1958/1965) wonderful notion of the capacity to be alone, which only develops in the presence of another. For us as clinicians, that might be a therapist, supervisor, consultant, or coach. I see an increasing need for reflective spaces, opportunities to process fast moving situations and to debrief from stress. Meanwhile, psychopathology moves more and more toward alienation, the development of schizoid defenses, pent up aggression and rage, and so on.

One of the questions that keeps me awake at night is the knowledge that although we have come quite far in our understanding of individuals, dyads, and small groups, we know very little about large group psychology. As we watch ongoing and seemingly unstoppable violence in many parts of the world, it seems crucial that we learn to understand what motivates people in large groups to lose their minds and commit appalling atrocities. How can we understand, prevent, and stop such humanly caused tragedies in the future? Some in group relations theory are tackling these questions, and I think if we in transactional analysis can use existing theory and develop new theory to understand these questions, we will be in a position to make a major contribution to the betterment of humankind.

Transactional analysis has been enormously enriched by including with it other theories and ideas. An important challenge for the future is to remain informed, abreast of, and in touch with current thinking so that we can integrate new ideas and information from such fields as brain research, cognitive science, emotions, psychopharmacology, psychoneuroimmunology, and infant research. We also need to look at expanding our existing theoretical models, especially, as I have already articulated, to include an understanding and appreciation of unconscious processes.

In conclusion, in transactional analysis we have an accessible, powerful model that lends itself to integration with many other approaches through its roots in core concepts. The challenge is to keep young, creative, innovative people who are initially turned on by transactional analysis within the ranks, contributing to its future development, and keeping it in the forefront of the field.

References

Berne, E. (1961). *Transactional analysis in psychotherapy: A systematic individual and social psychiatry*. New York: Grove Press.

Bollas, C. (1987). *The shadow of the object: Psychoanalysis of the unthought known*. London: Free Association Books.

Casement, P. (1985). *On learning from the patient*. London: Tavistocks.

Ernst, F. H., Jr. (1971). The diagrammed Parent ego state: Eric Berne's most significant contribution. *Transactional Analysis Journal, 1*(1), 49–58.

Gilbert, M., & Shmukler, D. (1996). *Brief therapy with couples: An integrative approach*. Chichester: Wiley.

Klein, M. (1959). Our adult world and its roots in infancy. In M. Klein (Ed.), *The writings of Melanie Klein* (Vol. 3, *Envy and gratitude*, pp. 247–263). London: Hogarth Press.

McDougall, J. (1986). *Theatres of the mind: Illusion and truth on the psychoanalytic stage*. London: Free Association Books.

Miller, A. (1980). *For your own good: Hidden cruelty in child-rearing and the roots of violence*. New York: Farrar, Straus & Giroux.

Tilney, T. (2000). Letter from the editor. *Transactional Analysis Journal, 30*, 178–181.

Winnicott, D. W. (1958/1965). The capacity to be alone. In D. W. Winnicott (Ed.), *The maturational processes and the facilitating environment* (pp. 29–36). London: Hogarth Press.

6

THERE AIN'T NO CURE FOR LOVE

The psychotherapy of an erotic transference

Helena Hargaden

The following case presentation involves the exploration of a psychotherapeutic relationship in which the emergence of Eros in the transference had to be taken into consideration. This relationship occurred prior to the publication of David Mann's (1997) *Psychotherapy: An Erotic Relationship*, in which the author explores the significance of sexual feelings in the therapy relationship. In fact, he views the therapeutic dyad as equivalent to two lovers. However, during the time I worked with the patient described in this article, I found a dearth of literature on the subject of erotic transference; this meant that I had to rely primarily on my intuition and imagination in working my way through this transference relationship. I think I did so with some success, and since then Mann's work has both confirmed some of my thinking and influenced me to consider other aspects of the transference.

This article presents the narrative about the case in four parts, each of which represents a phase of the transferential relationship. Each part describes the therapy process followed by a theoretical discussion. I have selected those aspects of the therapy that are most relevant to this discussion, but, of course, this is not a complete version of what took place. The theoretical model of psychotherapy used in this case is the relational model that I developed with Charlotte Sills (Hargaden & Sills, 1999, 2001), in which the transferential relationship is viewed as central to therapy.

Romeo and Juliet: in the beginning

When I opened the door for Noel on the day of his first session, he stood there, dressed in black and wearing sunglasses. At the time I lived next door to a pop music group, and my first thought was to wonder whether he had come to the right house. But he introduced himself and I invited him to come in. He walked into my consulting room; I sat down and invited him to choose a spot. He sat diagonally across from me and grinned: "Well, what happens now?" He seemed embarrassed, but before I could answer, he asked another question: "Do you mind if I smoke?" Having given up smoking only recently, I was particularly evangelical about the subject and replied immediately that maybe it would be useful to find out what he felt when he did not smoke. As soon as I said it, I realized that this rather threw us into the deep end. "You don't waste any time, do you?" he laughed, and I did too. In a sense this was the beginning of rapport between us, for he took my directness and played with it. And in that moment I experienced my first feeling of liking toward him.

Noel told me that he was 37 and that, although artistically creative and successful, he found himself with nothing much either materially or emotionally in his personal life. He wanted to change this. In particular, he declared himself to be deeply and passionately in love with a fellow artist, Anna, but he had messed up the relationship early on and now found it difficult to reconnect with her. He described her as a woman of intense femininity: She was not only physically beautiful, but also had a receptive spirit, a tender heart, and was bright and wise. In fact, it turned out that it was she who had suggested that Noel enter therapy. I was struck by his passion for her and immediately engaged in his dilemma. I liked the sound of her and felt her allure in the room; maybe I, too, was falling in love with her. The problem seemed to be that Noel was frightened of making a commitment or even letting Anna know of his love. There was no question in his mind and none in mine at this point about the reciprocal nature of the love.

As the therapy relationship unfolded, it was easy for me to like Noel. Our rapport continued. He was personable, intellectually curious, and politically observant and had an ironic wit that I enjoyed since I have a similar sense of humor. Many of our sessions involved him describing his feelings for Anna, his times with her (they did some work together), his fear of rejection, and the intensity of his desire and longing for her; he seemed to be hopelessly and completely in love. I became imbued with a passionate sense of how important it was that he communicate to Anna that he was in love with her. And while I had some misgivings at this stage—although I could not have articulated them then—I repressed them, somehow knowing that at that point I needed to accept Noel at face value. Thus, the first few months of the therapy were spent circling around his fear of commitment. After a while I began feeling somewhat restless. Noel did not seem to change, and the sessions seemed repetitive. I began to wonder about the nature of the problem and to reflect on what Noel might really be trying to tell me.

Discussion: In this initial stage of the therapy I believe that I was partly seduced by Noel into believing in his story of true love—a love that had been ill starred from the beginning, one fraught with misunderstanding and missed opportunities. He appealed to my romantic imagination. I found myself thinking of the great loves from literature—Romeo and Juliet, Troilus and Cressida—or the lyrics of love songs. Retrospectively, I ask myself why was I preoccupied with those myths, the stories of idealized heterosexual unions that go badly wrong. Did he need to *convince* me about his heterosexuality? Or was it about potency? As long as he did not tell Anna about his love, he could assume that she equally desired him and therefore retain his power in the relationship. This raised the question for me of how I could be powerful with him when pitted against such an idealized situation. In his fantasy life there were no ties, no commitment—not to others and not to me. He idealized but never got close. What was he avoiding? Noel seemed stuck with the desire and unable to transform it into anything more meaningful. Was he telling me of his impotence? I began feeling that I had been on a merry-go-round.

An aspect of my collusion may have been a fear that he would lapse into depression. If his love was an illusion, what would happen if the veils were dragged away?

I did not share my experiences of him at this stage because I thought he would find them intrusive and doing so would have been therapeutically ineffective. I knew I had to get to know him and that he was hiding behind his fantasy. At the same time, I never lost the feeling that contained within the fantasy was something essentially authentic about Noel. My feeling that I might be falling in love with Anna was, I think, significant in this respect. So while not inclined to be cynical about the romanticism, I was now more alert to my naive assumptions that this was a case of romantic love in the literal sense. But where was Noel? Who was Noel? I knew I had to find him.

Getting to know you, getting to know all about you

Noel continued to procrastinate about declaring his love to Anna, and as the story unfolded, I recognized that there *was* a considerable amount of fantasy in what he told me. Again and again he would revert to the story of Anna. Not only was she beautiful, intelligent, creative, and so on, but she was now also capable of profound therapeutic understanding. I began to feel that I had a rival. I felt envious of her, that I could never measure up to her. I began to be aware of other things, too. When not talking about Anna, Noel described some of his past relationships and how much he enjoyed making love to women. In particular, he spoke fondly and erotically about his last lover. At that point it became clear that he had been celibate for seven years, and I was aware of feeling shocked and thinking, "What a waste." I began to notice that Noel often sat directly opposite me in shorts with his legs open as he elaborated on how much he enjoyed making love to women. Partly I wanted to feel amused at the transparency of what he was saying and how he was behaving, but instead I was annoyed to realize that I felt sexually attracted by the idea that he was such a good lover.

As he learned to trust me more his story gradually unfolded. I learned that he had often been beaten by his father and had experienced his mother as ineffectual. His father had been religious and puritanical, a union man with a clearly frustrated passion that he expressed in envious attacks on his son. Noel's mother not only seemed subservient to his father, but she also used his father's violence as a way of keeping control of the children. Noel both admired and hated his father. He loved his mother yet felt rage and hurt at her betrayal. It was not until much later in the therapeutic relationship that I came to understand that Noel's father expressed a type of sexual passion in the beatings he gave his children and that Noel took some pleasure in first provoking an attack and then denying any pain. I was struck by the sadomasochistic dynamic, although it was not clear who was, in reality, beating whom. This dynamic had bred in Noel an intense love/hate feeling that had left a scar on his heart; his sense of how to love and how to express passion had been distorted and subverted.

Shortly after this phase of the therapy began, Noel embarked on his first sexual relationship in seven years. I thought this indicated that the therapy was working. However, his choice of a partner was disastrous (the woman sounded highly disturbed), and he had a truly dreadful time with her. Of course, she did not match up to Anna, and the reality and difficulties of the relationship threw Noel back into a prolonged examination yet again of why it should and needed to be Anna with whom he settled down.

Discussion: In this phase of the therapy I recognized two prominent features of my countertransference. I felt strongly invited, maybe even provoked, into feeling attracted toward Noel, and at the same time I felt intense resistance tinged with frustration at that idea. I felt that I was being teased. Was I being titillated and then denied since we both knew that sexual contact could not occur in the context of the therapy relationship? This made me reflect on my feelings with him. Maybe I was annoyed about being attracted to him because I felt that he was "turning me on" only to withhold. Even though rationally we both knew that this was a therapeutic relationship, I think we both bracketed those aspects of reality to allow the sadomasochistic dynamic to develop within the relationship. The fact that he knew there could be no sexual contact felt like part of the tease. This alerted me to the potentially sadistic aspect of his sexuality; in fact, this turned out to be his pattern with women: to make them interested and then withhold. At this stage I also wondered about Anna: Was she desperately waiting for him to get on with it? Or was that a fantasy?

My resistance was, in part, also due to my feelings of insecurity about sex rearing their head within the therapy relationship. The incest taboo is strong and has permeated our understanding of the therapeutic process so effectively that Mann's (1997) seminal work on the subject was not written until the late 1990s. Yet in my relationship with Noel, sexuality was intimately tied up with the problem that he faced in finding a companion with whom to spend his life. My resistance may also have been a response to picking up on his passive aggression: an "I will not be seduced" feeling or, "If I am, I will not let you know about it."

I also felt intimidated by his fantasy, as I said before. The idealized woman he described increasingly took on aspects of a goddess to whom one may aspire but with whom one may never compete. As I analyzed my countertransference, I recognized my sense of impotence when pitted against the reality of Anna. Was I being invited to experience how it had been between Noel and his father? I also wondered if there was a sexual element in his father's arousal—a sexuality that resulted in Noel's humiliation and brutality. Because of this, it seemed to me that to share my experience at this stage could be potentially brutal and humiliating to

Noel. As I said, part of me wanted to be amused, to laugh at him, and I feel sure that this was an unconscious manifestation of the original protocol.

In reflecting on my countertransference, it occurred to me that my position of amused detachment may also have been designed to protect me from feeling vulnerable and/or shamed because of having sexual feelings toward my patient. As I thought about these elements, it seemed that the question for me and for us was how I could have congruent, intimate contact with Noel. Together we had recreated an interpersonal dynamic that, in part, appeared to reflect the father–son relationship. Perhaps the task now was to find a way to transform this dynamic into an emotionally close and intimate one. Mann (1997) wrote about the transformational possibilities inherent in a creative analysis of the erotic countertransference. As I analyzed my countertransference, I became more accepting of my feelings. I recognized how much I liked Noel and what real attractive qualities he held for me. He was creative in the arts, and we shared a love of literature and art. I also came from a political background, so we met intellectually and politically as well. When researching the erotic transference I came across Diamond (1993), who emphasized the therapist's capacity and willingness to integrate fully and move fluidly between his or her own masculine and feminine attributes and his or her own heterosexual and homosexual responses. In this therapy I was now involved in the full scope of my own sexuality.

I need you to believe in me

In the third phase of the therapy I relaxed into the relationship, which was reflected in subtle changes in the dynamic between us. For instance, Anna became less of a focus, although if Noel felt too threatened, he would bring her into the conversation. I could recognize the extent to which I had made a therapeutic error by the amount of time spent on Anna. So, although often I experienced feelings of mutuality and warmth, I only had to misunderstand him or be misattuned in some way—perhaps by referring to the limitations of our relationship (i.e., overemphasize here-and-now reality)—and he would take refuge and suddenly become tangential by talking about Anna or rambling on about something else. I was often, therefore, reminded of the fragility of our relationship. Noel knew little about my personal life, but he inferred from my practice schedule that I have a family. He could also see some evidence of this when he looked into the garden outside my consulting room.

At about this time he came in with the following dream. He dreamed that he was in a regular session with me, and then in the next scene he was on a high building where a man was trying to kiss him. He recoiled and fell off the building. I arrived, dressed in white, to tend to him. In the next scene he and I are walking along with a child in a pram. Next he is trying to get into my house, banging on windows and doors. I am inside entertaining, unseeing and impervious to him. He spots a man, dark, in the garden (who could have been him) and feels caught and embarrassed so he leaves.

When reflecting on the dream, my analyst supervisor at the time suggested that the man represented Noel's latent homosexuality. But I wondered if it was representative of his relationship with his father—close but brutal (the jumping off the building). However, as already suggested, it could be that Noel's close relationship with his father, who was brutal, also contained elements of the homoerotic, which left Noel afraid of his homosexual aspects and ambivalent about his sexuality.

When talking about the dream with Noel, he particularly liked the part about us having the child in the pram, which we understood as symbolic of the product of our union. I also thought of it in terms of us bringing his Child into the relationship. One of the themes of our relationship was that he felt naked and defenseless in front of me. He often complained that he wanted to perform for me but I did not allow it: no sex, no art, no seduction. He bemoaned this frequently but somehow I always felt that he was saying, "Thank you for seeing me." I was confirmed in this shortly after the dream, for in discussing it I brought up more overtly some of the sexual feelings between us in a way that was bearable for him and for us. He seemed pleased and at the same time told me that he would be brokenhearted if I betrayed his trust and seduced him sexually. I turned this around and asked him if I should resist all his attempts to seduce me, thus letting him know that I had noticed him sexually. He seemed pleased with this interpretation and at the same time was still keen for me to understand that he resented the fact that he would be used sexually. I think his response reflected the quality of the impasse between us: I am to be seduced but not seduced and given all the responsibility for whatever happened. Linked to this was my realization that Noel wanted to impress me as a substitute for emotional relating, and yet he made it clear how important it was to him to be seen and valued just for himself. He grinned once and said, "I just can't pull the wool over your eyes, can I?" And he looked pleased. "I feel naked in here because I can't use the things I usually use to impress women."

Discussion: I think the vital issue in this phase of the therapy was that I had sufficiently analyzed my countertransference so that I could feel less frightened of the sexual feelings in the relationship and could understand the sadomasochistic element. Thus I did not either enact hostility toward him or become seductive with him. I became clearer in this phase about the role of his fantasy life, because whenever I was too blunt or assumed a more Adult ego awareness than was the case, he slipped into talking about Anna. At the same time, I allowed the ebb and flow of my own sexual responses either to him and/or to Anna to exist without trying to repress them. Noel and Anna were becoming increasingly fused in terms of my emotional and sexual responding.

The dream suggested many possibilities. Often one can see a thread and theme in a dream, but this one seemed particularly coded to me. I understood that it seemed to reflect his struggle with his core sense of who he was in the world. It seemed important for him to tell me about his sexual energy, but it was not clear how much he was in it versus how much he was observing himself in it. I thought the dream positive on several levels. It demonstrated that I was in his psyche, in his unconscious, and that in that place I represented the potential for closeness and procreation and therefore sexual intercourse and intimacy. In his dream I heal him, tend to him, and make him better, the result of which seems to be that we have a/our child together.

Does the dream refer to his fear of homosexuality; am I the person who will "cure" him and with whom he will have a baby? My white dress could suggest purity—maybe it was the immaculate conception—or did it mean I was idealized and/or an angel or goddess-type figure? What to make of the end of the dream? Was he unable to enter my house? Could he only observe? Was this about his potency? Could the dream be telling us about the obvious limitations of our relationship? Perhaps the exclusion from my house was a breakthrough of Adult ego in that somewhere he knew, understood, accepted, and even welcomed the boundaries and limitations of our relationship. For instance, one of the things I had come to understand by now was that an essential ingredient in his fantasy was that he never found out the truth about whether Anna (or other women) really found him as attractive as he imagined they did. By letting him know that I found him attractive, I broke through some of this, but then I felt the trap of not being able to enact it, which reflected a significant aspect of the fantasy: It kept women at a distance, waiting and hoping and never getting.

I want you

As the transference deepened, Noel's expectations of and demands on me increased. In this phase he replicated his feeling toward Anna in his relationship with me. The pull from his Child was so strong that I started to feel maternal toward him and inclined toward nurturing him and acting on his demands. For example, one day he came in rapidly, after a break, sat forward earnestly, opened his appointment diary, and said, "This can't go on. I need to see you more regularly." I was surprised and slightly anxious. I thought he meant that he needed to see me twice a week, but it transpired that he felt that he needed to see me during my holidays and expected me to make a special case of him. One of my initial responses was to say, yes, of course I will make a special case of you. I wanted to fold him in my arms, put him in a carry cot, and bring him away on holiday with us. I also wanted to make a joke out of it, perhaps in the sadistic fashion reflective of his father. Instead, I was able easily to show tenderness toward him and interpret his need for holding and loving without shaming him or acting on it.

After the break he chose not to come twice a week but started to become more hostile in the sessions, arguing with me about why it was my time, my house, and my agenda. He suggested that we meet halfway. I wondered if he wanted to deny the therapy relationship and make it into something else. But he persisted with his points, impervious to my reasoning. I stayed in the battle with him but remained firm. He vented his frustration and anger, "hitting" me in all my sore spots about equality, fairness, democracy, and so on. However, I kept myself anchored, believing that these were all ploys to subvert the therapy and attempt to make it into a friendship—or something else. In these moments he was forced to recognize the limitations of our relationship.

Noel's frustration with me manifested itself in a more conscious attempt to get his needs met elsewhere. After a break, he revealed that he had met a new woman. This time there was a different feeling. She was in a different career area and also in therapy. This sounded hopeful. He was hopeful. As their relationship progressed, we visited again the terrain with Anna. He reported feeling the gulf between his experience with Jane (his new girlfriend) and how she just did not compare with Anna. We seemed to have arrived at a pivotal moment in the therapy. He believed that he now really had to make a choice. He did make some overtures toward Anna, but what transpired made me realize that this love of his was not reciprocated and that his obsession was just that. However, I did not confront him about this, but instead we explored some of his feelings.

At this point he brought a piece of information into the therapy that offered insight into the nature of his obsession. His mother had had a stillbirth, his baby sister, just prior to his conception. As we talked about this he expressed a felt sense of having shared a womb with a ghost. Was it too fanciful to understand his obsessive need to fantasize in terms of the echo, the ghost of this sister who stalked his life in the form of Anna—who was perhaps just a convenient personification? Noel found this interpretation about his sister's ghostly influence on him useful; he connected with it and used it to help him ground himself in the new, evolving relationship with Jane.

Discussion: This phase of therapy clearly implicates Noel's experiences as an infant. My maternal countertransferential response was one of nurture and a feeling of needing to meet his needs; my paternal countertransferential response was to scoff at the need. I was immediately aware of the duality of my experience. Knowing this enabled me to respond with tenderness and to interpret his need without shaming him, thus avoiding reenacting the intrusive, controlling mothering or the sadistic fathering he had experienced from his parents. I think this was a critical moment in the therapy. In not getting the need met with me, Noel became frustrated enough to break through his fantasy and attempt to get his needs met in a more realistic way. Diamond (1993) wrote that the client's capacity to separate from the symbiosis depends, in part, on the therapist's capacity to experience both maternal and paternal identification.

The added information about the circumstances of Noel's conception and infancy is enormously significant; it is not difficult to imagine that Noel's mother was probably depressed and not very available to her infant son because of the stillbirth. Although the mother–infant dyad has traditionally been sanitized of its erotic content, there is evidence to suggest that conscious and unconscious eroticism is at the heart of this primary relationship (Kohut, 1971; Lichtenstein, 1970). When such love goes wrong, can it be put right? How will the psychotherapist understand the inarticulate speech of the injured heart?

In this case I think an accurate enough analysis of the countertransference was crucial to my staying emotionally available to be with Noel. It enabled me to avoid either behaving seductively, which was a huge temptation; laughing at him, which was also tempting at times; or becoming hostile toward him.

Is there a cure for love?

How successful was this therapy? If we judge it by Noel's behavior in the world, there was some degree of success because he was able to sustain an emotional

There ain't no cure for love   **93**

closeness with Jane, work at the relationship, and deal with the dissonance between his fantasy and reality. He was increasingly able to tolerate both his own and his partner's vulnerability. Through this process he became more confident in his material work and developed more realistic goals. Ultimately, however, he had to leave the therapy because he left town. I am not convinced that his dependency and/or sexuality needs were fully worked through with me, which I think left him vulnerable to his defences.

When reflecting on the work with Noel, one of the main areas in which there was some transformation and integration was between his masculine and feminine aspects as personified in the role of Anna in the therapy. My enthrallment and fascination with Anna intrigued me. I felt sure that she was more than a fantasy, and now I think back and wonder if Noel's depiction of Anna was so strong, passionate, and feminine because he was, in fact, describing those aspects of himself without knowing it. My theory is that she personified split-off aspects of himself that he had been forced to deny in the brutal relationship with his father. As he transferred some of those aspects of Anna onto me, he was then able to let go of her and integrate those parts of himself through me.

Frequently, we seem to create unconscious senses of self in relation to our earliest relationships, including relational stories and self-images that have some of those qualities that we currently believe to characterize our earliest relationships and earliest sense of self. In the therapy with Noel, I felt involved in the broad scope of my sexuality, including both heterosexual and homosexual connections and paternal and maternal identifications.

Perhaps one of the most significant transactions I did not make in the work with Noel was to confront his fantasy of Anna. Would it be too fanciful to consider that, as a result of therapy, the full beauty of Anna remained intact but no longer outside Noel—that now she was inside him?

References

Diamond, D. (1993). The paternal transference: A bridge to the erotic oedipal. *Psychoanalytic Inquiry, 13*(2), 206–225.

Hargaden, H., & Sills, C. (1999). The child ego state: An integrative view. *ITA News, 53*, 20–24.

Hargaden, H., & Sills, C. (2001). Deconfusion of the child ego state. *Transactional Analysis Journal, 31*, 55–70.

Kohut, H. (1971). *The analysis of the self: A systematic approach to the psychoanalytic treatment of narcissistic personality*. New York: International Universities Press.

Lichtenstein, H. (1970). Changing implications of the concept of psychosexual development: An inquiry concerning the validity of classical psychoanalytic assumptions concerning sexuality. *Journal of the American Psychoanalytic Association, 18*, 300–318.

Mann, D. (1997). *Psychotherapy: An erotic relationship*. London: Routledge.

7

PSYCHOLOGICAL FUNCTION, RELATIONAL NEEDS, AND TRANSFERENTIAL RESOLUTION

Psychotherapy of an obsession

Richard G. Erskine

Helena Hargaden's (2001) paper, "There ain't no cure for love: The psychotherapy of an erotic transference," is an example of a masterful psychotherapist's facilitation of an effective in-depth psychotherapy. In her article, Hargaden not only describes a client's emotional fixations, vivid fantasies, and ensuing transference, but she is also refreshingly forthcoming about her own countertransference. She, too, idealized the client's love object, found the client's stories erotically fascinating, and learned to make therapeutic use of both maternal and paternal countertransferential responses.

Although the contemporary psychoanalytic literature includes a number of case studies, written illustrations of clinical material usually rely on composite profiles that present a caricature of the personality or problem described. As a result, we are left to guess about what our colleagues actually do with their clients. Both gestalt therapy and integrative psychotherapy writings provide some examples of verbatim transcripts, but in the psychotherapy literature as a whole, thorough case studies or unedited transcripts of actual therapy sessions are seldom published. The transactional analysis literature also does not adequately reflect the therapeutic struggles, clinical methods, and resolution of therapeutic failures that are part of the daily work of clinical transactional analysts.

Therefore, Hargaden advances our understanding of the clinical process of transference, countertransference, and therapeutic resolution by exposing her work for critical review. This professional dialogue provides us with an opportunity to exchange theoretical concepts, engage in a meaningful discourse about therapeutic process, and arrive at new understandings of clinical involvement.

It is easy to criticize a therapist's approach when a psychotherapy is restricted by the therapist's narrow theoretical vision, or it leads to a reinforcement of the client's script beliefs, or it is handicapped by the therapist's failure to recognize and resolve therapeutic errors. However, it is difficult to criticize a psychotherapy that honors the client's natural vulnerabilities, respectfully facilitates the client in dissolving defenses, and results in the client's transformation and integration of fragmented aspects of the self.

Of course, it is always possible to criticize any approach or method used by a therapist if the colleague or supervisor merely addresses the clinical work from a different theoretical orientation or personal perspective than that used by the therapist. In this article I will share my current professional perspectives in the hope that they will facilitate a lively discussion and expand our collective knowledge of psychotherapy theory and methods. I will emphasize the elaboration of specific psychotherapy concepts as I might in supervision with an experienced psychotherapist: "The aim of supervision with an advanced psychotherapist is the development within the therapist of the ability to integrate multiple theoretical frames of reference and select various treatment plans based on observations and hypotheses about a particular client" (Erskine, 1997b, p. 223).

In actual supervision, an exploration of the psychotherapist's perspective, discussion of concepts, and further teaching are interwoven in the dialogue. In addition, a responsible collegial critique explores the therapist's reasoning, validates and/or challenges the therapist's assumptions, and provides alternative perspectives that enhance professional dialogue and the direction of future clinical work.

Psychological functions

It seems to me that Hargaden's case study is about the successful treatment of an obsession. There certainly is much material in this case study to facilitate discussion of erotic transference, narcissism, aspects of countertransference, and therapeutic methods. Each of these topics could lead to a fascinating and useful discussion. However, I will focus on the psychological functions and relational needs that underlie and are expressed in repetitive fantasizing and the use of the therapeutic relationship in curing obsession.

In this case, the client, Noel, was obsessed with Anna, a woman with whom he was peripherally involved. We can assume from Noel's consistent fantasizing that Anna served several psychological functions in his life. He described his Anna as a receptive spirit, as tenderhearted, bright, and wise. In fact, it was she who suggested the therapy.

Noel's Anna was, for him, a psychic entity—an internal image of another, a selfobject (Kohut, 1977)—that provided intelligence, creativity, and profound therapeutic understanding. Hargaden alluded to the psychological functions provided by the illusion of Anna when she described how Noel would bring Anna into the conversation if he ever felt threatened.

Noel's love and longing for Anna may have reflected a longing for a secure attachment. His attachment to his mother may have been disrupted by both "her betrayal" for using father's "violence as a way of keeping control of the children" and the implied depression in mother following the stillbirth of his sister just prior

96 Richard G. Erskine

to his conception. Noel's longing for Anna and his recurring fantasies about her provided for him the functions of stability, continuity, identity, and predictability. In healthy development, these psychological functions are provided within the relationship when there is a secure attachment (Erskine, Moursund, & Trautmann, 1999).

Obsessions, recurring fantasies, rigid behavioral patterns, and habitualized feelings are all maintained by an individual because they provide significant psychological functions. In an effective psychotherapy, the functions of the repetitive behavior, feeling, or fantasy must first be identified and appreciated by the client prior to any lasting growth or even change. For change to be lasting, it is essential that the psychological functions imbedded in the obsession, fantasy, or habitualized feeling be transferred into an actual relationship. In the life of a young child, these psychological functions were originally relational in nature.

As a result of relationship failure and the disruption of interpersonal contact, the functions became internalized, defensive, and attached to something intrapsychic, such as obsessive thoughts or feelings, the urge for compulsive behavior, or repetitive fantasy.

Predictability

As an elaboration of a biological imperative, humans have an internal urge to seek structure and predictability (Berne, 1963, 1966). When the urge for relationship is not satisfied, the failure of the relationship is often compensated for by the individual's increased attempts to structure experience, that is, to make meaning and predictability (Erskine, 1997c). Hence, repetition, compulsion, obsession, script beliefs, habitualized feelings or behavior patterns, and transference can all be seen as repetitive attempts to structuralize relationship failures.

As described in Hargaden's case study, Noel's obsessive fantasizing about Anna provided the psychological function of predictability. With Anna he could long for the secure attachment of a loving relationship with a receptive spirit who was tenderhearted, bright, wise, and understanding. Simultaneously, he retained an anticipation of no relationship or perhaps even rejection—a repeat with Anna of the disturbed attachment with mother through fantasizing about Anna. Noel spoke about Anna in therapy, but it seems from the case presentation that he did not speak to her directly. He did not court her or profess his love to her, although he reported in therapy that it was his desire to do so. By not talking with Anna and sharing his feelings with her, he passively created a non-relationship or, perhaps, in the fantasy, even rejection. But he was, through the fantasy, active and in charge of the prediction of rejection or of the non-relationship.

Identity

Noel expressed his unique identity in his fantasies about Anna. This identity was of someone who longed for a tenderhearted partner and yet unconsciously knew that he would be scorned—hence the conflict between longing for Anna's love and not communicating with her. "This is who I am!" is a felt sense that may be more affective and physiological than cognitive, one that often lacks words since the origin of this identity may be lost to awareness. Each fantasy of Anna was a further expression of Noel's unconscious identity—his life script. This archaic identity is maintained through fantasy rather than the ever-changing identity that occurs in active, spontaneous, authentic relationships. By maintaining a fantasy of Anna, Noel did not risk a new way of being in the world—the continually emerging "who I am" and the ongoing discovering of the other.

Continuity

By fantasizing about Anna, Noel maintained a psychological continuity with the past. If he had actually courted Anna and professed his love, most likely something dramatic would have happened. She might have responded in a loving way, thereby creating a juxtaposition between his current experience and his emotional memories of longing for an unrequited love. He would probably be filled with fantasies about the love he did not receive as a child. He would hurt again (Erskine, 1997a). Conversely, if Noel had developed a real relationship with Anna, she might not have wanted a loving involvement with him, and that might also have stimulated the emotional memories of the inherent rejection in mother's use of father's violence and/or her depression.

Stability

Obsessively fantasizing about what might occur is an attempt to remain psychologically stable and grounded. It is a false sense of living life today, a contact disruption from both the full remembering of the earlier emotional experiences and the pull to a therapeutic, healing regression. The unresolved early emotional experiences are unconsciously expressed in the fantasy. The hurt, rejection, neglect, or abuse may, through fantasy, be projected onto current or future relationships, thereby avoiding a full regression—a kind of being half in and half out.

Regression within a sensitive, caring therapeutic relationship is healing and growth producing. It is an opportunity for a reparative experience. Yet people fear the overwhelming flood of emotions often present in regression and therefore use obsessing and other psychological defenses as a desperate attempt to stabilize themselves. However, even in the presence of such defensive, stabilizing maneuvers there is always a pull to healing. Hence, transference and obsessing are expressions of both the repetitive and needed relationship and a defense against a full, vulnerable regression.

It is essential in an in-depth treatment of obsession to assess the origins and intrapsychic functions of the repetitive fantasizing and to validate how those multiple functions help the client to maintain psychological homeostasis. The psychological functions described in this article—predictability, identity, continuity,

98 Richard G. Erskine

and stability—are only four of a number of such functions. Many clients who are locked into a life script and use repetitive fantasizing as a means of maintaining homeostasis may use other psychological functions as well. Compensation, reparation, efficacy, integrity, and triumph are examples of other psychological functions used to maintain obsessions. The psychotherapy of obsessions is complex because of the compounded and continually reinforcing multiple intrapsychic functions. A respectful and patient inquiry into the client's phenomenological experience is required to learn the unique combination of intrapsychic functions.

Relational needs and transference

From a clinical perspective, transference is both an unconscious repetition of the past and an unconscious request in the present for a therapeutically needed relationship (S. Stern, 1994). Transference is the active means whereby the client can communicate his or her past. This includes the neglects, traumas, and needs that were thwarted in the process of growing up, as well as the defenses that were created to compensate for the lack of need fulfillment. In the unaware enactment of childhood experiences there is also an inhibition of full remembering. While this all constitutes a replication of previous relationships, often in coded form, also imbedded in the transference is the therapeutically needed relationship, the desire to achieve the satisfaction of relational needs and intimacy in relationship (Erskine, 1997d).

Perhaps what may be required for a more thorough understanding of script formation and transference is an appreciation of Bowlby's (1969, 1973, 1980) ideas about early bonding and the necessity of a "secure base," the psychological significance of disruptions in early attachment, and the psychological attachments that form a visceral and emotional core from which all experiences of relationship emerge.

Hargaden's sensitivity to both the repeated and needed relationship with Noel is reflected in her saying:

> I wanted to fold him in my arms, put him in a carry cot, and bring him away on holiday with us. I also wanted to make a joke out of it, perhaps in the sadistic fashion reflective of his father. Instead, I was able easily to show tenderness toward him and interpret his need for holding and loving without shaming him or acting on it.
>
> *(Hargaden, 2001, p. 217)*

The transference in everyday life that may occur in friendships and love relationships—for example, with one's children or on the job—also reflects the repetition of emotional experiences of past relationships and the unconscious desire for the other to repair the failures of past relationships. In the case presented by Hargaden, Noel's transference with Anna, presented in the context of a plausible real relationship, contained numerous and significant transferential idealizations of her attributes. His idealization was so compelling, in fact, that even Hargaden was caught up in the wonders of Anna.

In the first half of the case study, I anticipated that Noel's love for Anna would be transferred to Hargaden in some erotic form. As I continued to read I was reminded of Kohut's (1971, 1977) description of idealization as one of the dimensions of pathological narcissism. Although he identified mirroring, twinship, and idealization as the transferential expressions of pathological narcissism, he also attempted to distinguish relational, developmental needs that suffered disruption or rupture from classical transference based on a drive model of psychoanalysis. However, his methods remained psychoanalytic and did not make full use of a relational model of psychotherapy.

There may be evidence to support a diagnosis of narcissism in Noel's case: he sat provocatively in shorts while describing his sexual exploits with women, his self-centeredness and apparent lack of intimate connection, and his demands of entitlement to his therapist's schedule. However, as Noel's story unfolded it became clear that his idealized transference with Anna might reveal much more therapeutically useful material if perceived by the therapist, not from a pathological perspective (narcissism), but rather from the theoretical perspective that his idealized love was an expression of the relational need of a young boy for protection, security, and validation (Erskine, Moursund, & Trautmann, 1999; Erskine & Trautmann, 1996).

If I had been Hargaden's clinical supervisor during the early phase of Noel's therapy, we would have talked about Noel's relational needs and how they were unconsciously revealed through his general demeanor: initially in the stories he told about Anna, later in his history with his parents, and, importantly, in Hargaden's countertransferential response.

Countertransference has traditionally been viewed as the psychotherapist's unfinished business from the past (Racker, 1968). However, from a relational therapy perspective, countertransference refers to the feelings, images, fantasies, and reactions that a psychologically healthy therapist has as a unique reaction to the unconscious communication of a particular client (Bollas, 1979).

As her supervisor, I would have encouraged Hargaden to be sensitive to her own emotions and fantasies as a possible glimpse at perceiving Noel's relational needs. I would have continually raised questions about her feelings and fantasies as an identification with Noel's unconscious communication regarding his traumas, relational needs, and the psychological functions of his obsessions. Hargaden's "countertransference" reaction of also idealizing Anna may have been an indication of how profoundly Noel needed protection from a stable, consistent, and effectively protective other. Her caring feelings toward him and her nonjudgmental response set the stage for responding to Noel's need for security. She liked him and valued him, a necessary condition for attunement to affect, developmental level of functioning, and relational needs.

Attunement to the need for security involves the therapist being sensitive to the importance of this particular need and conducting himself or herself both emotionally and behaviorally in a way that provides security in the relationship. This includes respectful transactions that are nonshaming as well as an honoring and preserving of the individual's vulnerability. It involves the experience within the client that his or her variety of needs and feelings are human and natural. Security is a sense of simultaneously being vulnerable and in harmony with another. In my imagined supervision of Hargaden, the security aspects of the therapy with Noel would receive only a little attention since this is an area in which Hargaden seems so sensitive.

Early in the work I would also have focused on the unconscious communication of the need for protection as revealed in Noel's idealization of Anna. Idealization is the expression of a search for protection—the protection in early childhood from the emotional and physical impingement of bigger people. When manifested in psychotherapy, such idealization is the unconscious search for protection from a controlling and humiliating introjected Parent ego state and the resulting intrapsychic conflict. It may also represent the search for protection in the form of containment of an escalation of affect or fantasy or a secure setting of limits. Just as young children look to grown-ups for guidance and protection, so, too, was Noel searching for someone who could be strong, responsible, and protective. He most likely searched for the kind of protection that his mother failed to provide when she allowed his father to beat him.

Additionally, the consistency, dependability, and reliability of a stable mother was probably lost if mother was depressed following the death of Noel's sister. D. N. Stern (1985) writes of the importance of the mother's affect of vitality to the baby's emerging sense of self. If such maternal vitality is absent, as is often the case when mother is depressed, the result is an emotional abandonment, a lack of security and protection. Noel turned to an illusion to receive a sense of vitality and protection. Noel's description of Anna as strong, passionate, and feminine was not a description of himself, as Hargaden surmised, but a description of what was not provided in Noel's relationship with his mother and therefore was therapeutically needed in the psychotherapy relationship. I think that an essential therapeutic element was Hargaden's providing Noel with her attunement, involvement, and protection.

Hargaden's refusal to be seduced by Noel into a friendship or erotic relationship was also a necessary therapeutic response. He needed to be in the presence of someone who was stable, dependable and reliable; a friendship would not have provided the necessary protection. Hargaden's insistence on the structure of the therapeutic relationship provided the protection that allowed Noel to remember.

As Hargaden responded to Noel's need for validation, he was correspondingly more able to feel her provision of stability, dependability, and protection. Conversely, whenever she failed to validate Noel, he would bring Anna into the conversation as an illustration of both validation and protection. Since Hargaden is skillful at validating and affirming, in supervision I would not spend much time discussing various therapeutic responses to the need for validation. Rather, we would examine the inevitable therapeutic failure to provide perfect validation and the necessary repairs that reestablish contact-in-relationship (Erskine, Moursund, & Trautmann, 1999). (For a valuable discussion of the concept of "Failures in the therapeutic relationship: Inevitable *and* necessary?" see Guistolise, 1996).

Hargaden's failures to validate or affirm Noel's sense of being significant in the relationship stimulated his fixated early childhood need to depend on a stable other person while receiving security, validation, and protection. Bringing Anna into the conversation at such points served as an unconscious example of how to do it right. Noel's need to feel confirmed by the personal experience of another was responded to by Hargaden's shared delight in a similar sense of humor, art, literature, and political sensitivity, and perhaps also by her enchantment with Anna. Had Hargaden responded more behaviorally to Noel's demand for a shared experience, such as meeting socially or even telling him of her sexual fantasies, she would have overemphasized this need (perhaps acting out a need of her own) and missed the central importance of providing both validation and protection to a client whose Child ego states were active and vulnerable.

Even while sharing one's personal experience in response to the client's current relational needs, it is essential that the therapist remain mindful of the fixated relational needs of a traumatized child. The fixated archaic needs are either acted out in the transference or are expressed in fantasy. The unconscious behavior and/or fantasized expression of these needs demands an appropriate therapeutic response, one that may focus on providing either security, validation, protection, or initiation while also responding to the need to feel confirmed by the personal experience of another.

Noel attempted to have an impact on Hargaden by making demands for extra sessions during holidays and to meet some place other than the established therapy room. Certainly he had the need to make an impact on another person, but in the way he expressed this, his need for protection could have been overlooked if the psychotherapist allowed the relationship to become social.

Any child who has been neglected, rejected, and/or physically abused will have an intense need, later in life, to make an impact—to demand in some form or another "attend to me," "be sensitive to me," "don't hurt me." Often this need is acted out in the form of entitlement and/or takes subverted forms that overshadow other equally important needs (e.g., security, protection, self-definition, etc.); such was the case with Noel's request that he and Hargaden meet socially.

Hargaden demonstrated that she received the impact of Noel's presence and personal story when she initiated her interpretation about the psychological effects of Noel's dead sister and the depressing effect it had on his mother. Interpretation is psychologically transmuting (Kohut, 1977), not necessarily in its accuracy, but in demonstrating to the client that the therapist is stirred to think about him or her, that the therapist is taking the client's story seriously, and that the therapist is invested in the client's welfare. The accuracy of the interpretation may not be what is therapeutically important. A partially accurate interpretation leaves room for the client to correct the therapist, thereby creating an opportunity to make further impact. However, interpretations that accurately reflect a client's need or experience express an attunement and involvement that builds and strengthens the therapeutic relationship.

Noel's need to express love was evident in his affection for Anna—the Anna who in fantasy provided both validation and protection. Noel's current need to

102 Richard G. Erskine

express love was manifested in the establishment of a mature active involvement with an available partner.

Conclusion

I have enjoyed studying Hargaden's case presentation and appreciate her highly professional therapeutic acumen. However, in theory I disagree with one of her comments: "In not getting the need met with me, Noel became frustrated enough to break through his fantasy and attempt to get his needs met in a more realistic way." I have a different perspective: It is precisely because Noel had both his archaic and current relational needs therapeutically responded to by Hargaden that he could become involved with another woman. Because of Hargaden's attunement and involvement, Noel was able to transfer the psychological functions of predictability, identity, continuity, and stability into the therapeutic relationship and therefore establish a secure base from which to pursue a mature relationship.

Noel's obsession with Anna provided a pseudosatisfaction of his relational needs while alluding to significant relational failures in his childhood. The fantasies of Anna served to unconsciously reveal what was therapeutically needed: a receptive spirit, a tender heart, a person bright and wise. This was Noel's unconscious description of the therapeutically needed relationship that he brought to Hargaden. In providing Noel with therapeutic consistency, ethical responsibility, and dependable nurturing, the therapeutic relationship offered him an opportunity to relax his defenses, receive therapeutic responses to both archaic and current relational needs, and transfer the psychological functions imbedded in the obsession into the therapeutic relationship. Thus Hargaden's psychotherapy with Noel provided a protective, secure foundation for building a healthy mature relationship with another person. His healing was in the therapeutic relationship with Hargaden.

References

Berne, E. (1963). *The structure and dynamics of organizations and groups*. New York: Grove Press.

Berne, E. (1966). *Principles of group treatment*. New York: Grove Press.

Bollas, C. (1979). The transformational object. *International Journal of Psychoanalysis, 60*, 97–107.

Bowlby, J. (1969). *Attachment*. Vol. 1 of *Attachment and loss*. New York: Basic Books.

Bowlby, J. (1973). *Separation: Anxiety and anger*. Vol. 2 of *Attachment and loss*. New York: Basic Books.

Bowlby, J. (1980). *Loss: Sadness and depression*. Vol. 3 of *Attachment and loss*. New York: Basic Books.

Erskine, R. G. (1997a). Inquiry, attunement, and involvement in the psychotherapy of dissociation. In R. G. Erskine (Ed.), *Theories and methods of an integrative transactional analysis: A volume of selected articles* (pp. 37–45). San Francisco: TA Press. (Original work published 1993.)

Erskine, R. G. (1997b). Supervision of psychotherapy: Models for professional development. In R. G. Erskine (Ed.), *Theories and methods of an integrative transactional analysis: A volume of selected articles* (pp. 217–226). San Francisco: TA Press. (Original work published 1982.)

Erskine, R. G. (1997c). The therapeutic relationship: Integrating motivation and personality theories. In R. G. Erskine (Ed.), *Theories and methods of an integrative transactional analysis: A volume of selected articles* (pp. 7–19). San Francisco: TA Press.

Erskine, R. G. (1997d). Transference and transactions: Critique from an intrapsychic and integrative perspective. In R. G. Erskine (Ed.), *Theories and methods of an integrative transactional analysis: A volume of selected articles* (pp. 129–146). San Francisco: TA Press. (Original work published 1991.)

Erskine, R. G., Moursund, J. P., & Trautmann, R. L. (1999). *Beyond empathy: A theory of contact-in-relationship*. Philadelphia: Brunner/Mazel.

Erskine, R. G., & Trautmann, R. L. (1996). Methods of an integrative psychotherapy. *Transactional Analysis Journal, 26*, 316–328.

Guistolise, P. G. (1996). Failures in the therapeutic relationship: Inevitable *and* necessary? *Transactional Analysis Journal, 26*, 284–288.

Hargaden, H. (2001). There ain't no cure for love: The psychotherapy of an erotic transference. *Transactional Analysis Journal, 31*, 213–219.

Kohut, H. (1971). *The analysis of the self: A systematic approach to the psychoanalytic treatment of narcissistic personality disorder*. New York: International Universities Press.

Kohut, H. (1977). *The restoration of the self*. New York: International Universities Press.

Racker, M. (1968). *Transference and countertransference*. New York: International Universities Press.

Stern, D. N. (1985). *The interpersonal world of the infant: A view from psychoanalysis and developmental psychology*. New York: Basic Books.

Stern, S. (1994). Needed relationships and repeated relationships: An integrated relational perspective. *Psychoanalytic Dialogues, 4*(3), 317–345.

8

THE MAN WITH NO NAME

A response to Hargaden and Erskine

Charlotte Sills

As I read first Helena Hargaden's (2001) intriguing paper, "There ain't no cure for love: The psychotherapy of an erotic transference," and then Richard Erskine's (2001) lucid response, "Psychological function, relational needs, and transferential resolution: Psychotherapy of an obsession," I had the same sort of reaction that Erskine describes in his early pages. In a way, I felt I had nothing to add. I certainly did not want to deconstruct the work Hargaden and her client had done together, representing it as a perfect opportunity for cognitive behavioral therapy, for example.

Hargaden had gently mused and explored so many angles of her work with Noel, examining what the relationship brought and keeping her mind open to potentials of meaning, experience, and feeling. There was no rigidity or restriction in her approach, only opening and possibility, all within a carefully and securely held frame. In his paper, Erskine acknowledges this and then takes a view that, although within Hargaden's frame of reference as a relational therapist, is somewhat different, thus inviting her to see the case in a slightly different light. This is true "analysis" on the part of both of them. It captures the original meaning of the Greek word *analusis*—"a loosening of bonds"—for this is what they have done. I hope that my comments will also contribute to this process so that the story of the therapeutic dyad of Noel and Helena can be free to continue its evolution.

In the work Hargaden describes, her client, Noel, develops a strong attachment to her as his therapist. Hargaden understands this in terms of an erotic transference. On the other hand, Erskine sees it in terms of the idealizing component of a relational need. I intend to look at the complexity of this idealization and ask some questions about how we should respond to it.

To do so, I use a model of self-development that Hargaden and I developed (Hargaden & Sills, 1999, 2001, 2002) as a framework for understanding the many strands of thinking and feeling that occur in the therapeutic endeavor. The model has major implications for practice.

Therapeutic model

Clients enter therapy with difficulties arising from conflicts or tensions caused by early (and later) experiences, their lives restricted by lack of awareness and lack of choice. These problems are manifested in their relationships with people and the world that are stale repetitions of templates for thinking, feeling, and behavior developed early in life. How does psychotherapy help? Ideally, clients find in the therapist someone who both allows them to bring their original relational dynamics into the room and yet is sufficiently aware and willing to call them to a different sort of relationship. In transactional analysis terms, the therapist will not settle for cocreating a palimpsest (Berne, 1963, p. 228) of the original protocol.

The therapist must meet clients in real Adult–Adult contact that accounts for the relationship as it exists here and now in the consulting room. As part of and in addition to this, he or she also offers what Schore (2000) calls "the right brain connection," which involves responding to those ulterior transactions that Hargaden and I (Hargaden & Sills, 2001, in press) refer to as the *introjective transferences*. The therapist conveys to the client that he or she is strong, calm, protective, empathic, and accepting enough to receive all of him or her, that the client's feelings, needs (including early unmet needs), yearnings, assertions, and demands are more than fine with the therapist.

Hargaden and I locate these introjective transferences in C_1, the source of the core sense of self, which is established out of the infant's experience of the mutual interaction with a self-regulating other (Stern, 1985). We visualize this as being contained in a type of amniotic sac of the A_0 created by the interrelation between C_0 and P_0 (Sills, 1995). The C_0 is experienced as bodily-affective states that include the sense of being contacted by the environment (mother) represented by P_0.

From this theoretical stance, the introjective transferences are viewed as a normal part of being human. In this we follow the tradition of Kohut (1977), who suggested that what he described as selfobject needs continue throughout a person's life. This is also similar to the way Stern views the senses of self continuing as a central aspect of the individual and Bowlby (1977) identifies attachment needs that shape the behavior of both children and adults. Similarly, Berne offered the psychobiological hungers (structure, stimulus, incident, recognition (translated to relationship by Erskine (1998, p. 135)), power, and sexuality), which are an ongoing part of life, while Erskine (1993, 1998; Erskine, Moursund, & Trautmann, 1999; Erskine & Trautmann, 1996) in his integrative model also describes relational needs that bridge childhood and adulthood.

As a natural part of human functioning, we believe these needs arise from the necessity humans feel to manage the existential challenges of reality: that ultimately we will die, and meanwhile we are cast into a world apparently without order or meaning to live with millions of others. As Cohn (1997) puts it, "Human existence is always in the world, in space, in time, in the body, emotionally 'attuned' … intersubjective and limited by death" (p. 13).

However, we also see these introjective transferences as manifestations of unmet developmental needs. When the infant's needs are met and he or she is treated with appreciation and delight, his or her sense of self and others is good. When there are sufficient experiences of attuned interplay between the child and the environment, the child develops internalized representations of self-and-mother (C_0/P_0) to support the healthy development of a core self. When the infant experiences cumulative misattunement and/or nonattunement from the environment, then he or she has no way of dealing with this except by splitting off the "undigested" experiences (Klein, 1986). This can be understood as the schizoid process. In such cases, the child's A_0 remains, in a sense, incomplete and *unintegrating*, despite the fact that he or she may have a coherent and consistent, though limited, sense of self. The "split-off," unintegrated experiences are walled inside C_0 or form P_1 along with the internalized representations of the other (described by Goulding and Goulding (1976) as injunctions).

The therapist attempts to offer a response to the introjective transferences while at the same time being "ordinarily human"—making mistakes, acknowledging biases, disappointing the client in a myriad of ways that eventually allow him or her to accept the "good enoughness" of both of them. In that sense, the unmet needs of the client are potentially being met, but not by active parenting by the therapist.

Another vital element of the therapeutic dynamic involves the resolution of what Hargaden and I (Hargaden & Sills, 2001) refer to as the *projective transferences* and script material that the client brings from A_1 and P_1. These are replays of the original, unsatisfactory relationship "bonds"—repetitions of past ways of managing and controlling the self and the environment. They contain the ways the person has developed for managing C_0 yearnings, split-off aspects of the self, script decisions, and what Stern (1985) called "Representations of Interactions that have been Generalized (RIGs)" (p. 97). These are mostly out of awareness, and as Meier (1995) says of the activities of the unconscious, "They make themselves known indirectly and with peculiar effects" (p. 13). It is the therapist's job to offer "analysis" of these in the true sense, that is, by "loosening" these relational "bonds." He or she does this by raising awareness (both emotional and cognitive), by using his or her own responses to shed light on relationship patterns, by reflecting and inviting reflection, by confronting or by holding fast when the client accesses terrified or rageful ego states, by facilitating the discovery of explanations, and by offering a "safe container" in which the client can begin to integrate his or her various parts.

In addition to all of this, the therapist may act as a container for aspects of the client that are as yet disowned (*transformational transference*) and that can be integrated by the client through the transformational matrix of the therapeutic dyad. This process is eloquently described by Bollas (1987) and Ogden (1992). The therapist becomes aware of experiencing certain disowned feelings of the client and is required to accept and manage them so that eventually the client can recognize and own them as part of himself or herself.

This theoretical model can be a useful tool for organizing the complex dynamics involved in the psychotherapy relationship—with Adult–Adult representing the

The man with no name   **107**

here-and-now relationship, C_0 and C_1 conveying the relational yearnings (projective transferences), A_1 and P_1 being involved in the projective transferences, and any part of the Child ego state projected outward in the transformational transference.

The case of Noel

We can also use this theoretical framework to consider Hargaden's reflections as she muses on her client, Noel. For example, what was the meaning of the erotic in the relationship between Hargaden and Noel? Was it here-and-now Adult-to-Adult? Was it A_1 and P_1: a way of seducing and withholding, of punishing the mother? Was it a way to deflect real intimacy? Or was the erotic a manifestation of what Mann (1997) describes as the preoedipal erotic mother (or father) or, as Hargaden suggests, a blend of the preoedipal erotic mother and the oedipal erotic father?

What about the fantasy of the ideal Anna? What did she represent? A split-off part of Noel's self, as Hargaden suggests, the soft anima (female aspect) that is projected onto others until Noel can reown it? Or is it the C_0 yearning for the idealized mother who is kept ideal through distance? Or the idolized (as opposed to idealized) P_{1+} created by an A_{1+} who keeps himself feeling whole by carrying within himself his image of the perfect other (you are never alone with an introject)? Noel used his fantasy of Anna to judge real people and find them lacking, yet at the same time he maintained himself as unfulfilled and potentially rejected: The ideal was always out of reach.

This leads me to the major question I wish to raise here. How can we, as therapists, differentiate between a C_0 idealizing yearning, which needs to be validated, and an A_1 idolizing transference, which is an avoidance of intimacy and reality? Is it even possible and/or important to distinguish between them? And what implications might such a distinction have for therapy and therapist interventions?

I want to keep these questions in mind as I turn my attention to a consideration of Erskine's understanding of Noel. As I read Erskine's paper, I was captivated by the simple yet subtle notion of treating Noel as someone with an obsessional disorder. Of course, Noel was obsessed with Anna, and his ruminations about her fulfill the traditional elements of an obsession in that they contain both the seed of the real issue and the defense against it. Erskine highlights how Noel's presentation plainly contains what Hargaden and I would call the introjective transferences: the C_0 and C_1 yearnings. Noel's obsession with Anna served the selfobject function of meeting needs for stability, identity, and continuity, as Erskine describes, and also contained the repeated, defensive maneuvers for avoiding the deepest pain by keeping someone around yet at a distance. Erskine's understanding of Noel's obsession epitomizes Schiff et al.'s (1975) definition of a game: "Games are an attempt to reenact symbiotic relationships that the children did not resolve with their parents, or are an angry reaction to those relationships" (p. 7). Noel's seductiveness and his idolizing contain the unresolved issue of his early needs but also replay the invitation to persecute as well as (in unconscious anger) controlling his therapist's (and Anna's) closeness and distance. (Incidentally, I think that the Schiffs neatly resolve the argument between

108   Charlotte Sills

Berne and English with their definition. Berne thought games were played for the payoff. English thought they were played for the racketeering strokes available in the actual playing. The Schiffian definition explains that both are right.)

In his article, Erskine (2001) offers a coherent approach that helps the client go through the steps of integration to achieve lasting change. In particular, through a process of inquiry and attunement by the therapist, the "functions of the repetitive behavior, feeling, or fantasy must first be identified by the client." Then those functions need to be transferred into the actual relationship with the therapist so that, within a relationship that genuinely meets the client's relational needs, he or she can experience and understand the past pressure to create and maintain defenses. The client can then dissolve those defenses, leaving him or her free to make current relationships that meet relational needs.

I find Erskine's approach both internally logical and emotionally satisfying. However, I am interested to return to the question I asked earlier. Is it important to differentiate between introjective transferences and projective transferences? For example, how can we tell the difference between two types of idealization? On the one hand, there is the genuine relational need to be met and understood by a calm, competent other that arises from the unresolved infant need to have the other be a soothing and powerful extension of self. On the other, there is the desire to see the therapist as the powerful and wise parent figure who will confirm the person's A_1 image of self. Does it matter if the two are addressed together? In my view, doing so often does not create a problem. Clients enter therapy enacting their projective transferences, and analysis of these leads them to risk revealing their vulnerable introjective needs. The two are naturally resolved as a whole.

Nevertheless, I believe there can be a danger here. If the therapist meets a client's relational needs, he or she may be experienced by the client as meeting the A_1 needs and thus confirming the client's "false self" (Winnicott, 1984, p. 148). This might have the effect of rewarding the seductiveness, or perhaps of reinforcing the defense, so that those elements of the Child that have been split off and found unacceptable continue to be avoided. Further, even if the client feels truly accepted by the therapist, there is a danger that he or she will experience that in this relationship he or she has at last found the perfect other. What happens to the C_1 rage and pain at not having been met in the past if the client is being met in the present? I believe that when the therapist meets the client's relational needs, the client may feel consummately seen and appreciated in the consulting room, but only there.

The obvious safety mechanism for this possibility is that inevitably the therapist fails the client somehow: fails to be attuned, fails to be attentive, fails to be perfect. This failure then creates the opportunity for the client's grief and rage to emerge. However, even when such failures occur, some therapists continue to try to be so understanding—including about a rupture in relationship—that they nip in the bud any possibility of the client rekindling his or her infantile rage. Thus, outside the consulting room, in real life, when the client must deal with ordinary relationships, he or she continues to avoid them and/or to denigrate whoever lets him or her down.

It seems to me essential that therapists see the difference between the types of transference. I wonder if the clue to making such a differentiation can be found in Erskine's words (quoted earlier): "the functions of the repetitive behavior, feeling, or fantasy must *first* be identified by the client" (my emphasis). I believe that the differentiation between the demand of the vital introjective transferences and the pathological defensive ones (projective transferences) can be made only where there is Adult–Adult (and Adult–Child) relating, exploration, and understanding between therapist and client. While this occurs, the introjective transferences are addressed by an ulterior message from the therapist to the client's C_1. This message, usually nonverbal, is, in effect, "I'm OK, You're OK." In other words, "I am strong enough, calm enough, accepting enough, admiring enough, and you—with all your feelings, needs, moods, humor, everything—are fine with me." This blend of A–A with A–C$_1$ forms the basic therapeutic transaction and can normally be sufficient to meet both the here-and-now relational needs and the unresolved introjective transferences.

The fact is therapists are usually hypersensitive to their clients' unmet needs. That is why they become therapists. They intuitively recognize and empathize with the "inarticulate speech of the heart" (Morrison, quoted in Hargaden & Sills, 2001, p. 61). However, out of this develops a kind of self-imposed tyranny in which the therapist feels obliged to meet those needs. In my experience—both personal and with countless supervisees—it is a short step from there to either a sort of reparenting without a contract or (in the other vacant position on the drama triangle) to feeling resentful and angry with the client. Thus the therapist leads the way from the introjective countertransference into the complementary projective countertransference. That is, he or she takes the therapy in the wrong direction. As an antidote to this process, I am drawn to Hobbes' (personal communication, April 6, 2001) suggestion that if as therapists we move away from the phrase "relational needs" to the concept of "relationship processes," we may free ourselves from the imperative of responding actively to the client's yearning.

To return to Hargaden's case, one of the most successful elements of that work was that she allowed herself to feel the strong pull of both the introjective and the projective transference—and she acted out neither. She did not enter the game, and she left the process free so that new dynamics could emerge. For me the only missing piece was at the end. But I will get to that later. First I want to return to Erskine's paper.

As with all of Erskine's writing, this paper is full of gems to be savored and reflected on. For example, his comments about interpretation are very rich. The importance of an interpretation is not necessarily a result of its accuracy, although accuracy in understanding a client's need or experience builds the therapeutic relationship. Rather, interpretation, according to Erskine, shows that the client has made an impact, has made the therapist think and invest energy in the client. It is an invitation to the client to take himself or herself equally seriously. If the interpretation is only partly accurate, "it leaves room for the client to correct" it, as Erskine says. It requires him or her to reflect, to question meanings. I especially enjoyed the way Erskine takes the concept of

110   Charlotte Sills

interpretation out of the realm of objectification and "other-defining" into the juicy realm of relationship. I also see this as a fine example of the therapeutic transaction I described earlier.

I agreed with both Erskine and Hargaden in their understanding of the success of this psychotherapy. Interestingly, Erskine asserts that the success lay in the relationship, in which Hargaden provided Noel with "therapeutic consistency, ethical responsibility, and dependable nurturing" so that he could relax his defenses and allow both past and present relational needs to emerge. Noel was then free to make more fulfilling relationships in his current life. In contrast, Hargaden sees the fact that she did not meet Noel's need as enabling him to break through the fantasy and attempt to get his needs met in a more realistic way.

I believe that both are true. My view is that Noel (in his dark glasses and pop-star attire) presented as what the Jungians call a *puer aeternus* (Jung, 1972). This is a man who never grows up (e.g., Saint-Exupéry, Peter Pan), who splits off his hurt, vulnerable side and retains the idea that everything is all right and that he is in control. Such a man needs to make a relationship with another person to make a relationship with himself. Hargaden provided the necessary blend of right-brain connection and a relationship of mutual engagement and stable, boundaried psychotherapy in which Noel could achieve that task. However, I believe there was something important in the way she failed to meet his needs that pushed Noel to take the essential step of making real relationships with the world.

And this brings me to my last question. It is about the way in which Hargaden describes Noel's departure. Hargaden, as the reader will have noticed, is someone who uses herself and her imagination in understanding the therapeutic dynamics. She welcomes metaphor and imagery, coincidence and symbol. She allows her language to lead her, not just serve her.

How, then, did she come to use the following words in relation to the end of the therapeutic relationship: "He left town." He left town? For me that phrase conjures up images that have become part of twentieth century mythology. In my mind, I see the cool and taciturn cowboy who arrives in town, does what he has come to do, and then leaves. It is Clint Eastwood as "the man with no name." It is John Wayne. It is innumerable heroes who ride onto the scene, make their impact (maybe fall in love), but ultimately have to turn their backs and move on.

Why did Noel leave therapy? Was he a changed man as a result of his work with Hargaden? Or was he treating her as if she were the mother who was there to be used and left? Or was he turning away from the lover who risked capturing him? Was it script? Or had he, in the best tradition of the man with no name, done what he came to do, gotten what he wanted?

After all is said and done, I am left wondering whether there was something that Noel was not ready to do. In the early Western films, the hero left town and nobody questioned it, least of all the hero himself. Engagement and relationship were not expected of this sort of man. More recent Westerns tend to acknowledge that the cowboy hero has a flaw. He is tempted by the invitation to a real loving relationship (including the sexual, as Cornell points out in his commentary in

Chapter 9), the opportunity to settle down and make a life, have children, be part of the community. But he cannot. Perhaps Hargaden, by declining to step into the desired role, called Noel to make a commitment to a relationship that he was not quite ready to make.

And finally, I am compelled to consider what the significance is of what we are doing in these articles about the case of Noel. In the best tradition of the cinema there are film critics, people who analyze the plot, the screenplay, the characterizations. What impact do they have on characters in future episodes, on the film industry, on the film-going public? Here, we are all intrigued with Noel, analyzing him, understanding him, caring about him—without ever meeting him or knowing his real name. It is regrettable that we are not able to find out what ultimately unfolds for him. Is there a *Noel II—The Sequel?*

References

Berne, E. (1963). *The structure and dynamics of organizations and groups.* New York: Grove Press.

Bollas, C. (1987). *The shadow of the object: Psychoanalysis of the unthought known.* New York: Columbia.

Bowlby, J. (1977). The making and breaking of affectional bonds. *British Journal of Psychiatry, 130,* 201–210.

Cohn, H. (1997). *Existential thought and therapeutic practice.* London: Sage.

Erskine, R. G. (1993). Inquiry, attunement, and involvement in the psychotherapy of dissociation. *Transactional Analysis Journal, 23,* 184–190.

Erskine, R. G. (1998). The therapeutic relationship: Integrating motivation and personality theories. *Transactional Analysis Journal, 28,* 132–141.

Erskine, R. G. (2001). Psychological function, relational needs, and transferential resolution: Psychotherapy of an obsession. *Transactional Analysis Journal, 31,* 220–226.

Erskine, R. G., Moursund, J. P., & Trautmann, R. L. (1999). *Beyond empathy: A theory of contact-in-relationship.* Philadelphia: Brunner/Mazel.

Erskine, R. G., & Trautmann, R. L. (1996). Methods of an integrative psychotherapy. *Transactional Analysis Journal, 26,* 316–328.

Goulding, R. L., & Goulding, M. M. (1976). Injunctions, decisions, and redecisions. *Transactional Analysis Journal, 6,* 41–48.

Hargaden, H. (2001). There ain't no cure for love: The psychotherapy of an erotic transference. *Transactional Analysis Journal, 31,* 213–219.

Hargaden, H., & Sills, C. (1999). The child ego state: An integrative view. *ITA News, 53,* 20–24.

Hargaden, H., & Sills, C. (2001). Deconfusion of the child ego state: A relational perspective. *Transactional Analysis Journal, 31,* 55–70.

Hargaden, H & Sills, C. (2002). *Transactional analysis: A relational perspective.* London: Routledge

Jung, C. G. (1972). *Four archetypes.* London: Routledge & Keegan Paul. (Original work published 1959.)

Klein, M. (1986). *The selected Melanie Klein* (J. Mitchell, Ed.). London: Peregrine Books.

Kohut, H. (1977). *The restoration of the self.* New York: International Universities Press.

Mann, D. (1997). *Psychotherapy: An erotic relationship.* London: Routledge.

Meier, C. J. (1995). *Personality: The individuation process in the light of C. G. Jung's typology.* Einsiedeln, Switzerland. Daimon. (Original work published 1977.)

Ogden, T. (1992). *Projective identification and psychotherapeutic technique.* London, Karnac.

112 Charlotte Sills

Schiff, J. L., with Schiff, A. W., Mellor, K., Schiff, E., Schiff, S., Richman, D., Fishman, J., Wolz, L., Fishman, C., & Momb, D. (1975). *Cathexis reader: Transactional analysis treatment of psychosis*. New York. Harper & Row.

Schore, A. N. (2000). Minds in the making. Seventh Annual John Bowlby Memorial Lecture (CAPP), London.

Sills, C. (1995). From ego states and transference to the concept of setting in transactional analysis: Reviewing the healing relationship. Panel presentation at the annual ITAA conference, San Francisco.

Stern, D. N. (1985). *The interpersonal world of the infant: A view from psychoanalysis and developmental psychology*. New York: Basic Books.

Winnicott, D. W. (1984). Ego distortion in terms of true and false self. In D. W. Winnicott, *The maturational process and the facilitating environment: Studies in the theory of emotional development* (pp. 140–152). London: Karnac. (Original work published 1965.)

9

THERE AIN'T NO CURE WITHOUT SEX

The provision of a "vital" base

William F. Cornell

Helena Hargaden's (2001) case study, "There ain't no cure for love," is a frank examination of the erotic and sexual aspects of an intensive psychotherapy. As such, it provides the readers of the *Transactional Analysis Journal* with an opportunity that is rare in the transactional analysis literature. In her discussion of this rich and complex case, Helena offers a detailed account of her clinical thinking and countertransferential reactions as the therapy unfolded. Her case is further extended in fascinating ways by Richard Erskine (2001) and Charlotte Sills (2001) in discussant papers originally prepared for the 2001 Institute of Transactional Analysis (ITA) Conference in Keele, England. I am contributing a third discussant paper from a different diagnostic perspective.

Diagnosis

As I read the case of Noel, I considered, as did Richard, what I would say to Helena from a consultative point of view. I would start, as I typically do, with diagnostic impressions. In my reading of this case, I would diagnose Noel as a hysteric. From the opening scene as he arrived for his first therapy session with Helena—dressed in black, wearing sunglasses, evoking in Helena the question of whether he had come to the wrong door—Noel demonstrated the essence of the hysterical defense: Look, but do not touch (physically or emotionally). Viewing Noel's defenses as fundamentally hysterical is not inconsistent with Richard's and Charlotte's emphasis on the obsessional nature of Noel's functioning. In fact, I agree with Richard's observation that Helena's case study is "about the successful treatment of an obsession." However, I also suggest that Noel "left town" before his hysterical defenses and sexual avoidances were adequately addressed.

My thinking about Noel's diagnosis is deeply influenced by my Reichian training. Seen from a Reichian/bioenergetic perspective, obsession and hysteria

114 William F. Cornell

are two sides of the same coin, the "rigid" (Lowen, 1958; Baker, 1967) defenses that form during the oedipal period of development. This is the developmental crucible within which the young child learns what it means to love and to be aggressive. Earlier developmental processes tend to center on the experience of *being* loved (i.e., on receiving affection, nurturance, understanding, etc.), whereas in the oedipal period the young child wrestles with his or her capacity and right to *be loving*. Lowen (1975) characterizes the primary developmental task in this phase as internalizing the right to love. During the oedipal stage, the child begins to learn what it means to desire another and to show love for others. The capacity for desire, especially erotic desires, comes to life during these years.

The shadow of oedipal/erotic failure is evident throughout Helena's initial observations of and reactions to Noel: "In his fantasy life there were no ties, no commitment—not to others and not to me"; "He idealized but never got close"; "I began to feel I had a rival [in Anna], I felt envious of her, that I could not match up to her;" and "a scar on his heart; his sense of how to love and how to express passion had been distorted and subverted." Things go wrong when parents cannot receive a child's love, passion, and aggression. In Noel's case, his parents very likely repressed their own sexuality, denied the erotic aspects of family bonds, and denied or punished the emerging erotic expressions of their children.

Beyond my Reichian training, I have learned a great deal about hysteria from the writing of Khan (1979, 1989), Green (1986), and Bollas (2000). In her discussant article about the case of Noel, Charlotte Sills does not use the concept of hysteria, but she captures the essence of it in her description of the *puer aeternus*, the boy/man fleeing sexuality and reality. Bollas (2000) has written compellingly about this aspect of hysteria:

> For this *is* a performance: the good boy and the good girl are unreal manifestations of this internal world, even if they are celebrated by society. This little man and this little woman have leapfrogged into adulthood in such a way as to transcend sexuality in their childhoods. How can this be? If they have jumped into adult apparitions, would this not mean they have done exactly the opposite, that they have therefore rushed into the sexual? It would appear so, but by overtly expressing sexuality as performance—in the coquettish little girl or the macho little boy—the child presents, rather than experiences, sexuality. In adult life, these men and women may sustain the paradox of this accomplishment, appearing quite seductive and sexual, but when called upon by a lover to sustain sexuality, turning away from it and seeking to return to seductive presentations as an alternative to encountering sexuality.
>
> *(p. 76)*

Seen from a neo-Reichian viewpoint, failure in the oedipal period results in obsessional and/or hysterical defenses, that is, a shutting down of erotic desire or a splitting apart of heart (tenderness, idealization) and genital urges (aggressiveness, sexuality). Reich (1983) referred to the oedipal period as "the first puberty" (p.22), thereby recognizing these years (approximately three to six) as crucial to the child's first genitally centered, erotic awakenings. When things go wrong during these years, the capacity for mature, adult love is severely distorted. As Lowen (1958) observed, "If one attempts to reach the heart of the hysteric, to mobilize deep feelings of love, one will meet with the most determined resistance" (p. 240).

I would suggest that in Helena's work with Noel this is the central and determined resistance she came up against.

I wish that Helena's account of Noel had included more detailed history. We learn that his father was violent and his mother passive and controlling in her subservience. We see in this the underpinnings of what Helena characterizes as a sadomasochistic dynamic in which Noel's aggression is expressed as withholding or punishment, a turning away from passionate involvement. However, without more information about patterns of love and sexuality within the family system, my diagnostic impressions must be based largely on Noel's adult behavior in relation to his beloved but unfucked fantasy ideal of Anna, his relationship with Helena, his continual splitting apart of love and sex, and (as Bollas observes) his eroticization of absence rather than presence and involvement. I write here, intentionally rather crudely, "unfucked," so as to invite the reader to pierce the veil of the idealizing and romantic qualities of Noel's self representation in relation to his beloved Anna, and to language bluntly the reality of his unconscious invitation to look (and be looked at) but not touch (or be touched).

Hysteria is a controversial diagnosis (Bronfen, 1998; Dimen & Harris, 2001), very much out of fashion in the United States, where it is seen as a label that is too often used to pathologize and demean women. In Europe, however, an understanding of hysteria is alive and well, although it differs quite markedly from the caricatures presented within the American psychotherapeutic literature. As André Green (1986) observes,

> Nowadays hysteria is more discrete. It has not disappeared but it is hidden. ... Although a hysterical character no longer has attacks, he continues to make scenes, sometimes in the consulting room, but more often in the private space of the bedroom. ... That Freud discovered the unconscious, with hysteria at his starting point, is no accident—hysteria will always be associated with the question of Eros. The vast continent of sexuality was opened.
>
> *(pp. 220–221)*

In the treatment of hysteria, the "vast continent of sexuality" is opened up between therapist and client. If the hysterical avoidances of adult love are to be resolved, this continent must be explored overtly both within the client's actual love life and within the transference–countertransference dynamics.

In his discussant paper, Richard's emphasis on a diagnosis of obsessional character, viewed from the perspective of Berne's human hungers, stresses the function of obsessional defenses in satisfying relational and structure hungers. Richard outlines the functions of predictability, identity, continuity, and stability in understanding the psychological motivations of obsessions. In turning attention to the hysterical side of this coin, I suggest that the problems of stimulation hunger—such as eroticism, aggression, and passionate sexuality—are central in Noel's case and that the heart of treatment here is not so much the provision of a "secure" base (i.e., a stabilizing, predictable relationship) as it is the provision of the "vital" base of a challenging, unpredictable, lively relationship.

Games, projections, and transference

In her discussion of Helena's case, Charlotte makes the important distinction between "introjective transference" and "projective transference." In conveying a sense of being "strong, calm, protective, empathic, and accepting enough" (i.e., establishing a secure base), Helena addresses the introjective transference effectively. Treatment seems to run into trouble in unraveling the projective transference and games, as discussed by Charlotte.

In her prologue, Helena refers to the work of David Mann, whose book has had an important influence on my thinking as well. Mann (1997) stresses that the erotic pulls people toward "greater differentiation and individuation … to greater complexity and more diverse and complex structures" (p. 9). Such complexity did not seem possible with Noel. How was it avoided? I think in some way Helena was caught up in Noel's hysterical blindness toward genital sexuality. For example, she asked herself, "How could I have congruent, intimate contact with Noel?" This was an important question, but not sufficient. To my mind, what was missing was the question of having an *honest* relationship with Noel, within which erotic feelings, fantasies, and anxieties could have been made more overt and systematically explored. As a consultant I would have asked how Helena might have had an *in*congruent *and* intimate relationship with Noel, that is, one that comes to reflect differentness and conflict as aspects of intimacy. How could Noel's "balls-less" teasing and sadistic withdrawal have been addressed more consistently?

I respect the care with which Helena analyzed her countertransference, but in so doing she seemed to remove herself in subtle ways from more direct interplay with Noel. What might have happened if she had articulated her countertransference reactions to him while speculating that she was probably not alone in her reactions, just a bit more honest than most? What would have happened had she analyzed Noel's transference (games) more frequently and directly? From a clinical viewpoint, I found Helena too nice, too careful. From the first transactions in the first session, the games were set in motion. Noel asks, "Well, what happens now?" and then, without waiting for an answer, he says, "Do you mind if I smoke?" Helena replied by explaining that it would be useful to find out what he felt if he did not smoke. OK, but I would be really curious to know what might have unfolded if Helena had said something like, "No, it's not OK to smoke here. I don't allow it. Now, about your first question, what do you think will need to happen here in therapy with me?"

In a similar vein, later in treatment Noel grins seductively and appears to compliment Helena by saying, "I just can't pull the wool over your eyes, can I? ... I feel naked in here because I can't use the things I usually use to impress women." To my ears this has the ring of a false, deflecting con. I wonder what might have opened up if Helena had said something like,

> Actually, Noel, I think to manipulate and avoid me in here you've used many of the things you've used with other women. I rarely experience you as naked with me, though there have been some important moments. It seems terribly hard, frightening even, for you to expose yourself to me, to be too vulnerable, too excited, too real with me. Mostly I experience you cloaking yourself in one sort of costume or another. I imagine it's a lot like this with the other women in your life.

Erotic contagion/erotic avoidance

Helena's work with Noel was, from the beginning, inescapably erotically charged. Throughout the course of the therapy, Helena struggled with her sexual feelings and countertransferential reactions. I have great admiration for her process of self-examination in both the treatment itself as well as in her clinical writing about the case. Yet it remained difficult for her to bring Noel's or her own erotic excitements and anxieties consistently into the therapy. She seemed trapped in his hysterical avoidance: What would be too much, too intrusive, too sexual? In both his idealizations (of himself, Anna, and Helena) and his later regressive/demanding behaviors, Noel avoided the complexity of adult sexuality as well as the experiences of disappointment and differentiation that allow adults to discover differentness as an object of excitement and desire. In healthy erotic bonds—familial, therapeutic, or sexual—desire, vulnerability, conflict, aggression, and passion are continually intertwined.

A series of recent papers have been invaluable to my deepening understanding of working with erotic transference and countertransference (Tansey, 1994; Davies, 1994, 1998; Benjamin, 1995; Stein, 1998; Dimen, 1999, 2001; Bonasia, 2001). Jody Messler Davies (1994), for example, has written some of the most compelling material on work within the erotic transference–countertransference matrix. She observes:

> If we are to enter the clinical realm of erotic desire, confusion and inhibition, it would seem imperative that we gain access to this essential subtext of interpersonal relatedness as it effects [sic] both patient and therapist. Often this aspect of experience provides acces's to repressed and dissociated states of erotically charged experience, otherwise unavailable in the verbal discourse that dominates clinical inquiry. Yet, we are often taught to avoid such immersion in physicality, for the very reason that it is viewed as too primitive, too arousing, and therefore potentially too gratifying to the patient.
>
> *(p. 160)*

118   William F. Cornell

In writing about erotic transference and countertransference, I have wondered when we enter the realms of the erotic with our clients, do we court disaster or invite possibility? Do we dance on a knife-edge between the two? Do we allow the forces of erotic desire and fantasy to push against the familiar, established order of therapeutic limits? What is the nature of erotic transference? What is there to be gained by the client? The erotic is inherently contagious. It creates the confusions of desire: "Whose feelings are these? Who started it? Who are you to me? Who am I to you? Where are the boundaries between desire and action?" The erotic moves not only the client but also the therapist into realms of ambiguity, ambivalence, excitement, anxiety, and disgust.

This, I suggest, was the field of play between Helena and Noel. Helena's confusion, excitement, interest, and anxiety are evident in her presentation of this case, which she managed through self-examination and supervisory consultation. She invites us as readers into the field of play with her open self-reflection, questioning, and willingness to engage in dialogue with the discussants of this case.

At the erotic edge

Toward the end of treatment, Noel gave—as I would interpret them—important signals of his readiness to deal with the erotic, with differentiation and disappointment, and with the limits of the therapeutic relationship and Helena's love for him. Noel began to infer that Helena had a family. In bringing these inferences into sessions, I suggest that he was acknowledging that Helena had an important life outside of the office (e.g., his comments on the garden outside her consulting room) and a primary sexual partner who was not now and would never be him. Here may have been a doorway to dealing with the oedipal disappointments. Here, too, was an opportunity to explore the erotics of Helena and Noel's relationship, knowing that her actual sexual life was outside the consulting room. Actuality and fantasy could have been examined side by side.

And then there is the dream, a quite rich and fabulous dream. It is all there: the passions, confusions, and furies of the oedipal period. In a few short scenes from the unconscious, Noel recoils from his own and/or another man's desires, is rescued by one dreamed Helena (and a baby pops up), has his own desires/interests ignored by another dreamed Helena, and is caught and embarrassed by himself in the midst of his own desires. The dreamed Helenas are at once the white, rescuing angel/mother and then the blind and impervious wife-to-another. It does not get much better than this.

The dream is full of oedipal dilemmas and invitations to examine who cares about/loves whom (and why), who gets to stay with whom, who hurts whom, who stays and who leaves, and who gets to be fucked and live in the house. I think this dream represented the lowering of Noel's hysterical stance and a readiness to talk more directly about sexuality. Unfortunately, that did not happen. These issues, it seems, were touched on but not taken up directly or deeply enough. For example, in the dream Noel and Helena are walking along with a baby in a pram. They come to understand this dream image "as symbolic of the product of our union." Helena also wonders if the baby in the pram is symbolic of Noel's bringing his Child ego state more into the therapy. Perhaps this does foreshadow his subsequent regression and demands for more of her time. But I wonder what might have opened up if Helena had said something like:

> Well, Noel, if we going to be walking together with our baby in a pram, I guess we'll have to fuck. But nobody actually fucks anybody in this dream, so where did this baby come from? This dream is a lot like your waking life— opportunities not quite taken. You don't seem to ever actually get kissed or laid. What do you make of that?

Helena's analyst supervisor suggests that the repellent kissing man represented Noel's latent homosexuality, a hypothesis well worth taking up with Noel. I would raise that question along with another—that of his comfort/pleasure in his gender, in his own maleness. This brings to mind Offit's (1995) observation:

> One of the difficulties which must beset any therapist trying to determine whether these patients are troubled by their homosexuality is to distinguish between a personality problem and a dilemma concerning appropriate gender choice in a partner. Since such men are usually quite certain that they could not be happy with a woman as a mate, one must conclude that their major burden (like that of so many histrionic women) is characterological.
>
> *(p. 56)*

I would ask Noel what he makes of being repelled by a man's kiss (desire?). I would ask if he imagines that his desire to kiss is repellent to others. Does he kiss his mother? His father? Is he repelled by male desire, his own or that of others? And what about his penis, his desire to have a woman (a man?) with his cock, to penetrate?

By this point in the treatment, Helena had clearly established a strong working alliance with Noel—an alliance, I imagine, that was strong enough to tolerate and profit from disturbance. With a client like Noel, at this stage of therapy, I would intentionally use the language of fucking, kissing, cocks, and penetration to bring genital sexuality unavoidably into the room. I am not suggesting that Helena should have revealed to Noel her own sexual attractions to him, but that she might have brought adult, genital sexuality (and Noel's avoidance of it) directly into the work.

What was the transferential collusion (game) around Noel's coy avoidances? As I said earlier, I think that Helena was a little too careful and indirect. The fact is that Noel retreated and regressed. Helena writes that "as the transference deepened, Noel's expectations of and demands on me increased." I suggest that this increase of demands and expectations did not so much reflect a deepening of the transference as it did a shift in the nature of the transference from an emerging erotic transference into a defensive collapse backward into a regressive, more infantile transference. Noel shifted from acknowledging (and being a bit curious about) Helena's primary relationships outside of her work—a maturing transference relationship that was

120 William F. Cornell

beginning to allow differentiation—back into an anxious, demanding transference in which he wanted to be special and intrude on Helena's holidays (and, therefore, her differentiated, independent love life). Noel must have been rather good at this, as suddenly Helena felt, "Yes, of course, I will make a special case for you. I wanted to fold him in my arms, put him in a carry cot, and bring him away on holiday with us." For Noel, being cuddled and coddled seemed preferable to either fucking Helena (or at least acknowledging he had had passing thoughts about it) or being left by Helena (and thereby encouraged by her) to develop his own love and sexual life. This, to my mind, is hysteria in action.

Toward the end of treatment, Noel brought two new factors into the consulting room: information about a stillborn baby sister whose death just preceded his conception and news of a new woman whom, it seems, Noel actually took to bed (though she fell short of the ideal, unfucked Anna).

I wonder why Noel brought the information of the dead sister into treatment at that point. What was he trying to open up? In discussing the stillborn baby sister, Helena and Noel entered a world of unconscious fantasy, of ghosts, echoes, and obsessive shadow figures. These were important considerations, this dead figure at the start of his life, a dead body buried in the foundations of his script. Why did it come up, then, so late in treatment? I wonder if Noel's decision to give this information to Helena was an invitation to further address the ambiguity of his gender identification.

Traditionally, hysterical defenses are understood to be anchored in the oedipal period, but Bollas (2000) argues compellingly that hysteria is, in fact, rooted in infancy, in the parents' inability to celebrate the gender and genitality of their infant. The mother–infant relationship is an intensely erotic relation, the baby receiving its first knowledge of the erotic directly through the mother's body: her touch, pleasure, aversion, gaze, delight, disgust, voice. Bollas writes:

> The mother loves the infant with her whole body: her breasts for feeding, her chest for sleeping on, her lap for sitting, her knees for bouncing, her arms for enfolding, her hands for countless touchings. She suckles, caresses, wrestles, tickles, pokes and pulls the infant in hundreds of acts of physically delivered knowledge every day. If she is a "good-enough" mother she will translate not only her unconscious fantasies into body communication, she will also unconsciously interpret her infant's gestural requests through her body. Maternal body knowledge becomes part of the self's own body knowledge and is precursive to the self's own sensuality. … As the mother's intuitive body knowledge forms the base of erotic knowledge, it returns when lovers surrender to one another's bodies.
>
> *(p. 67)*

But this does not happen in the infancy of those raised in a hysterical environment. I have found Bollas's (2000) words echoed over and over again in the histories and experiences of my hysterical clients:

Specifically, the mother experiences intense ambivalence towards the infant as a sexual being, especially towards the genitalia, which cannot be sensorially celebrated. … If the mother then refuses the infant's genital sexuality—not sonically celebrating it, averting her gaze, stiffening her touch … she has removed the core of erotic life and sought surface sexuality as a defense against deep sexuality. … As maternal love is the first field of sexual foreplay, the hysterical mother conveys to her infant's body an anguished desire, as her energetic touches bear the trace of disgust and frustration, carrying to the infant's body communication about sexual ambivalence.

(pp. 46–48)

In a hysterical environment, genitals and gender are denied, disturbed, imbued with anxiety and disgust, sometimes subtly, other times dramatically and intensely. I wonder how Noel's mother received this boy baby born so shortly after the death of her girl baby. I wonder what happened to Noel's mother when she gazed on (or touched) his penis, missing (or imagining) the vagina of her dead daughter. How did Noel experience the meanings (conscious and unconscious) of being a boy and a someday-man within the losses and dynamics of this unhappy marital couple? What did it mean to Noel to have a penis and to want to use it?

I agree with Helena's observation that the rupture of Noel's not getting his needs met by Helena, as demonstrated in his grudging acknowledgment of her primary life outside of therapy, freed him of some of the depth of his fantasies to seek a love life in a more realistic fashion. The notion of a therapist "meeting the needs" of a client makes me cringe; when a therapist and client get caught up in that delusion, I think it kills any possibility of successful therapy taking place. In his description of the tendency toward "transference addiction" (p.146) in the treatment of hysteria, Bollas (2000) presents a particularly chilling rendition of this therapeutic trap. The therapeutic relationship should not be an end in itself but rather a means for the client's self-understanding and for developing real life and love outside the therapy office.

So Noel launched himself into the arms (and perhaps bed) of a new woman and out of Helena's consulting room. Helena is "not convinced that his dependency and/or sexual needs had been fully worked through with me." I agree that they were not, but I think that a great deal had been accomplished, which I hope laid the foundation for a gradually maturing sexual capacity in Noel and perhaps a return for more psychotherapy at a later date to further address his sexual and characterological defenses.

Conclusion

Work with hysteria is neither easy nor comfortable, but it can be richly enlivening for both therapist and client. The pressures and uncertainties of the erotic transference–countertransference matrix cannot be avoided with these clients: a blessing and

122   William F. Cornell

a curse. I have come to believe strongly that when we engage in therapy that is too nurturing, too careful, too sanitized, and de-eroticized, we do our clients a disservice (Cornell, 2000, 2003). The therapist becomes a kind of latter-day, hysteria-generating/-sustaining parent when he or she averts therapeutic attention from the gaze, conflicts, uncertainties, excitement, language, or activities of the erotic. It is our willingness to enter the arena of erotic anguish, desire, and delight with our clients that offers them the opportunity to restore the vitality of the body, to leave behind the deadness and distortion of parent–infant eroticism gone bad, and to open up to the world of passionate, adult intimacy and uncertainty.

I deeply admire Helena's honesty and self-scrutiny in the presentation of this case. I was excited and captivated by Helena's account of her work with Noel. In these discussant papers, Helena has invited us into an intellectual and I hope erotic interchange. I thank her for this opportunity.

References

Baker, E. (1967). *Man in the Trap*. New York: Collier Books.

Benjamin, J. (1995). *Like Subjects, Love Objects*. New Haven, CT: Yale University Press.

Bollas, C. (2000). *Hysteria*. London: Routledge.

Bonasia, E. (2001). The countertransference: Erotic, eroticised and perverse, *International Journal of Psychoanalysis*, 82, 249–262.

Bronfen, E. (1998). *The Knotted Subject: Hysteria and Its Discontents*. Princeton, NJ: Princeton University Press.

Cornell, W. (2000). Transference, desire and vulnerability in body-centered psychotherapy. *Energy & Character*, 30(2), 29–37.

Cornell, W. (2003). The impassioned body: Erotic vitality and disturbance in psychotherapy. *British Gestalt Journal*, 12(2), 97–104.

Davies, J.M. (1994). Love in the afternoon: A relational reconsideration of desire and dread in the countertransference. *Psychoanalytic Dialogues*, 4(2), 153–170.

Davies, J.M. (1998). Between the disclosure and foreclosure of erotic transference–countertransference: Can psychoanalysis find a place for adult sexuality? *Psychoanalytic Dialogues*, 8(6), 747–767.

Dimen, M. (1999). Between *Lust* and libido: Sex, psychoanalysis, and the moment before. *Psychoanalytic Dialogues*, 9(4), 415–440.

Dimen, M. (2001). Perversion is us? Eight notes. *Psychoanalysis Dialogues*, 11(6), 825–860.

Dimen, M. & Harris, A. (2001). *Storms in Her Head: Freud and the Construction of Hysteria*. New York: Other Press.

Erskine, R, (2001). Psychological function, relational needs, and transferential resolution: The psychotherapy of an obsession. *Transactional Analysis Journal*, 31(4), 220–226.

Green, A. (1986). Passions and their vicissitudes, in A, Green, *On Private Madness*, pp. 214–253. London: Hogarth.

Hargaden, H. (2001). There ain't no cure for love. *Transactional Analysis Journal*, 31(4), 213–219.

Khan, M.R. (1979). *Alienation in Perversions*. Madison, CT: International Universities Press.

Khan, M.R. (1989). *Hidden Selves*. London: Maresfield Library.

Lowen, A. (1958). *Physical Dynamics of Character Structure*. New York: Grune & Stratton.

Lowen, A. (1975). *Bioenergetics*. New York: Coward, McCann & Geoghegan.

Mann, D. (1997). *Psychotherapy: An Erotic Relationship*. London: Routledge.

Offit, A.K. (1995). *The Sexual Self: How Character Shapes Sexual Experience*. Northvale, NJ: Jason Aronson.

Reich, W. (1983). *Children of the Future*. New York: Farrar, Straus & Giroux.

Sills, C. (2001). The man with no name. *Transactional Analysis Journal*, 31(4), 227–232.

Stein, R. (1998). The poignant, the excessive and the enigmatic in sexuality. *International Journal of Psycho-analysis*, 79, 253–268.

Tansey, M.J. (1994). Sexual attraction and phobic dread in the counter-transference. *Psychoanalytic Dialogues*, 4(2), 139–152.

10

THE PLACE OF FAILURE AND RUPTURE IN PSYCHOTHERAPY

Carole Shadbolt

In this article I explore and describe a way of understanding, recognizing, and transforming experiences of failure and ruptures in transactional analysis psychotherapy. As my working definition, I regard failure as an occurrence that interrupts the therapeutic flow and leads to some kind of rupture in the therapeutic relationship. It involves the experience of a breakdown in relating. Both failure and rupture are attempts at communication

Many of the ideas I present are drawn from my clinical experience as both a psychotherapist and a client. I have also used material from colleagues, in whose writings I find similar dilemmas to my own.

My thesis is that when ruptures and failures are cocreated between client and therapist, rather than being regarded as pathologies that stand in the way of the work, they can be engaged with as therapeutic change opportunities, their resolution being the central therapeutic task.

In the following pages, I first offer some guiding principles to provide an ethical framework, then discuss the meaning of failure and rupture in a cultural and theoretical context, and finally offer reflections on all of this in a clinical context.

Ethical context and guiding principles

For any of us to work effectively as therapists, we must believe in ourselves and our work. That belief must rest on an ethic that has integrity and is trustworthy, one that we can sign up to with confidence.

Transactional analysis is just such a theory and psychology, built as it is on sound moral, humanistic principles. For example, there is the much-clichéd and often underestimated transactional analysis philosophy of "I'm OK, You're OK." Similarly, there is the tenet that most people, except perhaps those whose brains are hopelessly damaged, can think about their own situation, can have some power over their lives, and in most circumstances can bring about change. For the purpose of this discussion, I shall be widening and deepening these ethical principles, and in so doing, I lay the foundation for the theoretical and clinical discussion to follow.

As my first guiding principle, I take a nonpathologizing view of human nature and behavior, the opposite of considering behaviors, thoughts, and feelings as "wrong" or "crazy." I worked for many years in a psychiatric hospital, where I met many patients who were officially diagnosed and labeled insane, often by me, as a licensed mental health practitioner. As I came to learn their complicated stories, I realized that so-called "insanity" can take many forms. In transactional analysis, insanity or psychosis has been generally understood in ego state terms as an inability or failure to cathect the Adult ego state "on request" and/or to be unable to appreciate and understand a consensual reality. During my years working at the hospital, I met only one person who seemed unable to cathect, in some measure, his Adult ego state. I then discovered that he was an asylum seeker in the United Kingdom, the victim of torture in his own country, from which he had escaped and to which he was in danger of being forced to return. He understood not one word of English, and I could not speak his language, but when I discovered this one fact about his life, I understood with blinding clarity the language of not only his psychic pain and terror but his decision about how to survive the reality of his situation. It made perfect sense to me then that he should retreat somewhere beyond reach, an act of supreme sanity, in my view. This experience taught me that beliefs, behaviors, feelings, intuitions, emotions, and thoughts are usually explainable and probably understandable when all the facts are known. In other words, "I'm OK, You're OK."

I hasten to add that, of course, this does not mean that anything goes. It is undeniable that some of us manage psychologically in this life better than others—in other words, psychopathology does exist. Also, sadly, given the manner in which society is constructed, it is clear that some people do not survive psychologically intact without decompensating or dissociating. They do not fit, it seems, with what is called *consensual reality*. Nonetheless, I have often been reminded in my work that when a client's situation, presentation, and decisions, however bizarre they might seem initially, are understood, the behavior, thoughts, and feelings that I might at first pathologize or think are self-defeating can be seen as the client's unique and creative way of managing the unmanageable.

Eric Berne (1980) knew something of this, as we see from the opening words of his major scientific work on transactional analysis:

> Structural and transactional analysis offer a systemic, consistent theory of personality and social dynamics derived from clinical experience, and an actionistic, rational form of therapy which is suitable for, easily understood by, and naturally adapted to the great majority of psychiatric patients.
>
> *(p. 21)*

126 Carole Shadbolt

Implicit in Berne's understated, confrontational (in the transactional analysis meaning of confrontation) statement is his belief in a person's fundamental OKness. Berne was reaching for a nonpathologizing philosophy and therapy that can be used by clients and psychiatrists alike and together. He was addressing those of us who have the power in our hands to oppress by diagnosis, labeling, and soft patronage (i.e., not outright discrimination/prejudice but taking a position of superiority), sometimes dubiously incarcerating the most marginalized members of the society to which we belong. This can also occur in our treatment of clients who have come to be termed the *worried well* (i.e., clients who are functioning but anxious), and we need to be vigilant in the diagnoses we make.

My second guiding principle has to do with the nature of our existence. I take the view that we are not separate from one another. We impact and exert gross and subtle influences on each other. My experience is contrary to the old self-responsibility slogan so popular in the 1960s that someone else "cannot make us feel." Although I understand the political intention that underpins this liberating notion, it seems that we do, indeed, make each other feel. We can draw on research as well as our own experience to demonstrate this.

For example, however important sexuality is in human existence (as seen in Freudian ideas that human character is shaped solely by sexual drives), even more important is the need of human beings for attachment and recognition. This has been borne out by, among others, the work of John Bowlby (1973) and psychoanalyst Donald Winnicott (1965) concerning the development of the self. Similarly, we see the importance of the discoveries and applications of neuroscience explored within transactional analysis in the writings of Allen (2003, 2010). The transactional analysis theory of *strokes* bears this out, evidenced by our own knowledge and experience of how good we feel when someone strokes us and how bad we feel when we receive shaming negative strokes and experience a loss of attachment. What we do about those feelings and needs, and how we think about them, is perhaps a matter of choice and change (e.g., change of script). We are born and formed in relationship with each other, with ourselves, and with the environment and culture, and we seek to make and retain relationships and attachment at all costs. We are wounded in relationships and will most likely be healed in relationship. It is not difficult to appreciate that rupture, mistakes, and failure, seen through the lens of our relational existence and the influence of attachment, call forth from us the ideas of blame, shame, retribution, forgiveness, and redemption.

Dialectically juxtaposed with this idea is that human beings are also self-determining, separate beings with agency and a will of their own. In the context of psychotherapy, therapists and clients can make powerful, mutual partners and allies in healing and in the recovery of this lost facility for self-determination. Although the therapeutic relationship is usually asymmetrical, and power imbalances often exist within it, it is not always the case that the therapist is in the driver's seat. The idea of the therapist's vulnerability is a powerful and therapeutic notion, as I will discuss later. The medical model of psychotherapy, in which the therapist is "the doctor" who diagnoses the client and dispenses cure, sits uneasily within this principle.

My third guiding principle is based on the recognition that our theories are just that: theories. They are abstractions, hypotheses, ideas, or, as my transactional analysis trainer, Petrŭska Clarkson, would have said, "stories." In that respect, they are not the truth. We all have our favorite theories and stories, and our allegiances to them run deep. But however useful, even essential, theories are to containment for some people, to me they must be the servant of clinical experience and therapeutic relatedness, not the reverse. Otherwise, transactional analysis is in danger of becoming an intellectualizing, dogmatic exercise. At the same time, it is vital that we do not create a split between theory and practice (i.e., theory is bad, clinical practice is good, or vice versa). As Milton Erikson put it, "Each person is a unique individual. Hence psychotherapy should be formulated to meet the individual's needs rather than tailoring the person to fit the Procrustean bed of hypothetical theory of human behavior" (Erikson as cited in Price, 1987, p. 11). Although I would not go as far as Erikson, who seemed to reject theory and a systematic methodology, I strive to "hold my theory lightly," as the saying goes. That is, I bear in mind the uniqueness of each therapeutic encounter, in which what appears to fit as an idea and treatment plan to explain one person's situation may be entirely inadequate in another.

My fourth guiding principle is that failure or failing is akin to a human right. If this sits oddly in the mind and ear, observe the effects that failure, as it is popularly understood, can have on a person's life. That life can, in fact, resemble someone who has been denied or is denying himself or herself entry into the human race. Such individuals look and feel alienated, isolated, unworthy, and lonely. As I will describe later, when failure is viewed as bad (by self and/or others) or is in some way worthy of blame or censure, not surprisingly, those most undermining of human experiences—shame, disgrace, and betrayal—can ensue.

I remember from my training years Petrŭska Clarkson's approach to failure, which was, looking back, rather revolutionary. When someone felt he or she had failed or made a mistake, Petrŭska would say that it was "evidence that someone had tried to do something." I took her comments and observation as a permission, and I still do. My ethical point, and perhaps hers, is that we have a right to try something and not feel that we will be an outcast if we do not succeed. And here I would dearly love to rehabilitate the word *try* in our transactional analysis vocabulary and culture. I would like for it not to be followed by either the spoken or unspoken question, "Yes, but will you succeed?" This implies that in some way the person who has used the word "try" fully intends not to succeed, as we involuntarily invoke driver theory (Kahler, 1974). Of course, sometimes "Trying hard" is, indeed, a driver behavior, but thoughtless, dogmatic use of language can feel like the use of theory as a weapon. It can be distancing and distorting of the subtleties of meaning, and something is lost.

Fifth, since we ask our clients to take responsibility for themselves, to a certain extent, and to commit themselves to the work, likewise it is our responsibility to commit ourselves to our own psychological health by having at our disposal our own therapy and supervision. There we can reflect on our own emotional

128 Carole Shadbolt

growth and tread the path that we ask our clients to tread. Increasingly, as we study relational theory, we realize that the place of the therapist's experience, emotions, and disturbances during the therapeutic encounter and his or her ability to metabolize or "hold" and reflect on these in himself or herself are axiomatic to transformation (or change). Therapy and supervision are acts of commitment to both the work and the client. Supervision, but particularly personal therapy, enables the therapist to work, think, speak, and understand "from the depth of her own psychological life" (Basescu, 1990, p. 52). The ethical principles at stake are equality, mutuality, and integrity.

An anonymous quote on the wall of my training institute, which was founded by Petrūska Clarkson, Brian Dobson, and Sue Fish, remains with me to this day. It still has the power to invoke the spirit of OKness and attachment in the face of effort, failure, and mistakes.

> Every single human being, when the entire situation is taken into account, has always, at every moment of the past, done the very best that he or she could do, and so deserves neither blame nor reproach from anyone, including self. This, in particular, is true of you.

It is against the backdrop of these guiding principles that I offer the following reflections about rupture and failure.

The cultural context of failure and rupture

Some years ago in the United Kingdom, trainee transactional analysts spent many hours and much money making as sure as they could that they did not fail their Certified Transactional Analyst (CTA) or Teaching and Supervising Transactional Analyst (TSTA) examinations or the Training Endorsement Workshop (TEW). The thought of potential failure brought on such anxiety that for some it seemed that failure was not an option. Of course, it is perfectly understandable and desirable that we all do as well as we can, but the process of successfully learning was, I noticed, sometimes squelched by the dreaded thought of not passing exams.

Despite the approach to failure of some trainers (as described earlier) and also the use of the word *defer* rather than *fail*, I remember the dread of colleagues in my training group of being the first one to fail. For year upon year, no one failed as successes rolled out one after the other. The excellence of that training supported success quite rightly, but it felt, I must say, rather like a game of Russian roulette. It became increasingly scary as one person after the other pulled the CTA exam "trigger," and the day when the "failure gun" would go off came all the nearer with each success. The day came, of course, when someone failed. I recall it was every bit as shocking as I had feared, and the person never did retake her exam. She was a brilliant counselor, and I wonder now what happened to her, both publicly and privately, as she dealt with that failure. I imagine she felt shame deeply, that most unbearable, yet universal, human experience.

The place of failure and rupture **129**

I passed my CTA in Paris in 1992. I was relieved beyond words. I felt as if I had been "let in" to an exclusive club. However, there was a small thought that still arrives unbidden in me that it was some kind of unintegrated process that had shame and fear of failure at its heart. Later, as a transactional analysis trainer and supervisor, I noticed the same traumatic process in my supervisees and students. The joy and excitement of learning can be obliterated by the shame of possible failure. In our transactional analysis culture, exam success is, quite rightly, greeted with huge celebration. But there is another side to this that relates to my topic here. In transactional analysis, there seems to be a cultural meaning to failure and trying that is conflated with winning and losing, and transactional analysis loves winners.

As a result of my experiences as both a trainee and later as a supervisor and trainer, the shame and fear of failure has become of particular interest to me. I wonder what and/or who has failed, how that happened, and what the price is for that failure.

What is culturally at stake when we as transactional analysts put ourselves up for examination is nothing less than our position in the hierarchy. Reaching success, over and above the joy of personal achievement, also means acquiring status, prestige, and belonging within our profession and community. The driven aspect of passing exams can become an end in itself. It seems that it is not enough to reach the position of being trusted by clients or patients and to be assessed as competent to do that. So perhaps the cultural price of failure is the loss of status, of belonging and attachment, and of having and losing a position in the hierarchy of status, power, and influence.

Culture has a huge impact on who we are individually and collectively. We may barely glimpse these influences in our Adult ego state as they impact our thoughts and behaviors as therapists at an unconscious level. It follows, therefore, that the manner in which we are shaped by wider and particular cultures is central when thinking about failure and rupture in the somewhat isolated world of the individual therapy session. The failed intervention or the moment of misattuned rupture is filtered through the lens of the cultural view of failure. It is not difficult to appreciate what is ruptured in this cultural environment. The self is wounded in the loss of "face," in bearing others' perceived disappointment, of not meeting expectations, of being the one who "didn't make it." It can lead to anxiety and retreat from contact at the very moment when we need to engage further.

The theoretical context of failure and rupture

There are a number of ways within transactional analysis to look theoretically at failure and rupture. I examine three of them here, each based in a particular theory and method of transactional analysis.

The first is the so-called classical school or approach. From a classical transactional analysis perspective, we might think of failure as failure to make, complete, or achieve a behavioral contract or failure to protect adequately a client from what we have come to know as script backlash following a premature redecision. Or it

130 Carole Shadbolt

might represent those times when we neglect to confront a discount or we stroke an invitation to symbiosis.

Ruptures might be seen as evidence of a failure to be clear at the outset about what psychotherapy might involve. When the client experiences what might be ahead, this may come as a shock, and so trust may be lost in the therapeutic alliance. Additionally, a rupture may occur when our own script material "unhelpfully" breaks through into a client's time with us and takes our mind off the "real work." Or, as one long-running theoretical dispute in transactional analysis reminds us, our client has not closed his or her escape hatches (Holloway, 1973), and we are faced with holding anxieties about the person's "self-destructive" thoughts and feelings.

Classical transactional analysis is a proven psychology and psychotherapy whose therapeutic aim is clients' understanding of their internal dynamics and their capacity to change their behavior. It is a "systematic phenomenology," as Berne (1980, pp. 270–271), described it. Decontaminating the client's Adult ego state allows him or her to make informed, here-and-now choices about his or her behavior, thinking, and feeling. The therapist's role is to inquire and observe, to raise awareness of unacknowledged feelings, inconsistencies, discounts, and contaminations. He or she confronts by observing the client's behavior and transactions. He or she does not become emotionally involved as part of the work. This is not to say that as classical transactional analysis therapists we exclude our feelings during sessions, but these are seen as peripheral to the focus of the work.

There is an old story that a senior therapist once said that the test of effective classical transactional analysis practice was that if one TA therapist was substituted with another, the client would experience no interruption or change to his or her therapy. I hasten to add that this was a long time ago, but it does reflect the idea that the effectiveness of the therapy in classical transactional analysis is thought to reside in the theory and method more than in the person of the therapist or the relationship between client and therapist.

Another view is presented by integrative transactional analysis, which brings together transactional analysis, object relations theory, and developmental perspectives. The therapist offers a reparative emotional experience through empathy, attunement, and inquiry. He or she may even meet a hitherto unmet relational need. From this perspective, failure might be seen as the therapist failing to appreciate the relational needs of the client, and a rupture is experienced as a repeat in the here and now of the experience of unmet needs of a fixated archaic ego state. In both classical and integrative transactional analysis, the object of treatment and the source of the "problem" is the client's internal dynamics or script.

These two theories and methods are effective and respected therapeutic procedures, as are other transactional analysis theories and approaches, such as the redecision approach and the thinking of neo-Cathexis practitioners.

However, an enormous sea change has taken place within the world of psychoanalysis and psychotherapy in the last few decades concerning the nature and use of the relationship between therapist and client. Throughout the psychotherapy

The place of failure and rupture **131**

world, thinking has developed from what is known as a *one-* or a *one-and-a-half-person psychology* (Stark, 1999) to now include a *two-person psychology*. This movement is reflected in transactional analysis. *From Transactions to Relations* (Cornell & Hargaden, 2005) charted theoretical and clinical development with transactional analysis from a largely cognitive process to understanding and embracing, among other innovations, the importance of unconscious processes involved in decoding transference and countertransference communications.

This followed Hargaden and Sills' (2002) groundbreaking book, *Transactional Analysis: A Relational Perspective*, which repositioned, extended, and deepened the theory of deconfusion of the Child ego state into a contemporary relational process by making central the unconscious connections and communications between therapist and client.

Traditional transactional analysis, which includes classical, redecision, neo-Cathexis, and integrative transactional analysis approaches, largely involves cognitive-behavioral processes and thus one- and one-and-a-half-person psychologies. This refers to the degree of focus and engagement of the two people. A one-person therapy focuses on the client's individual experience, and the therapist is an observer or facilitator. A one-and-a-half-person therapy relies, to some extent, on the actions of the therapist. Relational transactional analysis, on the other hand, is a two-person perspective and has as its object the relatedness between therapist and client, which is intentionally used toward the goal of authentic mutual relating.

A two-person psychology, a term first coined by Michael Balint as long ago as 1968 (Safran & Muran, 2000, p. 38), contends that what transpires in therapy is cocreated by client and therapist. Both are viewed as co-participants and cocreators in the work. To Safran and Muran, for example, "The therapist can never be an impartial observer who stands apart from the phenomenon being observed" (p. 39). The therapist moves from being outside the work to becoming part of the process, from an objective position to a subjective one. The agent of change becomes the quality of relatedness that exists between the therapist and client.

Working from a two-person perspective requires therapists to shift their frame of reference and involves rethinking failure and rupture so it is not viewed as pathology, where something bad, un-therapeutic, unhelpful, or wrong has happened. Of course, there are unprofessional, unethical behaviors, breaches, and failures, but these are different because in such circumstances the other is treated as an object. Similarly, not everything that occurs in a session is cocreated by the working pair. The therapist and client each has his or her individual history and current preoccupations, but how each handles the other might be seen as cocreated.

This shift in thinking has major implications and exciting possibilities for understanding what occurs between two people in the course of their therapy journey together. What is immediately apparent is that there are now two persons in the room, two subjectivities, two script narratives, two internal processes, two unconsciousnesses, and two intersubjectivities, all of which were always there whether they were conscious or not. But now they become mutual components in the work. The therapist is not a neutral observer but becomes a participant observer. It follows, then, that as therapists, our own feelings, thoughts, and behavior become part of the work involved in both creating and resolving ruptures and failures.

Seen through a relational lens, the therapist's thoughts and feelings in session are not viewed as secret evidence of unresolved personal issues, although they may be. Instead, we can consider that our experience at that time, though it may also be a repeat of our own interpersonal patterns, is also being generated in the here and now with a particular client. Extraordinarily, there is usually some overlap, some interpersonal as well as intrapersonal dynamic or intersubjectivity to be taken into account. It seems almost inevitable that both conscious and unconscious patterns will be repeated in both client and therapist. Actively engaging to understand and explore that dynamic is the work rather than hiding, if you will, behind our theories of what might be going on in the client's intrapsychic world or script. From a one-person perspective, this dynamic is seen as a failure or rupture to the main therapeutic endeavor, an adjunct and hindrance to the work rather than the center of it. A two-person perspective requires us to move beyond this idea of mistake or failure. I suggest that what some call ruptures or failures are both forms of communication and an attempt at connection. They are signals that something has or has not occurred between the working pair, that something has been disturbing, angering, puzzling, or, alternatively, unexpressed or lost while at the same time wanted.

Safran and Muran (2000), citing Heather Harper, divided rupture into two types: *withdrawal ruptures* and *confrontation ruptures.* In a withdrawal rupture, the client, or sometimes the therapist, disengages. Some withdrawal ruptures are obvious and behavioral in nature. Others are less obvious as our clients adapt to or accommodate to us or we to them. Confrontation ruptures are more florid. Anger, resentment, fury, and dissatisfaction are often directly, loudly, and sometimes frighteningly expressed. Both types of rupture reflect the need for what Safran and Muran call *agency* and *relatedness* (p. 31). Agency is similar to the transactional analysis principles of autonomy and self-determination. Relatedness refers to the need for attachment. To Safran and Muran, a rupture denotes the tension between the possible loss of either one of these desires by having to choose one over the other, that is, either choosing autonomy or attachment. If the choice is autonomy, attachment is lost and vice versa, in other words, there is an impasse. They focused on the client feeling the rupture, but, of course, the therapist may as well.

Impasse theory in transactional analysis was originally based in a one-person frame of reference (Mellor, 1980). Then, in a groundbreaking article titled "Impasse and intimacy: Applying Berne's concept of script protocol," Cornell and Landaiche (2006) described the interpersonal nature of impasses and how they exist at a number of levels of consciousness and unconsciousness between client and therapist. They offered a relational and interpersonal perspective on what occurs between therapist and client as an enactment by both. Such enactments may communicate and illuminate through a rupture the seeming impossibility of both staying attached and being oneself. This tension, experienced sometimes as

The place of failure and rupture **133**

an inexplicable stuckness, is often unlanguaged, even unknown by therapist and client. It can be understood only through transferences and countertransferences or held bodily by both therapist and client at what Cornell and Landaiche call the *protocol level* of experience, that is, a third-degree or Type 3 impasse.

Game theory can be used to understand the cocreated dynamic of rupture and failure. Hine (1990), describing the bilateral nature of games, mapped the mutual hooking of con and gimmick in an ongoing game dance. Sills reconfigured game theory into a nonpathologizing perspective by quoting Keyes, who says a person's games contain at their heart "an inner flirtation with a core life question" (Keyes as cited in Sills, 2003, p. 283) that has not been addressed by childhood caretakers, which, of course, applies to both therapist and client.

My interest is in exploring the moment of crossup or switch in Berne's (1972) Formula G (game formula) (p. 443). I believe this is the moment when not only is there a crossed transaction and a moment of confusion but also when a rupture is revealed. In other words, the rupture is created in the con and gimmick stage but it is out of awareness. Combining these ideas, I suggest that games, in the switch or crossup, will be repeated until an answer is found to the original question.

The Clinical Context of Failure and Rupture

Whether we refer to ruptures as script, enactments, evidence of a cocreated impasse, an interpersonal or cocreated game, or an existential reality, it is when the rupture either bursts through dramatically into awareness or emerges gradually and half consciously that is at the heart of the therapeutic opportunity for change. As we realize we have become interpersonally embedded in each other's inevitably repeating dynamics, we create a different relational possibility. We reach a pivotal moment, within which lies the possibility of resolution and transformation. There is then the chance to work our way out of, or to resolve, the failure or rupture, the creation of which we have now become a part. This process involves genuine and profound change, not only of behavior but also of interpsychic and intrapsychic experience for both client and therapist. I view this communication and work as profoundly intimate, full of uncertainties and gambles. It is, as Nathanson-Elkind (1992) described it:

> the uniquely human striving for experiences of intimacy, connection, and attachment with others despite the impossibility of sustaining them. In the face of the impermanence and imperfection of all human relationships we yearn and strive for sustaining connections. But intimate relationships are like double-edged swords. They expose us not only to exquisite experiences of loving and being loved, of giving and receiving empathic understanding, but also to indescribably painful times of betrayal, hurt and loneliness.
>
> *(p. 1)*

Seen in this light, it is hardly surprising that what we most long for is what we most deny ourselves, until the longing becomes intolerable, usually unconsciously, and

134 Carole Shadbolt

we risk betrayal and loneliness. Sometimes in the risking it comes out all wrong, which is, to my mind, the experience of rupture.

So how do we recognize a rupture in the context of a therapy session? Aside from the obvious dramatic confrontational rupture described by Safran and Muran (2000), ruptures can be recognized because they are disturbing and have "shape." By this I mean that as we sit with our clients, we may become aware that the session has suddenly or gradually developed a different mien. We may become aware of some subtle discomfort inside us that suggests that things are not running as smoothly as we had first imagined. The client's face has or has not changed expression, and we know that he or she is experiencing something that was generated between us. Somehow we have sailed into a different and unknown place, and suddenly we are not sure of anything. We have made a mistake. Alternatively, a client may appear in our dreams or may be on our minds between sessions. We feel worried or dissatisfied with ourselves over a small, seemingly inconsequential comment by the client.

Working through ruptures is not easy or comfortable for the therapist or the client. Surprises can feel like attacks, and uncertainty can feel like failure, and both risk triggering the shame I mentioned earlier. The therapist must stand ready to engage authentically in the moment with what is happening in the room. There are no specific techniques or "how to's" but rather a set of relational attitudes and values as described earlier. All the therapist's experience, training, supervision, and personal therapy and his or her resulting expertise, wisdom, steadiness, and plain humanity are required at such times. The therapist's job is to be curious rather than interpretative or evaluative, inquiring and reflective about the client's and the therapist's subjective experience and truth. It is important to be attentive and willing to engage with what is occurring, not an easy task when the therapist's own material may be part of what is causing the rupture.

As an intersubjective rupture reveals itself, the therapist's vulnerabilities become evident. As Aron, citing Benjamin, described it, "The feeling that we must either submit or resist is the hallmark of the doer/done-to relationship" (Benjamin as cited in Aron, 2012, p. 207). To submit to or resist the client or he or she to us is traumatic, and the impasse described earlier between self-agency and attachment is keenly experienced by both. One way through this relational impasse, referred to by Benjamin as the third perspective (as cited in Aron, 2012, p. 225), is to reach an understanding of the client's position without losing our own awareness— in other words, to keep our own mind. This is what gestaltists call "inclusion" (Joyce & Sills, 2001, pp. 46–48) and Fonagy, Gergely, Jurist, and Target (2004) termed "mentalization" (p. 23). At such moments the therapist can experience being "in" and "out" of the work at the same time. Part of the task is to own and reflect on the transferences and countertransferences and then carefully and thoughtfully self-disclose real dilemmas and own one's mistakes. Although this may be uncomfortable for the therapist, it is, in my view, indicative of the third perspective and so therapeutically desirable. During this process, Benjamin (2006) suggested, the therapist is doing the changing and the psychological work. It seems related to the process of partially "giving up" to the client described by Maroda (2004). This involves allowing oneself to become vulnerable while at the same time holding on to one's integrity. At these moments, we as therapist are genuinely, authentically impacted by the real mutual power of the relational pair without having to choose between agency and attachment. As a result, meaning is explored, and the experience of both client and therapist is validated from the standpoint of cocreating an alternative, a fresh and new third experience.

Fisher (1990) described this type of therapeutic relatedness as "the shared experience" (p. 11) and asserted that ultimately such an experience cannot take place among unequals. To him, the withholding from others of thoughts and feelings lies at the root of what we understand as psychopathology (p. 10). Stricker (1990) also described an asymmetrical shared experience in which the "climate of self-revelation is valued and acceptable" (p. 278) and, like Fisher (1990), believed that the opposite of such a shared experience is alienation (p. 10).

Self-disclosure

Self-disclosure is the cornerstone of the shared experience or cocreated dynamic, and if it is successful, both individuals discover, or perhaps rediscover, hope in their joint, relational endeavors. As transactional analysts, we may recognize this as the recovery or creation of intimacy, which Fisher (1990) referred to as "a state of grace" (p. 3). To Stricker (1990), "self disclosure lies at the heart of psychotherapy" (p. 277). Since ruptures also appear to lie at its heart, there is a fundamental and special healing place for self-disclosure and its potential to transform failure and rupture in psychotherapy.

Despite the fact that we reveal ourselves to our clients in myriad ways during the course of psychotherapy, self-disclosure may feel counterintuitive to those who have been trained in a one- or a one-and-a-half-person mode and who have held a medical model of psychotherapy.

Self-disclosing from within such a frame of reference may feel like creating a rupture in itself, and, in a way, it is, but there is a world of difference between intentional, thoughtful self-disclosure and disclosure that comes about simply by way of being with another human being. Basescu (1990) described it as the difference between "showing" and "telling" (p. 47). In such thought-about or reflected-upon self-disclosures, the work moves from an authoritative or neutral mode to being collaborative at its heart (p. 51).

Self-disclosure in the therapeutic relationship is still controversial, however. There is general agreement about not "assuming it should be done on a regular basis" (Maroda, 2010, p. 120) and that each therapeutic relationship calls forth a different response concerning self-disclosure. The uncertainty of self-disclosure requires the therapist to ruthlessly, sometimes contemporaneously, examine his or her own motivations for revealing thoughts, feelings, and behaviors brought about during the work. Ill-thought-out, exploitive, or narcissistic self-disclosure or self-disclosure that is done continuously or to ward off anxiety or vulnerability about a client's

136 Carole Shadbolt

anger functions as a defense that is unlikely to result in genuine transformation of a rupture, except perhaps to make it worse. Essential to the vital process of self-inquiry and reflection is a reliance on and belief in the ethical principles I outlined earlier. Without the support of an ethical stance, the work has no frame and thus has the possibility of unraveling.

A relational approach to rupture

A relational therapeutic stance embodies the therapist's attitude toward failure and rupture from theoretical, cultural, clinical, and ethical perspectives. It is not adequately described by techniques or formulaic interventions, but it can be in terms of a sequence of phases, including acknowledgment, space, and meaning making (as described by W. Cornell, personal communication, 9 February 2004), to which I add transformation.

Acknowledgment

This recognizes that something has occurred between us and offers a thoughtful speaking to the real situation. This is the moment and process of self-disclosure.

Space

Space is made for genuine interpersonal exchange and awareness in a nonretaliatory or defensive manner in the context of which we describe experience rather than define the other and inquire rather than interpret. It can also be a private space of silence in which no self-disclosure or words are exchanged, but there is a growing into and a development of the here-and-now dynamic.

Meaning making

Making meaning of the rupture may include hearing about feelings of betrayal, disappointment, blame, and loss, which can lead eventually to the relational construction of the new or third reality.

Transformation

The relational search for meaning leads sometimes to a transformation in which the multiple perspectives within the therapeutic relationship are discovered, felt, and accounted for, and there is a shift in meanings and feeling. To me this is the real meaning of change, felt in the micromovements of experience in a here-and-now relationship. As Stern (2004) wrote:

> The basic assumption is that change is based on lived experience. In and of itself, verbally understanding, explaining, or narrating something is not sufficient to

The place of failure and rupture **137**

bring about change. There must also be an actual experience, a subjectively lived happening. An event must be lived, with feelings and actions taking place in real time, in the real world, with real people, in a moment of presentness.

(p. xiii)

Returning to Formula G, I believe that what is transformed in this process is the script payoff. Both therapist and client move away from needing to win or lose in the impasse. They no longer must choose between self-agency and attachment. What is gained is the experience of at last "feeling felt," that beautiful phrase coined by Siegel (2001), and a release from the need to repeat the process yet again.

I offer the following sequence as an expansion of Formula G in order to account for the relational aspects I have been exploring in this article:

Formula (G +1): C + G = R $\rightarrow$ S $\rightarrow$
X $\rightarrow$ R $\rightarrow$ (P) $\rightarrow$ A + S + Mm = T

Con + gimmick leads to response, which leads to a switch, crossup, and rupture, which then leads to the potential payoff leading to acknowledgment, space, and meaning making followed by transformation.

Case vignette

The case I describe here is based on an event from a number of years ago, one that ultimately led me to think about rupture, games, and Formula G from the relational perspective. It began when, to my mild horror, I opened the door to my first appointment of the day to find that the person standing there was not the one I was expecting. I had an appointment with a supervisee, but before me stood a client who was due an hour later. She had driven some distance, so, seeing her smile, in that moment I did not have the heart (or the wit) to say she had the wrong time. In any case, at that point I was not certain that she did, even though I knew we met weekly at 10 am. I also wanted to avoid having a doorstep conversation about who could come in and who could not as I saw my supervisee's car approaching. I asked my client in, knowing that at any moment my supervisee would arrive. So far, so game theory: the con, the gimmick, the first discount (mine), easy now to spot!

As the bell rang, I asked my client to take a seat, saying that I would return in a moment. On the doorstep, I hurriedly explained to my supervisee that I had made a mistake, and a client had arrived at the wrong time. Would she mind waiting for an hour? "Not at all, quite all right, happens to the best of us." But already it was far from all right with me. In a matter of moments, my unconscious, we might say, had arranged it so that I had a client inside my consulting room at the wrong time and my expected supervisee outside at the right time. I felt caught and less than professional. It ought to have been straightforward to sort out, a simple mistake by one of us, but looking back, it already had a quality of confusion and uncertainty. In a few transactions, in less time than it has taken to write this sentence, I had already made one mistake on top of another.

I returned to my client, who sensed that something had occurred and so had not taken her seat. She inquired if all was well. I told her about the mix-up.

"Have I come at the wrong time then?" she asked, reaching for her diary to check (con). "Well, perhaps," I said, "but let's start, shall we?" She did not sit and my heart started pounding (gimmick).

"Look," she said, no doubt sensing my discomfort, "I can easily wait. I don't want to take someone else's time" (con).

"It's fine," I said (gimmick).

"Are you sure?" she continued, looking worried and still standing (response).

"It's really OK," I said and then added, "Don't panic" (response).

Back came her out-of-character reply: "I'm not the one who's panicking!" (crossup and switch). She then metamorphosed into a person I had not seen before: stern, critical, haughty, and frightening.

I knew right away we were in choppy waters. Out of a clear blue sky the unconscious process between us emerged in the rupture that had occurred. I was totally unprepared for the switch. I felt upended, unsure how to respond, anxious, and shamed for sure (payoff).

The work we had been doing together up to that point had appeared straightforward, but looking back, it held within it all the depths of disturbance and shame about making mistakes that I was about to feel, that, relationally speaking, had found a home in me.

My client had previously described a time when she sent her authoritarian, punctilious father a small parcel without a stamp on it. He had paid for its delivery and turned on her for her "stupidity and inconsiderate behavior" with a venom that surprised her. She burned with shame and fury but made no response to his outburst. No intervention by me about small slips helped her. Now, as I sat in front of her as she had in front of her father, shamed and feeling stupid, a sense of panic and fear came over me.

This feeling and the dynamic between us occurred in a number of subsequent sessions, and I began to dread our meetings. I felt distracted, and the panic I had felt in that session rose each time our next session together approached.

I addressed these concerns in supervision and therapy and variously diagnosed them as script, games, rackets, and so on. This did not relieve my distress. But back then, before relational transactional analysis had really developed, I had not yet learned about the power of unconscious process, the mystery of countertransference and enactments, or the involvement of my own subjectivity. It did not seriously occur to me to acknowledge my experiences with my client, partly because I was ashamed of the realization that I was afraid of her and of my mistake. Also, I was working in a different mode of therapy, a one-person mode, we might say.

The place of failure and rupture   **139**

Nevertheless, I dimly realized that to heal this situation, I would probably need to acknowledge to my client something of what was going on between us. Eventually, and reluctantly, I did speak of my experiences with her (acknowledgment). There followed a most astonishing moment between us that itself felt all wrong, but in the space that we made later for reflection and meaning making, she used what had occurred to transform her experience of herself, and I learned about the importance of the therapist's vulnerability.

I started out, "I am aware of feeling afraid in our sessions …" A bubble seemed to burst. She looked dumbfounded and was silent, but a space opened up between us. I went on, emotion clearly on my face, "… since the mix-up in appointments." She rose from her chair after what seemed a long time and came toward me with her arms outstretched. She gathered me in her arms and drew me to her. I was mortified, my head raced again with unhelpful thoughts about touching clients, losing therapeutic distance and power, of the therapist being the consoler of the client not the reverse, and so on. "I hope I haven't been the cause of that," she said, and then she added, "It was nothing, nothing at all." We were both surprised at what had occurred, spontaneously, authentically, both fully feeling and accounting for our subjectivities. There followed a time and space in which we understood that the care she showed me over the potential shaming and the betrayal and panic I had felt at my mistake and her censure, escalated many times over, was what she had needed from her father but had not been given. The payoff between us in that process was transformed into learning a life lesson not understood by her own father: that mistakes are understandable and forgivable.

Conclusion

As I hope I have shown, the therapeutic task is for the client and therapist to survive, if at all possible, a rupture with all its twists and turns, not to regard it as a failure but rather as a necessity, an open door to deeper understanding. The therapist is supported in this endeavor by ethical principles, a culture of experiment and learning, and a theoretical framework that offers a relational approach.

References

Allen, J. (2010, 30 October–7 November). Neurosciences, psychotherapy and transactional analysis: A second look. International Association of Relational Transactional Analysis Colloquium. Retrieved from http://lists.topica.com/lists/iarta2010

Allen, J. R. (2003). Biological underpinnings of treatment approaches. *Transactional Analysis Journal, 33*, 23–31.

Aron, L. (2012). Analytic impasse and the third: Clinical implications of intersubjective theory. In L. Aron & A. Harris (Eds.), *Relational psychoanalysis* (Vol. 5, pp. 205–239). New York, NY: Routledge.

Basescu, S. (1990). Show and tell: Reflections on the analyst's self-disclosure. In G. Stricker & M. Fisher (Eds.), *Self-disclosure in the therapeutic relationship* (pp. 47–59). New York, NY: Plenum.

140 Carole Shadbolt

Benjamin, J. (2006, 9 October). Our appointment in Thebes: The analyst's fear of doing harm. Paper presented at the CONFER Conference, London, UK.

Berne, E. (1972). *What do you say after you say hello? The psychology of human destiny*. New York, NY: Grove Press.

Berne, E. (1980). *Transactional analysis in psychotherapy: A systematic individual and social psychiatry*. New York, NY: Grove Press. (Original work published 1961.)

Bowlby, J. (1973). *Attachment. Vol. 1 of Attachment and loss*. New York, NY: Basic Books.

Cornell, W. F., & Hargaden, H. (Eds.). (2005). *From transactions to relations: The emergence of a relational tradition in transactional analysis*. Chadlington, UK: Haddon Press.

Cornell, W. F., & Landaiche, N. M., III. (2006). Impasse and intimacy: Applying Berne's concept of script protocol. *Transactional Analysis Journal, 36*, 196–213.

Fisher, M. (1990). The shared experience and self-disclosure. In G. Stricker & M. Fisher (Eds.), *Self-disclosure in the therapeutic relationship* (pp. 3–15). New York, NY: Plenum.

Fonagy, P., Gergely, G., Jurist, E., & Target, M. (2004). *Affect regulation, mentalization, and the development of the self*. New York, NY: Other Press.

Hargaden, H., & Sills, C. (2002). *Transactional analysis: A relational perspective*. Hove, UK: Brunner-Routledge.

Hine, J. (1990). The bilateral and ongoing nature of games. *Transactional Analysis Journal, 20*, 28–39.

Holloway, W. (1973). Shut the escape hatch. In M. M. Holloway & W. H. Holloway (Eds.), *The monograph series* (No. 4, pp. 15–18). Medina, OH: Midwest Institute for Human Understanding.

Joyce, P., & Sills, C. (2001). *Skills in gestalt counselling and psychotherapy*. London, UK: Sage.

Kahler, T. (with Capers, H.). (1974). The miniscript. *Transactional Analysis Journal, 4*(1), 26–42.

Maroda, K. (2004). *The power of countertransference*. Hillsdale, NJ: Analytic Press.

Maroda, K. (2010). *Psychodynamic techniques: Working with emotion in the therapeutic relationship*. New York, NY: Guilford Press.

Mellor, K. (1980). Impasses: A developmental and structural understanding. *Transactional Analysis Journal, 10*, 213–220.

Nathanson-Elkind, S. (1992). *Resolving impasses in therapeutic relationships*. New York, NY: Guilford Press.

Price, R. (1987). The legacy of Milton Erikson: Implications for TA. *Transactional Analysis Journal, 17*, 11–15.

Safran, J. D., & Muran, J. C. (2000). *Negotiating the therapeutic alliance: A relational treatment guide*. New York, NY: Guilford Press.

Siegel, D. (2001). Interpersonal neurobiology of the developing mind. *Infant Mental Health Journal, 22*(1–2), 67–94.

Sills, C. (2003). When the whole group plays a game. *Transactional Analysis Journal, 33*, 382–387.

Stark, M. (1999). *Modes of therapeutic interaction: Enhancement of knowledge, provision of experience, and engagement in relationship*. Northvale, NJ: Jason Aronson.

Stern, D. N. (2004). *The present moment in psychotherapy and everyday life*. New York, NY: Norton.

Stricker, G. (1990). Self-disclosure and psychotherapy. In G. Stricker & M. Fisher (Eds.), *Self-disclosure in the therapeutic relationship* (pp. 277–289). New York, NY: Plenum.

Winnicott, D. W. (1965). *The maturational processes and the facilitating environment: Studies in the theory of emotional development*. London, UK: Hogarth Press.

11

TRAVERSING THE FAULT LINES

Trauma and enactment

Jo Stuthridge

Beginning in September 2010, Christchurch, New Zealand, my home town, suffered a terrible series of earthquakes. In the wake of these, the image of the *fault line* became a powerful metaphor in my work with trauma. The fault line symbolized my thoughts about dissociative cracks, enactment, and ruptures in relationships. I begin this article with a personal example and a brief overview before describing each of these concepts in more depth.

My use of theory explores the interface between transactional analysis, relational psychoanalysis, and the literature on trauma. Transactional analysis offers a unique perspective on the wider dialogue regarding trauma, dissociation, and enactment and can, in turn, be enriched though this encounter with other perspectives.

This article began life as an address to a small conference in London put on by the International Association of Relational Transactional Analysis (Stuthridge, 2011). When I was initially invited to speak, I felt waves of panic welling up within me. The waves gathered momentum and formed a small flood of anxiety. I felt the anxiety as an amorphous, nameless pool of dread. My mind leapt into a hypervigilant state in the early hours of some mornings, alerting me to imminent peril. I was convinced there was danger ahead.

We might say that a minor fault line had opened up within my psyche. In this state of anxiety, I lost connection with the competence I enjoy in other contexts. It was as if I had never known competence nor ever would again. Continuity within my sense of self was broken. My mind unconsciously separated these feeling states in order to protect against danger perceived in the future instead of integrating them into a narrative of the past. Self-coherence in this instance represented a threat to self-stability (Bromberg, 2008). Van der Kolk (1995) described how this system of dissociation works like a smoke detector, sounding the alarm at the slightest whiff of

142 Jo Stuthridge

danger. The isolated state of anxiety I was experiencing warned me against repeating earlier trauma, perhaps fear and shame associated with exposure.

Unfortunately, such rifts in the mind, and the rigid self-narratives whose boundaries they preserve, tend to bring about the feared outcome. Sleepless nights made it difficult to write, confirming my fears of incompetence. This is the teleological process that Eric Berne (1961) described as *script*. In the narrow sense employed by Berne, script is a self-protective process that shapes the future according to the past. As Bromberg (1998a) observed, danger is always felt to be around the next corner.

My experience is an example of what is often referred to as *developmental trauma* (Bromberg, 2008; Stolorow, 2011). My mind was scanning the horizons ahead for trauma that had its roots in formative relationships. Developmental trauma results from the cumulative effect of a caregiver's repeated failures to recognize aspects of a child's emotional experience. We can all be vulnerable to developmental trauma in this sense; it is a matter of degree.

For survivors of severe developmental trauma, such as childhood sexual or physical abuse, protecting oneself means anticipating danger in intimacy. Relationships become dangerous ground.

These ideas grew from my clinical experience over 25 years with survivors of child abuse. More recently, I have worked with survivors of the Christchurch earthquakes. The title of this article was inspired by Adam, a client who was caught in the major Christchurch earthquake in February 2011 and then 10 days later in the Japanese earthquake. Adam became hypervigilant to sudden movement and low noises. He scanned buildings for exits and checked walls for structural safety. Mostly he was terrified of the future. He said he felt fragile, as though the ground within his internal landscape had shattered. Memories of the past had also begun to haunt him. It seemed that recent events had ruptured old fault lines within his psyche. He felt flooded by painful feelings that sprang from a childhood history of family violence.

I am using the term *trauma* here to refer to this whole range of experience: gross violation of the self, as in child sexual and physical abuse; adult onset trauma in the wake of overwhelming horror, such as an earthquake; and developmental trauma that results from invalidation by a caregiver. I believe the consequences of these experiences are interrelated. In my work with earthquake survivors, I noticed that in every case in which posttraumatic stress symptoms escalated over time rather than subsiding, the client revealed a history of childhood trauma. The events of the earthquake collided with early trauma creating a nightmarish present. For example, in Adam's case, the frequent aftershocks triggered the sound of his father's approaching footsteps and a state of terror.

I began to wonder about the processes underlying these diverse experiences. To make sense of my clinical experience, I have looked increasingly to theories of dissociation and enactment (Bromberg, 1998a, 2006, 2008; Davies, 2004; Davies & Frawley, 1994; Stern, 2003, 2010) along with the clarity provided by a transactional analysis framework. This article proposes that the healthy mind moves fluidly between ego states, providing continuity between past and present and across various affective states. Trauma and its aftermath shatter the mind, creating self-states that harden and cleave into separate parts of the self, like tectonic plates. Bromberg (2006) and Ogden (1994) described, in different ways, how we readily trade psychological stability for the price of continuity within the self. Stolorow (2011) described how trauma destroys temporal continuity, that is, our lived experience of time. Berne (1964) insisted that the human mind seeks psychic stability or homeostasis above all else. We unhappily (but predictably) spend our lives waiting for dreaded events that have long since passed.

Ultimately, trauma in the absence of recognition creates an incoherent sense of self. Unbearable bits of experience are cut off and banished from any link with the subjective "I" felt as one's identity. These "not-me" (Bromberg, 1998a; Sullivan, 1953) fragments, once exiled from consciousness, then tend to intrude in the present as dysregulated affective experiences (Schore, 2009) or transferential enactments (Bromberg, 1998a; Stern, 2003). When internal fault lines are externalized, relationships are prone to rupture.

Integrating the fractured self requires an emotionally transformative process and often involves the unconscious participation of client and therapist in a series of shaky encounters. These collisions between two minds allow dissociated experience to be enacted, symbolized, and linked to a broader sense of "I." We discover "not-me" through an act of recognition (Benjamin, 1990; Ogden, 1994): feeling seen and felt in the eye of an other. When client and therapist resolve an enactment, the interpersonal connection facilitates internal connections. Bridging the fault lines in the interpersonal realm increases continuity within the self and expands possibilities for affect regulation and intimacy.

The multiple mind

Transactional analysis ego state theory lends itself to a contemporary interpretation of the mind as a multiplicity of discrete self-states that form a nonlinear dynamic system (Stuthridge, 2010). This model suggests that a healthy mind develops when differentiated self-states are integrated to create a complex, flexible, coherent system (Siegel, 1999). The assumption of multiplicity is shared by relational psychoanalysts such as Bromberg (1998a), Davies and Frawley (1994), Harris (1996), Mitchell (1993), and Stern (2010); neuroscience researchers such as Le Doux (2002) and Schore (1994); and cognitive science researchers such as Bucci (1997). These writers from diverse fields draw on Pierre Janet's (van der Kolk & van der Hart, 1989) ideas about the centrality of dissociation and Fairbairn's (1992) concept of multiple ego states. Berne's (1961) structural model likewise assumes that the mind is comprised of multiple ego states that are more or less integrated. Berne (1972) cited Fairbairn's work as "one of the best heuristic bridges" (p. 134) between transactional analysis and psychoanalysis.

This conception of the mind has implications for the way we think about script and ego states. Following Cornell (1988), I view script as "an ongoing process

144 Jo Stuthridge

of self-defining and sometimes self-limiting psychological construction of reality" (p. 281). Where he uses the term *life plan* to distinguish a healthy process, I retain the term *script* to signify the whole range of possibilities, thus avoiding a dichotomy between health and pathology. I think of script as an unconscious self-narrative that organizes the mind, life experiences, and a sense of identity. This narrative construction can be flexible, coherent, and complex or rigid, narrow, and self-limiting. My definition draws on nonlinear systems theory (Allen, 2010; Stuthridge, 2010) and builds on a constructivist perspective of script evident in the writing of Allen and Allen (Allen, 2003; Allen & Allen, 1997), Cornell (1988), English (1988), and Summers and Tudor (2000).

While there are important conceptual differences between Berne's (1961) understanding of the ego and contemporary ideas about self-states, I do not want to digress in that direction (see Allen, 2003; Cornell, 2003; Novak, 2008, for further discussion). Suffice it to say that I will retain Berne's terms *Parent* and *Child ego states* as lively metaphors. Berne's personified terms capture the essence of a state of mind as an emotional, relational, and embodied way of being derived from early experiences of self and other.

We tend to experience Parent and Child ego states as nonreflective ways of relating that feel automatic, compelling, or instinctive. These states involve highly selective perceptions of self and other, thus creating transference.

Parent and Child ego states are like actors in a play. These characters, with their own behaviors, feelings, and thoughts, represent all the different "me's" that together create personality. A flexible script allows the actors to interact or associate freely in both internal and interpersonal contexts. However, within a rigid script, these characters remain more or less dissociated, acting without awareness of each other.

In contrast, an Adult ego state allows a more reflective consciousness. I think of the Adult ego (Erskine, 2003; Tudor, 2003) as the script writer: a metaphor for the subjective "I" or agentive self who authors experience. This is the part of the self that constructs meanings and mediates between internal experience and life events. The Adult ego allows us to see from multiple perspectives and play with alternate meanings of events, expanding the possibilities for perception. Fonagy and his colleagues (Fonagy, Gergely, Jurist, & Target, 2002) described this reflective capacity as *mentalizing* while Bromberg, 1998b referred in one of his chapter titles to the ability to "stand in the spaces" between self-states.

Multiple self-state theory assumes, to quote Bucci (2011), that "some degree of dissociation is normative and necessary to allow us to function smoothly" (p. 50). The healthy mind moves with ease between a relatively stable but fluid arrangement of discrete ego states, adapting appropriately to the moment. Bromberg (2006) suggested that this stability allows us to feel like a unitary self, while normal multiplicity allows us to be creative and spontaneous. This formulation is reminiscent of Berne's (1961) concept of the *moving self*.

A flexible mind is capable of containing conflict by integrating disparate experiences into a coherent sense of self. A coherent script, like an orchestra score, creates harmony from a diverse range of instruments and notes. Phenomenologically, this might feel like living with Puccini's gentle harmonies in the background of the mind.

A less flexible arrangement leads to rigid ego state boundaries and an incoherent sense of self. Fractures within the mind obstruct the ease of movement from one self-state to another, creating a range of symptoms, from incongruity to character disorders. Trauma leads to discontinuity within the self, dissociation, and dysregulated affect. Living with a background of trauma might feel like living with discordant music (Siegel & Cozolino, 2005). Imagine for a moment, living with the theme from Hitchcock's (1960) film *Psycho* as background music. A client, who worked with film, taught me that while you cannot change the events in the movie of your life, you can change the background music. We can rewrite the script.

Recognition and continuity

In a chapter titled "A theory of social contact," Berne (1961, p. 77) proposed that "the ability of the human psyche to maintain coherent ego states seems to depend upon a changing flow of sensory stimuli. This observation forms the psychobiological basis of social psychiatry." He went on to define the "flow of sensory stimuli" as social recognition, initially met through "social handling and physical intimacy" and later sublimated into a need for symbolic forms of recognition, such as words. In this chapter, Berne sketched his theory of psychological hungers, which provides the foundations of transactional analysis as an interpersonal theory or social psychiatry.

Recent research in the fields of attachment and neuroscience concur with Berne's assumption: that social recognition is crucial to healthy development and continuity within the self. Schore (1994) and Fonagy et al. (2002) articulated systems of affect regulation determined by patterns of recognition within early relationships. Both systems influence the degree of continuity between self-states, ultimately shaping the development of the self. Schore (1994) described how right-brain to right-brain emotional attunement between two individuals "integrates a sense of self across state transitions, thereby allowing for a continuity of inner experience" (p. 33). Fonagy et al. (2002) argued that coherence within the self is a developmental achievement dependent on contingent attunement from caregivers.

With adequate recognition from caregivers, painful experience and ruptures can be symbolized and internalized as intrapsychic conflict. The capacity to symbolize bodily affect as a conscious feeling is acquired through certain kinds of mirroring (Fonagy et al., 2002). Redecision methods work well with ego states that represent symbolized but conflicted parts of the self. Inadequate recognition from others will compromise the Adult capacity to mentalize and lead to pockets of unsymbolized experience, which linger as dysregulated affect in dissociated self-states. Continuity within the self is reliant on recognition from the other.

146 Jo Stuthridge

The failure of recognition: dissociation and discontinuity

A cumulative failure of recognition leads to developmental trauma and pathological patterns of dissociation within the mind (Erskine, 1993; Schore, 1994). When a caregiver fails to recognize certain elements of a child's subjective experience, these parts of the self become dissociated or not-me. Rather than being integrated into a conscious self-narrative, this experience remains "unformulated" (Stern, 1983) or "unsymbolized" (Bucci, 1997) and unlinked from the subjective "I." These alien or not-me elements remain isolated in the outer islands of nonconscious Child and Parent ego states. Most of us can recall a moment of self-revelation when we utter something like, "That is so not me." Actually, it is. But there is often no place for not-me in a defensive narrative.

Stern (2003) distinguished between passive dissociation, which results from selective attention, and a more active form of dissociation that is defensively motivated. Passive dissociation occurs when a parent selects some aspects of the child's self to validate while disconfirming others. Nonrecognized affect remains unformulated and outside awareness. Selective perception from a caregiver narrows the possibilities for self-narrative, producing a self-limiting script. Stern used the term "narrative rigidity" (p. 129) to describe this weaker form of dissociation. The child learns to define himself by the way he feels seen in his parents' or caretakers' eyes. The script then acts like blinkers and prevents other meanings about the self from being articulated (Stern, 2010).

We employ active dissociation in the context of severe trauma to reject specific meanings and feelings. Stern (2003) described this strong form of dissociation as an unconscious refusal to formulate certain meanings rather than an attempt to avoid conflict (as in splitting, disavowal, denial, or repression). Fonagy et al. (2002) described a similar defensive process as a refusal to mentalize.

Stern (2010) and Bromberg (2011) agreed that defensive dissociation is unconsciously motivated by attempts to maintain a stable identity and needed ties with caregivers. We dissociate those states that are incompatible with the self as seen by our parents. The aim is to avoid being the person who experienced unbearable feelings, such as terror, humiliation, shame, despair, or abandonment. We defend against this dreaded state of being, unconsciously perceived as a threat to selfhood, by separating these not-me states from our conscious identity.

It is the absence of recognition that creates trauma, not a painful experience per se. Affect becomes unbearable and overwhelming when the recognition a child needs in order to symbolize and integrate a feeling is missing. Stolorow (2011) made this point clear:

> It cannot be overemphasized that injurious childhood experiences in and of themselves need not be traumatic (or at least not lastingly so) or pathogenic, provided that they occur within a responsive milieu. *Pain is not pathology.* It is the absence of adequate attunement to the child's painful emotional reactions that renders them unendurable and thus a source of traumatic states and psychopathology.
>
> *(p. 27)*

When the child's inchoate distress finds no safe haven in the mind of another, the mind splinters, defending sanity through dissociative processes. We sacrifice parts of the self, continuity, and coherence to safeguard psychic stability. Interpersonal failures of recognition form fault lines within the mind. Developmental trauma leads to subtle fissures while chasms divide the mind in conditions of abuse or neglect.

Dissociation: the new black?

It might be argued that words such as dissociation and enactment are trendy new words for old concepts. I will make some brief observations about this complex issue. From a constructivist perspective, dissociation and enactment (Bromberg, 2006; Stern, 2003; Stolorow, 2011) are embedded in a relational context. The interpersonal context determines which experiences can become conscious and which remain unformulated. This idea is consistent with the importance of interpersonal dynamics in determining intrapsychic structures within transactional analysis theory. Repression, disavowal, and splitting, in contrast, are anchored in a Freudian (Freud, 1959) perspective of trauma that views the mind as an isolated entity, vulnerable to internal flooding. These traditional concepts arise from intrapsychic processes (McWilliams, 2011), implying that something once "known" or symbolized has been banished to the unconscious. Splitting provides a defensive solution to internal conflict by separating self-states so they cannot be simultaneously experienced. Dissociation is a more primitive solution to trauma that prevents conflict from being symbolized or formed within the mind (Bromberg, 2011; McWilliams, 2011; Schore, 2009; Stern, 2003, 2010; Stolorow, 2011). Dissociation "is not conceived in interpersonal theory as disavowed intrapsychic conflict. It is rather the subjectivity we never create, the experience we never have" (Stern, 2010, p. 95). Trauma in the absence of recognition forecloses possibilities for symbolism and internal conflict.

This distinction becomes significant when we consider the clinical implications of working with trauma. Unsymbolized experience is enacted because it has never been symbolized and cannot be contained as conflict. For example, the experience of violence or sexual abuse from a loved father is so disjunctive that the mind's best defense is a refusal to formulate, or mentalize, the experience. In a therapy dyad, instead of being experienced within one mind, the dissociated experience is enacted between two minds, "like the broken halves of two plates" (Stern, 2010, p. 95). This model of dissociation assumes that enactment precedes symbolization and internal conflict. Splitting, disavowal, and repression assume that "unconscious internal conflict ... *precedes* enactment" (Stern, 2010, p. 9).

This constructivist perspective on dissociation and enactment (Stern, 2003) offers an alternative understanding to Cornell and Landaiche's (2006) thoughts on enactment as the externalization of a Type III (Mellor, 1980) or protocol-level impasse.

148 Jo Stuthridge

Between a rock and a hard place: a clinical vignette

While watching the movie *127 Hours* (Smithson et al. & Boyle, 2010) with my son, I was reminded of my work with Ella, a client. The movie tells the true story of a young rock climber, Aron, who falls down a deep narrow canyon and becomes trapped with his arm jammed between a rock and the canyon wall. After 127 hours, Aron decides that the only way to escape is to amputate his arm. Aron's predicament, the grueling tone of the movie, and the visual images of the vertical fall held several meanings for me. I realized that this is what it felt like being stuck in a fault line with Ella when conflict erupted between us. It was as if intersubjectivity collapsed, and we both fell into an abyss. In these moments we lost any sense of mutual understanding. I felt trapped, with no way out. I wondered if this is what it felt like for Ella as a child: a feeling of terror, entrapment, and impossible choices. Ella had also been forced to cut off a part of herself to survive.

Ella and I arrived at this stuck place repeatedly during the first year of our work together. I will recount one such sequence of events, which occurred the day after the first Christchurch earthquake. The client I was expecting had already arrived and was seated when I heard someone come into the waiting room. Oh shit, I thought, I've double booked the session. I went out and found Ella standing outside the door. Her face went white with shock when I explained my mistake. I felt guilty and embarrassed. It was a dreadful moment.

We agreed to meet early the following morning. Ella was still devastated. She said she had sat for an hour in the car after the incident, in a state of shock, unable to move. She had only recently decided to come twice a week, and this was to have been the first of her second sessions. She felt convinced that I had forgotten her because I did not want to see her twice weekly. She feared that she was "too much" for others, and for Ella this moment was proof. She was too much for me also.

Ella stared at me with wide, accusing eyes and said she did not want my apologies, she wanted an explanation. She described the state of abjection she had left with, feeling like an "aborted thing," utterly unwanted. Why had I chosen the other client and not her? she demanded. I said I could not tell her the reason, as it would compromise the other client's confidentiality, but I made the best decision I could in the circumstances. I made various attempts to explore her fantasies and feelings in the moment, but Ella's feelings escalated rather than abated. The tension between us soared.

Ella said, "There's no way back from here. I can't recover from this. I will have to leave. When you turned me away, I felt slapped in the face." She was distraught and unrelenting. Nothing I said made any difference. It felt like a stalemate. As the session veered toward an uncertain ending, I could feel myself withdrawing to a defensive distance. Her implied threats to end the therapy seemed unreasonable, and I could find no way through the impasse. I felt trapped "between a rock and a hard place."

Just then there was the sound of little feet running downstairs. I work in rooms built onto the third story of our home. Ella looked surprised. She asked if I had children in the house. I said, "Yes, there's been an earthquake," my exasperation leaking. She smiled at the irony and the rift between us narrowed slightly. I explained that family had arrived the previous night. She seemed to weigh this up, pausing. There was a glimmer of momentary shame in her facial expression but also distrust. I felt myself softening and told her I had had a sleepless night, disturbed by both events. There was silence as Ella began to rearrange her mind. She relaxed visibly. In those few unspoken seconds we both experienced a deep sense of mutual recognition. She saw that I had no intent to forget her; I saw her terror. Later she told me it was my willingness to be vulnerable, like her, that made the difference. When I spoke of my disturbance, she saw that her distress had made an impact. The shared feeling created a bridge over the abyss. In the moment of the double booking she saw me as an abandoning mother, impervious to her horror. And I objectified her. I saw her as a demanding child who felt entitled to my attention and concern. This tangle of transference and countertransference is an example of a mutual enactment.

In subsequent sessions, Ella linked this experience with me to an early memory of herself at five years old clamoring and clinging to her mother at the door while her mother tried to leave. We both understood that the double booking had re-created the scene at the door. Ella had felt repeatedly abandoned by caregivers as a child.

This pattern of enactment returned several times during the therapy in different forms. On each occasion, the relationship seemed to teeter on the edge of a sudden ending, a traumatic repetition of early abandonment. I felt pushed to the edge of rejection each time by Ella's attempts at coercion. She described feelings of terror, desperation, and unbearable despair. Part of me wanted out, but I did not want to acknowledge this rejecting self-state. It was not me. Good therapists do not feel like this. Shame clouded my ability to see a way through the deadlock.

Ella and I survived the repeated ruptures, and over time we constructed new and richer meanings from the debris. It seemed that a fearsome Child ego state in Ella emerged when internal terror threatened to overwhelm her, provoking in me the reaction she feared most. She experienced this behavior in herself as out of character and contrary to her usual adaptive, pleasing nature: not-me. The movie image offered a glimpse of Ella's predicament. She could either "cut off a limb" and avoid feelings of rage and terror to maintain her attachment to me (as she had with her mother) or risk losing the relationship by unleashing the monstrous child. With each enactment there was a risk of either reinforcing or transforming Ella's experience of trauma.

The dilemma for the abused child is that the person she depends on is often the person who is hurting her. She lives in a reality that is grossly invalidated by others. Any self-state that threatens the needed attachment must be dissociated from the core sense of self as it is defined by the caregiver (Bromberg, 2006). Fairbairn (1992) captured this dilemma poignantly when he wrote, "It's better to be a sinner in a world ruled by God than to live in a world ruled by the Devil" (p. 66). The child internalizes badness as self-blame in order to keep the parent good. The abused child maintains attachment at the cost of continuity in her own mind. Incompatible

150 Jo Stuthridge

experiences of terror, loss, or rage are cut off and banished to unlinked Child and Parent ego states. This is what it means to "cut off a limb" in order to survive.

Will you be there for me?

Desires, tender feelings, and needs for loving recognition are all too often split off from consciousness, just as we isolate affects like rage and terror. Needy feelings can be perceived as a threat to the caregiver just as much as hate can. The hunger for recognition is sequestered within the mind, like an area marked with fluorescent danger tape. This barrier also wards off the pain of betrayal and shame that follows a breach of trust. Thereafter, one's identity and relationships must be structured in a way that keeps unwanted affects, such as tenderness, desire, or need, firmly out of bounds. Trust in the other becomes a no-go area.

For example, Ella had developed a sense of identity as a highly independent, self-contained person. She functioned very successfully in her solitary way. The desperately needy Child ego state that emerged in our work represented an unwelcome not-me feeling. For Ella, neediness was experienced as dsytonic to her scripted identity.

Working with traumatized clients ultimately involves rebuilding trust and the possibility of depending on the other. Mazzetti (2008) vividly described the loss of trust in humanity that arises from severe trauma. The interpersonal context is crucial not only to the development of trauma but also to the therapeutic process.

Traversing the fault lines: enactment

During an enactment, fault lines within the self erupt in the therapy relationship. Stern (2010) defined enactment as "the interpersonalization of dissociation" (p. 14). Self-states that are dissociated tend to be enacted unconsciously between client and therapist in behavioral expressions of transference and countertransference. In an attempt to avoid dissociated states, we either act out or elicit the intolerable feeling in the other person. The client exerts subtle forms of pressure that prod, push, or pull the therapist to act or feel a certain way. Davies (2004, p. 719) compared the frenzied struggle to get rid of malignant selves as like playing the card game Old Maid (in which players try to get rid of pairs of cards until the loser holds the last or Old Maid card). We desperately arrange the relationship to find not-me parts of the self in the other person.

In transactional analysis terms, an enactment can be defined as an intersection between two scripts. These interactions are scenarios that arise at the point at which the unconscious relational patterns of client and therapist meet. Dissociated Parent and Child ego states are tossed about in an unconscious drama in which each person is enlisted to play a role in the other's script. The vulnerabilities, anxieties, and defenses of client and therapist become interlocked in an emotional tangle.

It might be argued that the clinical events I am describing could be understood as projective identification. I prefer to use the term *mutual enactment* as distinct from *projective identification* because I do not consider the therapist to be an empty container for the client's bad object. When a therapist becomes caught in an enactment, she or he dissociates an aspect of herself. In effect, the therapist becomes the new bad object (Cooper, 2011) not the old one. We each get drawn into enactments according to our unique vulnerabilities. My experience with a particular client will be different from yours. We are uniquely recruited into the other's script. We might speak of an enactment being one-sided if the client's activity fails to evoke a reciprocal action from the therapist. A therapist who does not share the required script vulnerability may be able to retain an Adult ego capacity to mentalize even under pressure. Using a model of projective identification, a therapist's unconscious behavior might be considered a failure of containment. Theories of enactment, in contrast, view these events as opportunities for dissociated experience to be symbolized. (For further discussion of the differences between these models, see Gabbard, 2004; Mitchell, 2008; Stern, 2010.)

I use classical transactional diagrams to illustrate mutual enactment and cocreated transference. Figure 11.1 diagrams the enactment between Ella and me. This diagram implies that the therapist is an active part of the unconscious process rather than a neutral observer, as in Berne's (1961) or Moiso's (1985) depiction of transference. Moiso's diagrams, which locate the therapist behind a blank screen, elegantly depict a projective process.

Dissociation and enactment offer a powerful form of self-protection while compromising the potential for intimacy. Berne's (1961) script theory elucidates this Faustian bargain. By externalizing our broken internal world through games and enactments, we maintain internal stability. When we enact dissociated parts of the self, we tend to elicit a response that confirms the script. These not-me parts of the self ultimately run the show, and our behavior inadvertently leads to the dreaded outcome. Ironically, dissociation leads to repeated patterns of trauma. Despite my conscious efforts to avoid being untrustworthy, adversarial, seductive, or whatever the client's script demands, I often find myself identifying with, or worse, behaving like the actual parent. For example, while consciously I encouraged Ella

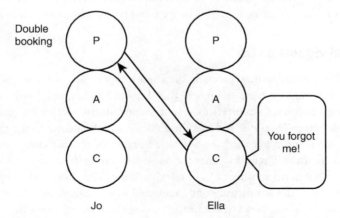

FIGURE 11.1 Diagram of enactment

152 Jo Stuthridge

to come twice weekly, unconsciously I double booked her session. In this moment I became the abandoning parent.

In work with trauma survivors, enactments can evoke dire feelings of shame, betrayal, envy, and aggression in either participant. These characters can be ugly. Parent and Child ego states may include identifications with the abuser and intensely shame-based Child ego states. Ferenczi (1988) vividly captured this experience: "The time will come when he [the therapist] will have to repeat with his own hands the act of murder previously perpetrated against the patient" (p. 52).

Therapy often begins with intense idealizations as Parent–Child ego state dyads (Stuthridge, 2006) are enacted through a Victim–Rescuer transference. The client in a Child ego state longs for the loving mother whom she never had. Incest survivors often describe a leaning toward the father in reaction to a rejecting mother. Many therapists carry a fairy godmother introject within, ready to rush to the Rescue.

The going becomes more difficult once the abused child and the abuser appear in the transferential mix. Client and therapist take turns at playing both parts of this painful relational dynamic. In a Child ego state, the client enacts the abused child's experience and provokes the therapist to react like the abuser, thus re-creating the trauma. Alternatively, the client activates a Parent ego state and recruits the therapist to play the abused child or Victim role by hooking some aspect of the therapist's vulnerabilities. I think a sudden game switch, typically from Child to Parent, occurs in a moment when an unwanted self-state threatens to become conscious. For example, to avoid the pain of humiliation, I humiliate the other. To avoid feeling manipulated, I manipulate. The main thing is to avoid being not-me and to maintain a sense of "I" that is syntonic with the scripted identity. Benjamin (2004), Davies and Frawley (1994), Ehrenberg (1992), Mitchell, 2008, and Stern (2010) have all described similar transferential dynamics involving representations of self and other as abused and abuser.

In the transactional analysis literature, Little (2006) has also observed that Parent and Child ego states operate as relational units in the transference. However, he described patterns of externalized internal conflict rather than the dynamics of dissociation and enactment, which in my mind typify work with trauma.

Clinical vignette: Lisa

I am often stunned at how precisely the client's experience of trauma is re-created, always drawing out parts of myself that I would rather not know about. The following enactment occurred in a split second during a therapy group. It was the week before I was due to leave for a conference. Someone in the group made a joke that I might get stuck on a beach because of the ash clouds interrupting flights at the time. There was laughter, but it felt wrong. It chafed, as Stern (2010) would say, but in the moment I laughed with them: "Well, how bad would that be?" Immediately as the words were out I regretted it. Lisa called out, "Don't say that!" She spoke about her dread of the break, voicing the fear and anger that the group's laughter hid. At the close of the group, Lisa left abruptly.

Lisa was an extraordinary young woman who was sexually abused by her father from her earliest years until she was 16 years old. The abuse included perverse acts, rape, and violence in the context of a very manipulative and affectionate relationship.

In the individual session that followed the group just described, Lisa told me about a dream. In it she turned up to her session as usual, but I was not there. While sitting in the waiting room, she was sure I had been killed in a plane crash or earthquake but no one had thought to tell her. No one would know she was there. She associated the dream imagery with volcanic ash clouds, volcanoes, fire, and earthquakes. She guessed this was about rage.

We wondered together if her relationship with me felt secret just as her relationship with her father had. I tried to think myself into being Lisa's father, which was difficult. My mind flicked to the moment of laughter in the group. I knew in that moment that my laughter was painful to Lisa, and I had not stopped myself. I felt a sick, sinking feeling of shame as I realized what had happened. In that split second, Lisa had encountered the sadist within me. I have no doubt she was looking quite selectively.

I asked, "Did you see me a bit like Dad in group when I laughed with the others?" She said, "Yes, I thought you were hurting me on purpose. That is exactly like Dad. I know you weren't, but that's what I felt. I wanted to walk out." I agreed that there was something hurtful in my laughter. I thought about plane crashes and clouds of volcanic anger and asked, "Do you ever want to hurt me? I was thinking about that plane crashing in your dream." Lisa was horrified:

> Oh, like I'm so angry I want your plane to crash? That is so not me. I would hate it if you died. But I do hate it that I will be hurting so much while you are having fun. … That is what I hate most about break. I do want to spoil your fun. I suppose it is like those dreams of watching Dad on fire.

We talked further. She told me that her suicide fantasies were usually about trying to hurt me. She hated that I had so much while she had so little. It was the only way she could take something from me, a desperate defense against envy. She knew that killing herself would hurt me.

I was forced to recognize Lisa's hatred for me and forgo being the loved therapist while she had to acknowledge her desire to hurt me, a frightening echo of her father. Lisa had secured a place in my heart from the start of our work together. In retrospect, I think I made no space for her hostility. While Lisa needed to keep her anger from damaging her safe place in my heart, I needed to avoid feeling hated. I wanted to be the heroine of this story, not the villain. We were enacting a classic Victim–Rescuer impasse. We both needed to exclude hatred. Woods (2007) warned against games soaked in positive strokes that avoid recognition of the ugly parts of ourselves. He wrote, "The stroke that really counts is the recognition of what is really going on with the client" (p. 34).

Slochower (2011) cautioned against the therapist's need to idealize the client and be idealized in return. Such jointly constructed dynamics can seriously inhibit

154 Jo Stuthridge

a therapeutic process. The unconscious deal is "I'll love you if you love me" (p. 8). My admiration for Lisa and her need for a good mother had taken us a good way down the path of this therapeutic dead end.

A sadistic self-state was tossed between Lisa and me during this series of events. In the moment when I laughed, we both fell into the abyss. I lost my reflective ability, and intersubjectivity collapsed. However, through the enactment and our talking, the unbearable became bearable. I had to find the sadist in me before I could see it in Lisa. My sadistic feeling was nothing like her father's behavior, but it was similar enough to reactivate the fault line. Lisa's dissociated rage began to find images and words. The impossibly conflicted love and hate she felt for her father inched a little closer within her. In this brief act of recognition, Lisa's rage was seen and felt. The bridge between us formed a tentative bridge between Lisa's estranged selves.

While I was away, Lisa sent me an e-mail. The subject line read "BEWARE: I be angry." She was risking anger with me, albeit from a safe distance. Lisa coped with this break without cutting herself for the first time in the three years we had worked together. More importantly, her rage began to find words rather than being enacted between us or trapped in dreams. The unsymbolized experience, which included a complex mix of envy, rage, and a desire to hurt, became conscious and knowable. I discovered more about that persistent desire to be the loved other, which perhaps motivates many of us who do this work (Slochower, 2011).

Bridging the abyss: an act of recognition

I think of enactment as inevitable and necessary. This nonconscious mode of communication is often the only way a dissociated self-state can find a voice (Bromberg, 1998a; Stern, 2010). The experience can be enacted but not told. Methods of conscious attunement, inquiry, and empathy (Erskine, 1993), while essential to building an alliance, may not reach this implicit, wordless story. The fault lines need to be reactivated but in a way that allows the unconscious affect to be felt, tolerated, and integrated. Enactments risk a fine line between repeating and containing trauma. However, this edgy emotional landscape is the place where healing happens. Schore (2009, p. 132) argued that interactive affect regulation occurs at the boundaries between two windows of affect tolerance. The space where one subject rubs up against another creates an active fault line, allowing unformulated experience to emerge and be transformed into symbolic feelings and words. Enactments frequently occur around the boundaries of the therapeutic frame because that is where the client will encounter the therapist's subjectivity.

Enactments are a little like aftershocks. The dreaded feeling that was at one time experienced as too dangerous surfaces in a safer relational context. Bucci (2002) wrote, "The threatening dissociated affect must be activated to some degree but in trace form" (p. 787). When the intolerable feeling can be tolerated, the client expands his or her ability to regulate affect. Bromberg (2006) emphasized the need for a working relationship that is "safe but not too safe" (p. 189).

During an enactment we cast the other in a role prescribed by our script. We objectify the other and selectively perceive those aspects that fit our script expectations. Ogden (1994) and Benjamin (1995) both argued that during a deadlock in therapy, the subjectivities of both participants are negated. An act of recognition is required to reestablish intersubjectivity. (I am referring here to Benjamin's, 1990, use of the term *intersubjectivity* as meaning mutual recognition, the ability to recognize and feel recognized, which she sees as a developmental achievement.) Instead of perceiving the other as the locus of not-me or as an object to be feared or controlled, we begin to perceive the other as a separate subject. The other is suddenly seen as more human, an equal subject with separate feelings and thoughts rather than an object of script fantasy. Most importantly, there is a shift in the emotional tone of the relationship. Things begin to feel different.

In the language of transactional analysis, an act of recognition can be defined as a *crossed transaction* (Berne, 1961). For example, with Lisa I named her desire to hurt me, crossing the complementary transactions immersed in idealized feelings. This transaction was disturbing to us both and created a disjuncture typical of a crossed transaction. These moments are often unsettling because we find ourselves reflected in ways that are at odds with our conscious identity. During an enactment, we seek to organize the relationship to conform to our script. We nudge the other into seeing those aspects that are syntonic with our scripted identity and keep not-me out of the picture. A crossed transaction will disrupt this expected flow of communication, bringing to light script dystonic elements of the self. In these moments we become visible to each other as human subjects.

In practice, there is no particular technique for arriving at this point of recognition. Sometimes the therapist is able to create a shift by reflecting on his or her countertransference. The dissociated experience is found within the therapist rather than through determined attempts to attune and empathize with the client. This process requires a willingness to accept that we might be part of the problem. An open, receptive attitude is helpful, as is curiosity about feelings that disturb us. Deadening, boredom, discomfort, heated conflict, or feelings of dread can all be clues that an enactment is operating beneath one's conscious awareness. Stern (2010) suggested we pay attention to emotional "snags and chafing" (p. 81). This expression brilliantly evokes the vague discomfort of a feeling that we do not want to know about.

When we find a way to name and communicate this new understanding, the client often experiences a profound sense of being recognized. Once a feeling becomes sharable, it can be integrated and linked with the subjective "I." It is no longer felt as a threat to one's sense of identity. Finding a way to introduce not-me to the client in an acceptable manner is the therapist's art.

In my work with Lisa, movement out of the enactment began when I reflected on my uncomfortable moment of laughter. In that instance, reverie and an active attempt to mentalize invited recognition of the dissociated self-state in each of us. The implicit became explicit, knowable, and speakable.

156 Jo Stuthridge

Sometimes an enactment is resolved through action in the interpersonal field and insight follows. There is a shift in the way we relate to each other, but it is hard to know what happened. Most of the choices we make in therapy occur in nanoseconds through subsymbolic modes (Hoffman, 2001). This is quite contrary to what I learned as a trainee. In the example of Ella, the shift was serendipitous. The children's feet introduced a third element and a new perspective for us both. Ella initiated a shift in perception when she saw me as vulnerable rather than threatening.

As enactments are repeated and resolved, the client's script becomes more complex and coherent. The goal is not so much related to content but to increasing one's capacity to sustain paradox, conflict, and the ambiguity of human experience. Disconnected parts of the self begin to talk to each other. Bromberg (1998a) and Stern (2010) both argued that the goal of resolving enactments is to increase the client's tolerance of intrapsychic conflict. Enactment occurs in the absence of internal conflict, not as a by-product. With resolution, not-me can be integrated into a broader sense of "I" rather than being enacted in interpersonal conflict. We expand the Adult ego's capacity for creative authorship of one's script. We can create new realties or stories for our lives.

Conclusion

We might conclude that an encounter with otherness is essential to free up a mind that has become fractured and frozen as a result of trauma. Returning to Berne's thesis, recognition in the face of the other fosters coherence between ego states. Moments of recognition are needed to disrupt a static script and facilitate internal movement from fragmentation to fluidity. Enactments in therapy provide an opportunity to discover the lost parts of oneself for both client and therapist. When we remain stuck in these interpersonal fault lines, we risk reinforcing trauma and rigid script patterns. When we manage to haul ourselves out of these chasms, we create a more flexible script and new possibilities for intimacy.

Trauma destroys continuity within the self, creating a rigid script and a dissociated self-structure. Healing takes place when unconscious affects or disconnected ego states find a home through an act of recognition. As we integrate these unwanted parts of ourselves, we develop our capacity for subjectivity and intersubjectivity. For the survivor of child abuse, healing is ultimately about taking a risk with intimacy. Ella put this task into words for me when she said, "It's like you are asking me to cross a chasm on a tightrope with my hands tied behind my back and a blindfold on." I think that image sums up the feeling of what it means for a trauma survivor to trust that the other will be there in a moment of need. For therapists, working with trauma means watching our own step on the tightrope and being prepared to fall occasionally. It means being willing to be vulnerable.

References

Allen, J. R. (2003). Concepts, competencies and interpretive communities. *Transactional Analysis Journal, 33*, 126–147.

Allen, J. R. (2010). From a child psychiatry practice. In R. Erskine (Ed.), *Life scripts: A transactional analysis of unconscious relational patterns* (pp. 151–178). London, UK: Karnac Books.

Allen, J. R., & Allen, B. A. (1997). A new type of transactional analysis and one version of script work with a constructionist sensibility. *Transactional Analysis Journal, 27*, 89–98.

Benjamin, J. (1990). An outline of intersubjectivity: The development of recognition. *Psychoanalytic Psychology, 7*(Supp), 33–46.

Benjamin, J. (1995). *Like subjects, love objects: Essays on recognition and sexual difference.* New Haven, CT: Yale University Press.

Benjamin, J. (2004). Beyond doer and done to: An intersubjective view of thirdness. *Psychoanalytic Quarterly, 64*, 5–46.

Berne, E. (1961). *Transactional analysis in psychotherapy: A systematic individual and social psychiatry.* New York, NY: Grove Press.

Berne, E. (1964). *Games people play: The psychology of human relationships.* New York, NY: Ballantine Books.

Berne, E. (1972). *What do you say after you say hello? The psychology of human destiny.* New York, NY: Grove Press.

Bromberg, P. (1998a). *Standing in the spaces: Essays on clinical process, trauma and dissociation.* Hillsdale, NJ: Analytic Press.

Bromberg, P. (1998b). Standing in the spaces: The multiplicity of the self and the psychoanalytic relationship. In P. Bromberg (Ed.), *Standing in the spaces: Essays on clinical process, trauma and dissociation* (pp. 267–290). Hillsdale, NJ: Analytic Press. (Original work published 1996.)

Bromberg, P. (2006). *Awakening the dreamer: Clinical journeys.* Mahwah, NJ: Analytic Press.

Bromberg, P. (2008). Shrinking the tsunami: Affect regulation, dissociation and the shadow of the flood. *Contemporary Psychoanalysis, 44*(3), 329–350.

Bromberg, P. (2011). *The shadow of the tsunami and the growth of the relational mind.* New York, NY: Routledge.

Bucci, W. (1997). *Psychoanalysis and cognitive science: A multiple code theory.* New York, NY: Guilford Press.

Bucci, W. (2002). The referential process, consciousness and sense of self. *Psychoanalytic Inquiry, 22*, 766–793.

Bucci, W. (2011). The interplay of subsymbolic and symbolic processes in psychoanalytic treatment: It takes two to tango but who knows the steps, who's the leader? The choreography of the psychoanalytic interchange. *Psychoanalytic Dialogues, 21*(1), 45–54.

Cooper, S. (2011, 30 June). Heart/mind theft and the dilemma of psychoanalytic engagement: The analyst's fantasy of becoming a good internalized object. Paper presented at the International Association for Relational Psychoanalysis and Psychotherapy Annual Conference, Madrid, Spain.

Cornell, W. F. (1988). Life script theory: A critical review from a developmental perspective. *Transactional Analysis Journal, 18*, 270–282.

Cornell, W. F. (2003). Babies, brains and bodies: Somatic foundation of the child. In C. Sills & H. Hargaden (Eds.), *Ego states* (Key concepts in transactional analysis: Contemporary views) (pp. 28–54). London, UK: Worth.

Cornell, W. F., & Landaiche, N. M., III. (2006). Impasse and intimacy: Applying Berne's concept of script protocol. *Transactional Analysis Journal, 36*, 196–213.

Davies, J. (2004). Whose bad objects are we anyway? Repetition and our elusive love affair with evil. *Psychoanalytic Dialogues, 14*, 711–732.

Davies, J. M., & Frawley, G. M. (1994). *Treating the adult survivor of childhood sexual abuse: A psychoanalytic perspective.* New York, NY: Basic Books.

Ehrenberg, D. B. (1992). *The intimate edge: Extending the reach of psychoanalytic interaction.* New York, NY: Norton.

English, F. (1988). Whither scripts? *Transactional Analysis Journal, 18*, 294–303.

Erskine, R. G. (1993). Inquiry, attunement, and involvement in the psychotherapy of dissociation. *Transactional Analysis Journal, 23*, 184–190.

Erskine, R. G. (2003). Introjection, psychic presence and the parent ego state: Considerations for psychotherapy. In C. Sills & H. Hargaden (Eds.), *Ego states* (Key concepts in transactional analysis: Contemporary views) (pp. 83–108). London, UK: Worth.

Fairbairn, W. R. D. (1992). *Psychoanalytic studies of the personality.* London, UK: Tavistock/Routledge. (Original work published 1952.)

Ferenczi, S. (1988). *The clinical diary of Sandor Ferenczi* (J. Dupont, Ed.; M. Balint & N. Z. Jackson, Trans.). Cambridge, MA: Harvard University Press. (Original work published 1932.)

Fonagy, P., Gergely, G., Jurist, E., & Target, M. (2002). *Affect regulation, mentalization, and the development of the self.* New York, NY: Other Press.

Freud, S. (1959). Inhibitions, symptoms, and anxiety. In J. Strachey (Ed. & Trans.), *The standard edition of the complete psychological works of Sigmund Freud* (Vol. 20, pp. 77–175). London, UK: Hogarth Press. (Original work published 1926.)

Gabbard, G. O. (2004). *Core competencies in psychotherapy. Long-term psychodynamic psychotherapy.* Arlington, VA: American Psychiatric Publishing.

Harris, A. (1996). The conceptual power of multiplicity. *Contemporary Psychoanalysis, 32*, 537–552.

Hitchcock, A. (Producer & Director). (1960). *Psycho* [Motion picture]. Los Angeles, CA: Paramount Pictures.

Hoffman, I. Z. (2001). *Ritual and spontaneity in psychoanalytic process.* Hillsdale, NJ: Analytic Press. (Original work published 1998.)

Le Doux, J. (2002). *The synaptic self.* New York, NY: Viking.

Little, R. (2006). Ego state relational units and resistance to change. *Transactional Analysis Journal, 36*, 7–19.

Mazzetti, M. (2008). Trauma and migration: A transactional analytic approach toward refugees and torture victims. *Transactional Analysis Journal, 38*, 285–302.

McWilliams, N. (2011). *Psychoanalytic diagnosis: Understanding personality structure in the clinical process* (2nd ed.). New York, NY: Guilford Press.

Mellor, K. (1980). Impasses. *Transactional Analysis Journal, 10*, 213–220.

Mitchell, S. (1993). *Hope and dread in psychoanalysis.* New York, NY: Basic Books.

Mitchell, S. (2008). *Influence and autonomy in psychoanalysis.* New York, NY: Psychology Press. (Original work published 1997.)

Moiso, C. (1985). Ego states and transference. *Transactional Analysis Journal, 15*, 194–201.

Novak, E. (2008). Integrating neurological findings with transactional analysis in trauma work: Linking "there and then" self states with "here and now" ego states. *Transactional Analysis Journal, 38*, 303–319.

Ogden, T. (1994). *Subjects of analysis.* Lanham, MD: Jason Aronson.

Schore, A. N. (1994). *Affect regulation and the origin of the self.* Hillsdale, NJ: Lawrence Erlbaum.

Schore, A. N. (2009). Right brain affect regulation: An essential mechanism of development, trauma, dissociation and psychotherapy. In D. Fosha, D. J. Siegel, & M. F. Solomon

(Eds.), *The healing power of emotion: Affective neuroscience, development and clinical practice* (pp. 112–144). New York, NY: Norton.

Siegel, D. (1999). *The developing mind*. New York, NY: Guilford Press.

Siegel, D., & Cozolino, L. (2005, 24–25 June). Weaving hearts, merging minds and changing brains: The interpersonal neurobiology of psychotherapy. Seminar sponsored by PsychOz Publications, Melbourne.

Slochower, J. (2011). Analytic idealizations and the disavowed: Winnicott, his patients and us. *Psychoanalytic Dialogues, 21*(1), 3–21.

Smithson, J., Colson, C., Boyle, D., Kelly, J., Falcone, L. M., Ivernel, R., … McCracken, C. (Producers), & Boyle, D. (Director). (2010). *127 hours* [Motion picture]. Los Angeles, CA: Fox Searchlight Pictures.

Stern, D. B. (1983). Unformulated experience: From familiar chaos to creative disorder. *Contemporary Psychoanalysis, 19*, 71–99.

Stern, D. B. (2003). *Unformulated experience: From dissociation to imagination in psychoanalysis*. New York, NY: Routledge.

Stern, D. B. (2010). *Partners in thought: Working with unformulated experience, dissociation and enactment*. New York, NY: Routledge.

Stolorow, R. (2011). *World, affectivity, trauma: Heidegger and post-Cartesian psychoanalysis*. New York, NY: Routledge.

Stuthridge, J. (2006). Inside out: A transactional analysis model of trauma. *Transactional Analysis Journal, 36*, 270–283.

Stuthridge, J. (2010). Script or scripture? In R. Erskine (Ed.), *Life scripts: A transactional analysis of unconscious relational patterns* (pp. 77–100). London, UK: Karnac Books.

Stuthridge, J. (2011, 1 October). Traversing the fault lines: A relational approach to the treatment of trauma. Speech delivered at the International Association of Relational Transactional Analysis Conference, London, UK.

Sullivan, H. S. (1953). *Conceptions of modern psychiatry*. New York, NY: Norton.

Summers, G., & Tudor, K. (2000). Cocreative transactional analysis. *Transactional Analysis Journal, 30*, 23–40.

Tudor, K. (2003). The neopsyche: The integrating adult ego state. In C. Sills & H. Hargaden (Eds.), *Ego states* (Key concepts in transactional analysis: Contemporary views) (pp. 201–231). London, UK: Worth.

van der Kolk, B. A. (1995). The body, memory and the psychobiology of trauma. In J. A. Alpert (Ed.), *Sexual abuse recalled* (pp. 29–60). Northvale, NJ: Jason Aronson.

van der Kolk, B. A., & van der Hart, O. (1989). Pierre Janet and the breakdown of adaptation in psychological trauma. *American Journal of Psychiatry, 146*(12), 1530–1540.

Woods, K. (2007). The stroking school of transactional analysis. *Transactional Analysis Journal, 37*, 32–34.

12

THIS EDGY EMOTIONAL LANDSCAPE

A discussion of Stuthridge's "Traversing the fault lines"

William F. Cornell

Jo Stuthridge's "Traversing the fault lines" (2012) offers a rich, evocative, and provocative discussion of the place of trauma in the genesis of therapeutic enactments and the centrality of the therapeutic relationship in the reworking of unacknowledged and unresolved trauma. Her article also traverses another fault line, one too common in contemporary transactional analysis: the fault line between what is often cast as classical, "Bernean" transactional analysis and the current valorization of "relational" transactional analysis.

I will start my discussion of Stuthridge's article with her theoretical traversing of this theoretical fault line in transactional analysis theory. I will then go on to present two differing points of view.

Stuthridge roots her clinical perspective within the contemporary, relational theories of trauma and dissociation, theories that virtually did not exist when Berne was creating his model of transactional analysis. Nevertheless, she repeatedly draws links and similarities between Berne's thinking and the contemporary theories that underlie her article. For example, when quoting Bucci's statement that some degree of dissociation is a normative and necessary element of a fluid self-experience, she links this to Berne's conceptualization of the *moving self* (p. 240) as the fluid capacity to shift experience among differing states of the ego.

Later, Stuthridge eloquently evokes the dilemma and dialectic of dissociative mechanisms and their enactment in the psychotherapeutic relationship:

> Dissociation and enactment offer a powerful form of self-protection while compromising the potential for intimacy. Berne's (1961) script theory elucidates this Faustian bargain. By externalizing one's broken internal world through games and enactments, we maintain internal stability. When we enact dissociated parts of the self, we tend to elicit a response that confirms

the script. These not-me parts of the self ultimately run the show, and our behavior inadvertently leads to the dreaded outcome.

(pp. 245–246)

In this passage we see the theoretical reach and implications of Berne's original script theory set side by side with a more contemporary, relational model. Where I think Stuthridge most profoundly differs with Berne is that while he argued that therapist and client must share the responsibility for *solving* the problem, Stuthridge further suggests that therapist and client must also share responsibility for *having* the problem. This is an example of one of the things I most admire about her writing, that is, the way she reflects on the richness of classical theory while exploring new ground.

There are two areas where my thinking diverges from the frame of reference Stuthridge articulates in her article. The first has to do with the limits of the trauma and dissociation model, as I see it. The second has to do with her emphasis on the necessity of recognition by another in healing trauma and establishing a continuity of mind.

There is no doubt that the recognition of trauma and dissociative reactions to trauma has profoundly informed and enriched clinical theory and practice. It has required a couple of generations to grasp fully the ubiquity and frequency of traumatic failures and intrusions in the developmental histories of many who seek psychotherapy and counseling and for mental health practitioners to generate techniques that make links between trauma and dissociative mechanisms.

Van der Hart, Nijenhuis, and Steele (2006) used the concept of *structural dissociation* to designate the dissociative reactions that occur "during confrontations with overwhelming events when mental efficiency is too low" (p. 43). They observed that "childhood abuse and neglect are major factors in the development of trauma-related disorders in adults following their exposure to extremely stressful events in adulthood" (p. 43). This description of trauma and dissociation emphasizes that the genesis of trauma lies in the intrusion and profound disorganization created by external/environmental factors that overwhelm the individual's psychological and emotional capacities. This description, as I read it, is consistent with Stuthridge's understanding of the relationship between trauma and dissociation. However, as is so often the case with emergent theoretical models (as, for example, with definitions and applications of attachment theories and countertransference), dissociation has become a multi-headed theoretical beast. As van der Hart et al. observed:

> *dissociation* is the key concept to understanding traumatization. Virtually everyone in the trauma field uses dissociation in different ways, and there are many disagreements about its causes. ... The symptoms considered to be dissociative vary tremendously from one publication to the next.

(p. 2)

While I found Stern's (2010) differentiation of weak and strong dissociation— which is similar to Bromberg's (2011) distinction between normal and pathological dissociation—interesting, I think these definitions stretch the concept

162 William F. Cornell

of dissociation so broadly that it begins to lose its focus and meaning. In his description of strong dissociation, Stern (2010) wrote, "The disallowed experience is so intolerable that, despite its presence within the very broad bounds of subjectivity, it is not acknowledged as a part of the self (it is not me) and therefore cannot be articulated in awareness" (p. 153). Here, I think, the conceptualization of dissociation begins to become stretched beyond useful bounds. For her part, Stuthridge asks, "Dissociation: the new black?" There is a risk of the dissociative model being stretched to become a descriptive theory to account for everything,

To my mind, dissociation conveys a sense of aspects of experience that have been blown apart by overwhelming circumstances in such a way and to such an extent that these aspects of experience cannot come together again. What I find Stern to be describing in his notion of strong dissociation is a different process, one in which rather than being blown apart, experiences are unconsciously not allowed to come together. In my clinical experience, notions of dissociation do not adequately capture the sense of the forceful expulsion of aspects of one's self-experience. In such instances, I think we are witnessing the impact of a kind of unconscious, psychotic denial or disavowal. I think here of a number of my clients for whom the not-me is better described as "NOT ME, NEVER, EVER!" and "Don't you fuck with it." Models of dissociation just do not cut it in my clinical experience of this level of disavowal.

Stuthridge roots her clinical discussions in the work of Donnel Stern (2010) and Philip Bromberg (1998, 2011), both of whom have based their models on the interpersonal theories of Harry Stack Sullivan. His model, described in *The Interpersonal Theory of Psychiatry* (Sullivan, 1953), foreshadowed many of the challenges raised in Berne's theories of a social psychiatry. Sullivan introduced the idea of dissociative defense mechanisms. He described a category of self-experience that he called "not-me" (p. 316), which he held in contrast to "good-me" and "bad-me." For Sullivan, good-me and bad-me are split-apart aspects of one's sense of self, but both "are the basis of lifelong ingredients of consciousness" (p. 316). Not-me, however, is dissociated, as Sullivan used the term, that is, not allowed into the conscious experience of self in the face of intense expressions of dread, loathing, and horror:

> The not-me is literally the organization of experience with significant people that has been subjected to such intense anxiety, and anxiety so suddenly precipitated, that it was impossible for the then relatively rudimentary person to make any sense of, to develop any true grasp of, the particular circumstances which dictated the experience of this intense anxiety. … It tends to erase any possibility of elaborating the exact circumstances of its occurrence, and about the most the person can remember in retrospect is a somewhat fenestrated account of the event in the immediate neighborhood.
>
> *(p. 314)*

The "immediate neighborhood," that is, the "edgy emotional landscape," as it is described by Stuthridge (p. 248), is the field of enactment that she so richly describes as a form of unconscious, enacted memory and the opportunity for repair of early developmental failures. Sullivan, Bromberg, and Stern have situated the genesis of dissociative defenses squarely within the interpersonal field. More traditional trauma theorists, such as van der Hart, situate trauma and dissociation in the face of massively overwhelming external events. Stuthridge and those authors she draws on emphasize the environmental intrusion in reaction to/against a child's expression of internal self-states. Hence, an emphasis on relational repair is at the heart of her article.

Stuthridge argues that "this constructivist perspective on dissociation and enactment … offers an alternative understanding to Cornell and Landaiche's (2012) thoughts on enactment as the externalization of a Type III or protocol-level impasse" (p. 243). I think she offers an additional, rather than an alternative, understanding to what Landaiche and I were attempting to delineate. Seen from the perspective of impasse theory, not all enactments are necessarily mutual, and one can occur at any of the three levels of impasse. The protocol-level of impasse that we were attempting to describe is inevitably mutual, and Stuthridge's dissociation model can extend our understanding of what is allowed at the level of protocol as a me or not-me experience.

I agree that dissociation is significantly different from repression and that repression is a defense mechanism that arises in the face of the experience of intolerable internal conflict, which occurs within the mental capacity for verbal symbolization. I do not agree, however, with Stuthridge's suggestion (quoted from Stern, 2010, p. 9) that the concepts of splitting and disavowal "assume that 'unconscious internal conflict … precedes enactment'" (p. 243). I would argue that splitting and disavowal preclude any possibility of internal conflict in that these are such fundamental and radical defense mechanisms that they disallow the coexistence of aspects of self that could ultimately come to be experienced as conflictual.

From a technical viewpoint, this difference underlies another area of disagreement I have with Stuthridge's clinical thinking. She writes, "I prefer to use the term *mutual enactment* as distinct from *projective identification* because I do not consider the therapist to be an empty container for the client's bad object" (p. 245). Mutual enactments are not a matter of projection and projective identification. Relational models have brought important recognition to the mutuality of unconscious patterns of influence within the therapeutic dyad. There are, however, times in the face of a client's disavowal and/or psychotic levels of projection when the therapist is, indeed, both the object and the container of the client's disavowed aspects of self. These moments are not mutually constructed or co-created.

These theoretical biases and differences may, of course, consciously and unconsciously be influenced by the nature of the practices Stuthridge and I each have and the types of clients we see. My practice involves work with a significant number of people who struggle with psychotic levels of splitting, disavowal, and disorganization. I have visited this terrain myself in my own psychotherapy. These are not mutually constructed arenas of relatedness. These are arenas of profound disturbance in which the therapist may spend years providing a containing function, absorbing and surviving intense projections, disorientation, and psychic

164 William F. Cornell

worlds often teetering on the edge of disintegration. In these realms of my work, I have found the writings of Michael Eigen both informative and grounding. In describing his work with a young psychotic man, Eigen (2011) vividly captured the lived realities of a mind at the psychotic edge:

> A problem in psychosis is that commands are taken "literally". You must do this, must not do that. They could not be taken as invitations to change, messages, or announcements: more exists, more is on the way. … It is hard, if next to impossible, to re-shift the pull, the centre of gravity. The command sticks with unimpeachable authority. One is judged by them. If one does not follow them, one is doomed, lacks courage, lacks faith, lacks the courage of one's faith. There are no shades, no continuum, no variation through which one mutates.
>
> *(p. 88)*

The notion of strong dissociation does not capture the nature of this experience of self. There is barely a self, let alone another. As our theories embrace new ideas, such as dissociation, I am concerned that earlier concepts that have truly captured and conveyed aspects of the human dilemma will be replaced with "the new black." The emergent understandings of dissociative mechanisms can be greeted enthusiastically and then overgeneralized in their applications, obscuring important nuances of human experience and behavior.

To offer, perhaps, another example from a more "normal" field of human experience than that of psychosis, let us look at sexuality. Not all good sex necessitates the attentiveness, or even the presence, of another person. Even when making love with a truly beloved partner, there are aspects of our sexual experience, sexual arousal, and sexual satisfaction that have little or nothing to do with the other. There is a fundamental autoerotic aspect of sexuality operating alongside of, but quite distinct from, mutual delight and satisfaction.

I suggest that there are many times over the course of our lives when we are too much for ourselves, that is, when our somatic and psychological capacities to process experience are overwhelmed by the intensity and force of life within ourselves. We do not always need an intense, invasive intrusion from others and the outside world. Our internal world can be deeply unsettling on its own.

Reading Eigen (1998) has had a great impact on my thinking in this regard. As he put it:

> The psyche lacks equipment to bear what it produces. The capacity to experience and process states breaks down. To some degree, one gives up contacting self out of fear of the unmanageable. One builds a second self expert at circumventing incapacity.
>
> *(p. 55)*

We are, by the very fact of being alive, in essence, a threat to ourselves, at risk of being too much for ourselves. The forces of human development constantly push us past our capacities to maintain a self in equilibrium. This can be experienced as traumatic, regardless of the recognition and attention of another. I fail myself, and I want to set myself right. At times we turn to others, need others, to help us regain equanimity. There are times when we must have the engagement of another. But often we are quite capable and content to "do" ourselves by ourselves. This seems to be discounted or altogether forgotten in the relational turn. There is an exquisite and deeply satisfying dialectic between undoing and redoing one's self.

I think also, in this regard, of clients I have had who were born with congenital diseases. Often they were kindly and competently attended to by parents and professionals, but this did not eliminate the trauma of a body constantly in trouble with and failing itself. Relational attentiveness is not a universal solvent to trauma.

As infants, of course, we all need an other (or if we are lucky, many others) to help us process what our young psyches cannot yet manage. There are, without a doubt, times in our lives when the recognition, responsiveness, and/or accountability of another is life saving and life giving. As psychotherapists, counselors, teachers, and consultants, we derive deep meaning and pleasure from being that person. But people do not always need others, and we do not live our lives in perpetual, intersubjective matrices.

Children do not always need their parents, nor do they always want their parents or other people around. Children find great developmental satisfaction in discovering and cultivating their own somatic and psychological equipment for managing and enlivening all that goes on inside of them. Adolescents demand it, in spite of repeatedly being overwhelmed and screwing things up. Even adult clients in psychotherapy and counseling, given the opportunity, sometimes like to do things on their own and to develop their own capacities independently of the professional other. It can be gratifying, sometimes essential, to have someone else around, but it is not always essential for self-development or continuity of mind.

Undoubtedly, my perspective here is informed and shaped by my training as a body psychotherapist, through which I have come to know the importance of the development of the body in relation to itself, the body as a foundation for a coherent and resilient sense of self. It is further informed by work with my consultant and last analyst, each of whom was a serious student of Buddhism and, in his own way, introduced me to the discipline of self-encounter.

Stuthridge brings her paper to a close by suggesting, "We might conclude that an encounter with otherness is essential to free up a mind that has become fractured and frozen as a result of trauma" (p. 249). I would not argue with her conclusion, but I would suggest that "helpful" might be a more accurate word than "essential." I would further suggest that we not underestimate the power of an encounter with one's own self, independent of others, as a means of freeing a fractured and frozen mind.

References

Berne, E. (1961). *Transactional analysis in psychotherapy: A systematic individual and social psychiatry*. New York, NY: Grove Press.

Bromberg, P. (1998). *Standing in the spaces: Essays on clinical process, trauma, and dissociation*. Hillsdale, NJ: Analytic Press.

Bromberg. P. M. (2011). *The shadow of the tsunami and the growth of the relational mind*. London, UK: Routledge.

Cornell, W. F., & Landaiche, N. M., III. (2006). Impasse and intimacy: Applying Berne's concept of script protocol. *Transactional Analysis Journal, 36*, 196–213.

Eigen, M. (1998). *The psychoanalytic mystic*. Binghamton, NY: esf Publishers.

Eigen, M. (2011). *Contact with the depths*. London, UK: Karnac.

Stern, D. H. (2010). *Partners in thought: Working with unformulated experience, dissociation and enactment*. London, UK: Routledge.

Stuthridge, J. (2012). Traversing the fault lines: Trauma and enactment. *Transactional Analysis Journal, 42*, 238–251.

Sullivan, H. S. (1953). *The interpersonal theory of psychiatry*. New York, NY: Norton.

van der Hart, O., Nijenhuis, E. R. S., & Steele, K. (2006). *The haunted self: Structural dissociation and the treatment of chronic traumatization*. New York, NY: Norton.

13

ARE GAMES, ENACTMENTS, AND REENACTMENTS SIMILAR?

No, yes, it depends

Edward T. Novak

This article had its origins in the 2014 World Transactional Analysis Conference held in San Francisco and titled "TA Now: A Game Changer." The conference provided many opportunities to review game theory and the similarities between games and enactments as defined by transactional analysis and psychoanalysis. During the conference, I noticed that many practitioners, including me, seemed to use the terms *games* and *enactments* interchangeably. As the conference progressed, I began questioning this assumption. I engaged in many conversations about how we might have been too quick to conflate the two terms without examining the possible differences between them. When I asked colleagues if they thought games and enactments were similar, most had a knee-jerk reaction that yes, they were similar, followed by a reflective pause that indicated possible doubt, and then further discussions, with no definitive answer emerging.

In this article, I want to consider these constructs—games, enactments, and reenactments—and the ways they may be seen as similar or different depending on which definitions and theories are used for the comparisons. I believe that despite having many similarities, there are meaningful clinical differences that suggest the importance of clearly distinguishing between them.

Untidy definitions of games and mutual enactments

When games and enactments are evaluated through the lenses of transactional analysis and psychoanalysis, the similarities or differences depend on which definitions are used for comparing them. More liberal definitions create greater similarities than do narrow definitions.

Since Eric Berne's *Games People Play* was published in 1964, game theory has been one of the fundamental constructs of transactional analysis. Games have a rich

168   Edward T. Novak

history in describing patterns of relating and behaving as well as their motivations not only in therapeutic relationships but also in groups and everyday life. Berne's primary definition of a game was clear and straightforward: "an ongoing series of complementary ulterior transactions progressing to a well-defined, predictable outcome" (p. 48). He suggested that the defining features of a game are its ulterior quality and the payoff.

Since then, other writers have expanded our understanding of why a game is played. English (1977) suggested that games are played for a payoff of strokes rather than a payoff of bad feelings. Her emphasis was on the process of the game leading to these strokes, which she called "racketeering" (p. 130). Joines (1982) also distinguished between games and rackets. He believed a person settled for playing a game to evoke unpleasant feelings when racketeering was not possible.

Zalcman (1990) noted that although games are usually described as being played between two people, "a game does not necessarily require two players, but instead can be carried out by one player single-handedly in transactions with another person who is not playing a complementary game and does not collect a payoff" (p. 10). Berne (1970) referred to these types of games as *skull games.* Zalcman viewed one-handed games "as intrapsychic processes which parallel but are not the same as transactional games" (p. 10).

Cornell (2008) has written about the limitations of Berne's idea that games are preconscious experiences that can be easily brought into consciousness. Cornell believes there is also a deeper unconscious experience and advocates for pushing the frame of games to include such unconscious processes. He suggested that within the Child ego state there is a level of organization "that is learned at a body level and lived, experienced, and expressed not in the words of an internal dialogue, but in somatic organization, in unconscious fantasies and wishes, and through the styles of our contemporary relationships" (p. 97).

Whether games and enactments can be viewed as similar depends on whether one believes that the definition and theory of games can be expanded to include the processes Cornell described. For my part, I favor retaining the more traditional ways of defining games and placing the deeper unconscious experiences within the construct of enactments. Keeping games and enactments separate allows us to distinguish between preconscious relational patterns as found in games and unconscious processes often discovered through enactments.

Unlike games, enactments are not well defined and do not lead to predictable outcomes. In fact, enactments within a therapeutic relationship have the potential for creating what Bromberg (2006) described as "safe surprises" (p. 198). These safe surprises occur when, following the initial experience of pain and discomfort within the enactment, there is a new experience between the client and therapist in which the unsymbolized emotions and ego states of the past are recognized and processed by them together. This is where I see the primary difference between games and enactments: Games tend to support the individual in defending against unconscious experiences, whereas enactments tend to reveal unsymbolized unconscious experiences.

This distinction centers on my belief that some experiences are defended against, whereas others have never been formulated and therefore require no defense. I came to this understanding after reading Stern's (2003) views on unformulated experiences. For him, experiences that are outside consciousness may not require action or effort for them to remain there. Rather, action may be required to bring these experiences into consciousness. From this perspective, rather than primarily looking for and trying to disable defenses in therapy, the client and therapist work to uncover unsymbolized experiences. One way this can occur is through enactments. Stern compared these unformulated experiences to boulders on the bottom of the ocean. For him, working to bring these experiences into consciousness is like "lifting a rock from the bottom and hauling it to the surface" (p. 86).

I think the difference between payoffs in games and safe surprises in enactments is that, generally, the exploration of games leads to an understanding of how known experiences became split off and defended against, whereas enactments lead to the discovery of unformulated experiences within both the client and the therapist. Keeping games and enactments as separate constructs provides transactional analysts with a way to theorize and work with both.

To date, most exploration of enactments in psychoanalysis and transactional analysis has been limited to the analytic dyad, although Aron (2003) noted that family therapists (e.g., Minuchin, 1974) have developed the construct in work with families. A standard definition of enactment remains elusive, and it is likely that enactment will continue to have multiple definitions and meanings. For my purposes here, however, Chused's (2003) definition can be used as a starting point. She identified the bidirectional nature of enactments, which are generally thought to originate within the transference–countertransference field (Bass, 2003). She described enactments:

> as occurring when a patient's behavior or words stimulate an unconscious conflict in the analyst, leading to an interaction that has unconscious meaning to both. Conversely, an enactment [also] occurs when an analyst's behavior or words stimulate an unconscious conflict in a patient, productive of an interaction with unconscious meaning to both.
>
> *(p. 678)*

Chused further noted that not all of the analyst's countertransference reactions are elicited by the patient and that only those countertransference reactions that appear to be elicited by the patient fit within the construct of enactment (Chused, Ellman, Renik, & Rothstein, 1999, p. 11).

Historically, McLaughlin (2005) was one of the earliest psychoanalysts to write about enactments. He believed the construct offered a new way of thinking about countertransference and the therapist's impact on the patient. His views were consistent with Ellman's (Chused et al., 1999) idea that countertransference should not to be viewed as a deficiency in the analyst that revealed that he or she was not fully analyzed but as a natural part of the analytic process. This shift created opportunities to explore the mutual influences between patient and analyst, including enactments.

With the development of a more relational approach in psychoanalysis (Greenberg & Mitchell, 1983) and a less pejorative view of countertransference, analysts were now able to make therapeutic use of their countertransference. Enactments became an important part of the therapeutic experience, a space in which patient and analyst are engaged within transference and countertransference processes. In addition, with a deeper understanding of trauma and dissociation (LeDoux, 1996; van der Kolk, McFarlane, & Weisaeth, 1996; van der Kolk, van der Hart, & Marmar, 1996) as well as psychotic processes (Eigen, 1993), enactments are now seen as an almost necessary part of treatment. They have been referred to as "potholes in the royal road" (Bromberg, 2000, p. 7) to the unconscious and, like dreams, are first experienced and then explored to understand unconscious and/or dissociated parts of the personality.

A primary issue in defining enactment is the understanding to what degree it describes both specific moments of interpersonal interaction in treatment and a broader sense of relating. The challenge is to guard against defining it either too narrowly or too broadly. For example, Jacobs (1986) originally defined enactment as "any unconscious interpersonal communication in which gestures, body language, and nonverbal communication play significant roles" (p. 134). This is quite a broad definition. McLaughlin (2005) anticipated such issues when he wrote, "Soon we shall have packed it with analytic meanings, only to come to the sad conclusion that we have a term utterly lacking in the precision that would satisfy those who like their theory neat" (p. 185).

Aron (2003) viewed the difficulty in creating a neat definition of enactment as something positive in that it creates an "important tension" (p. 623) between narrow and broad uses of the term. He suggested that enactment can represent both "episodic discrete events" (p. 623) as well as ongoing interactions in treatment. While Aron valued both sides of this tension, he cautioned that the broader definition can result in "turning all of analysis into one huge enactment" (p. 623).

Bass (2003), a psychoanalyst, distinguished between ongoing and specific enactments by using a lowercase "e" for the former and a capital "E" for the latter. The former describes "enactments that form the daily ebb and flow of ordinary analytic processes" (p. 660), whereas the latter "are phases of both unusually high-risk and high-potential growth for analyst and patient alike" (p. 660).

Davies (1997), used the term "therapeutic enactment" (p. 246) to describe certain moments in treatment that she referred to as "wrinkles in time" (p. 246). These collapse both past and present into "a co-constructed organization of the transference–countertransference matrix that bears such striking similarity to an important moment of the past that patient and analyst together have the unique opportunity to exist in both places at the same time" (p. 246).

As had happened in psychoanalysis, the development of a relational approach in transactional analysis (Hargaden & Sills, 2002) created an interest in ways client and therapist enact unconscious parts of both of their personalities. In this context, the term *enactment* has been used to describe work with trauma and dissociation by authors such as Little (2006), Stuthridge (2006, 2012), and Oates (2012). In the transactional analysis literature, there is limited exploration of the tension Aron (2003) described between enactments that are discrete events and those that are ongoing interactions. This may be a fruitful area of study within transactional analysis.

Stuthridge (2006) has written about enactments in relation to her work with trauma and dissociation. She described how early relational interactions a child experiences with primary caregivers are internalized within a "Parent/Child ego state dyad" (p. 271). She added, "the intrapsychic structure then shapes the view of self, others, and the world outside so that the adult survivor of abuse continues to see monsters long after they are gone" (p. 275). She suggested that through the therapeutic relationship, including enactments, these "implicit relational patterns formed in the abusive context inevitably emerge in the therapy relationship" (p. 277).

Stuthridge (2006) also described the difficulty in reconciling traditional transactional analytic theory with the concept of enactments. Because Berne's methodology was primarily a one-person approach, the detached therapist usually remains outside the relationship. From this position of a detached observer, he or she would refuse to engage with the client's transference. Instead of viewing the transference as part of an enactment that needs to be experienced in a two-person relationship, the one-person approach views such transference as a game to be confronted.

I am arguing here that games have a much broader reach than enactments. The concept of games has been explored and used effectively beyond the therapeutic dyad in such contexts as social action (Joines, 1982), families (Massey, 1990), couples (Karpman, 2009), and organizations (Summerton, 1993). Thus, whereas an enactment may be another form of a game, there are many other ways to make use of game theory that fall outside the realm of enactments.

Sometimes clients are unable to work within a two-person model (Stark, 1999) or their issues need to be addressed more intrapsychically than is possible through an interpersonal approach. In such cases, the client is unable to recognize that what is occurring in the therapeutic relationship is not a continuation of past childhood trauma, and a fuller immersion in the client's emotional world within a co-created experience may be not only less effective but ill advised. This type of experience seems better defined as a *reenactment* rather than an enactment or a game.

Reenactments

The recent emphasis on enactment in the clinical literature seems to have engulfed the term *reenactment* in a way that blurs the distinctions between the two. In addition, the distinction between games, enactments, and reenactments has not been discussed in much detail in the transactional analysis literature. I believe there is important therapeutic, if not theoretical, value in distinguishing between these terms.

Schwartz (2000), who has written about trauma and dissociation, stated that reenactment and enactment are often used interchangeably. However, he delineated between the two by defining reenactment as a specific type of enactment that is trauma based. He cited Miller (1984), who defined reenactment as containing "elements of the original trauma in posttraumatic symptoms, behaviors, and/ or interpersonal patterns of relating—all characteristic of trauma survivors' functioning" (p. 134). For enactment, Schwartz took what he described as an egalitarian perspective, defining enactments as having "not only elements of the patient's psyche but elements of the therapist's psyche as well" (p. 134).

As with games and enactments, how one differentiates between reenactment and enactment depends on the ways each is defined. To my way of thinking, an important difference is that often in a reenactment the client's experience of traumatic memories makes it more difficult for him or her to make use of the therapeutic relationship. In many cases, the client is unable to separate the traumatic memory being evoked in the therapy from the actual past trauma. In such instances, the therapist may be seen as a stand-in for a past abuser or unprotective caregiver.

Davies (1997) took a similar position, noting that in an enactment there is a joint reliving of a traumatic experience as opposed to a more one-sided reliving of a trauma as in reenactment. She believes this joint reliving is what makes an enactment distinct from a traumatic reenactment. She wrote, "A joint reliving of what was originally experienced in psychic desolation and traumatizing isolation is the only way to categorically differentiate the therapeutic reprocessing of previously inexpressible horror from a traumatic reenactment of the abusive events" (p. 247). Using language that sounds similar to transactional analysis, she added, "It is only in relationship to an analyst who feels for and with him that the abused child within the adult survivor may come to struggle once more with emotional desire and yearning" (p. 247).

Davies' (1997) thoughts on relating more directly to and with the abused child within the adult survivor are consistent with the ways I use transactional analysis when a client is able to work more relationally with his or her trauma. However, when the person is in the throes of a reenactment, the work may need to focus more on the client's intrapsychic processes. Often this requires a shift from a two-person approach (Stark, 1999) to a one- or one-and-a-half-person mode of therapy. The primary focus then becomes what is being triggered within the client's traumatized ego states rather than what is being evoked in the here-and-now relationship.

The clinical difference between reenactments and enactments is subtle but significant. In a reenactment, the client's experience in session is not being co-created with the therapist as it is in an enactment. Rather, the origins of the reenactment are usually in the client's trauma memories. Although the therapist's words or body language may be triggering the traumatic memories, those stimuli

Games, enactments, and reenactments **173**

are generally not originating in the therapist's countertransference or unconscious processes. In fact, the client may be misreading the therapist.

At such moments, the therapist's training and his or her own self-awareness are crucial in helping him or her to discern whether the current situation is more of a reenactment or an enactment. Davies (personal communication, 30 March 2012) believes that the therapist must be able to self-reflect on his or her own countertransference when the patient is accusing or attacking rather than becoming reflexively defensive or assuming that an enactment is taking place. It is through understanding the therapist's contribution (an enactment between client and therapist) or lack of one (a reenactment based on past traumatic experiences) that the client develops a greater ability to distinguish between experiences that are either primarily interpersonal or intrapsychic. (This distinction is illustrated in one of the clinical vignettes described later in this article.) Reenactments can then be seen as originating primarily in the client's transference and intrapsychic experiences that are being triggered and symbolized in the therapeutic relationship. It is important to note that not all reenactments are the result of a negative transference; a positive transference can create a reenactment around loving or longed for individuals from the past.

Keeping the idea of reenactments separate from games and enactments provides us with a specific term and clinical construct with which to distinguish them from the kinds of trauma repetitions we see in games and enactments. Speaking to the lack of consensus on the meaning of enactment, McLaughlin (2005) speculated that "probably the best we can do is to declare our preferences and attempt to justify these as best we can on both clinical and theoretical grounds" (p. 186). As stated, my preference is to keep games, enactments, and reenactments separate because I think each construct describes a different experience or process.

Clinical reasons for separating games, enactments, and reenactments

Unlike the familiar relational patterns in games and the familiar intrapsychic processes in reenactments, enactments are relational moments in which both client and therapist experience a way of relating that is new for both of them. What seems to be evoked in the client is a part of the self that has been so deeply split off that it is usually not revealed in either games or reenactments. Often such unconscious experiences are revealed within intense enactments. (The second of the case vignettes later in this article touches on this process.)

Another reason for keeping the three constructs separate is the difficulty of integrating constructs from different periods or different theories. Soth (2013) expressed concerns about "stretching a framework" (p. 132) when that framework is rooted in an earlier historical period. For example, Berne's game theory was developed well before the recent surge of interest and writing in transactional analysis about trauma and dissociation (Caizzi, 2012; Cornell & Olio, 1992; Erskine, 1993; Stuthridge, 2012). His references to unconscious processes were consistent with his

174 Edward T. Novak

psychoanalytic training and the theories of unconscious process of his time. Today, both relational psychoanalysis and transactional analysis heavily emphasize enactments that originate in issues of trauma and dissociation, ideas that were not being discussed in Berne's era. I agree with Soth (2013) that while there are benefits to an integrative approach, there may be unintended consequences, one of which might be an oscillating by the therapist "between contradictory principles, thus unwittingly giving double messages to … clients" (p. 132).

In my own case, my training in contemporary psychoanalysis occurred many years into my career, which until that point had been primarily based in transactional analysis. At the time of my psychoanalytic training, I also began to learn more about trauma and dissociation. A long-term client of mine began to recognize how my ways of working were changing. In some sessions I saw his issues as trauma based and worked within my understanding of reenactments. At other times I worked as though we were in an enactment. At still other times, my work was informed by my understanding of game theory. While his presenting issues did not change, my way of working with them did. I thought this was affording us many different ways to look at his issues, but I missed the confusion I was causing him. One day, in an exasperated tone, he said, "Jesus! When I started therapy with you, you used TA. Then you added trauma theory. Now you've added this psychoanalysis stuff. It seems you try something different every session. You're driving me crazy!" I thereby discovered the importance of keeping the constructs of games, enactments, and reenactments separate and using them in more informed ways.

In a previous article, I (Novak, 2013) took the theoretical position that games were similar to enactments when I was working clinically with trauma and dissociation. I fell into the trap Soth (2013) mentioned of appropriating a word or construct in a "taken-for-granted" (p.132) fashion.

When I was introduced to game theory over 20 years ago, I was taught that all clients play games, and part of my job was to recognize the game, label it, and work to help the client stop playing it. Usually this involved some form of confrontation. In group supervision, often with the use of tape recordings of sessions, I was taught to look for the first con or discount, which could alert me that my client and I might be in the terrain of a game. This way of working had already put me at odds with my client. I viewed him as being up to something, trying to con me and get me to feel bad at the end of a game, so I needed to be on guard. This is hardly conducive to creating potential space for co-creative experiences. In addition, this way of working with games usually foreclosed the development of the type of potential space in which enactments generally occur.

A parallel issue in classical psychoanalytic theory is the distinction between manifest content and latent content (Fosshage, 2011). The analyst listens to the patient's words and stories (manifest content) as if they represent a defense and attempts to uncover what meanings they carry at deeper unconscious levels (latent content).

Both these ways of working can create situations in which the therapist may listen to the client with suspicion or actually not believe what the client is saying.

I would argue that minimizing manifest content might be the first discount, and it comes from the therapist.

The historical technique of game analysis is ingrained in me at a deep procedural level, and when I use it in treatment I recognize myself working more within in a one- or one-and-a-half- rather than a two-person experience. I think my more intuitive clients sense this shift.

Because games, enactments, and reenactments have different origins and require different treatment approaches, rather than integrating them, I have found myself using each construct independently at different times over the course of treatment. In this regard, I have found the ideas of Howard Bacal (2011) and his specificity theory to be useful. He wrote, "Each analyst-patient dyad constitutes a unique, reciprocal system" and that "therapeutic possibility is co-created in the specificity of fit between the patient's particular therapeutic needs and that therapist's capacity to respond to them, both of which will emerge and change within the unique process of each particular dyad" (p. 267). Specificity theory captures the way I make clinical use of games, enactments, and reenactments because my client and I may at different times be involved in any of the three. My challenge as the therapist is to decide which seems to being going on within the therapeutic relationship at any given moment. This is not an integrative or eclectic approach. Rather, it involves identifying which process is underway and then choosing the corresponding treatment approach.

For example, when I sense a client and I are working within a reenactment, I think in terms of trauma theory (Schwartz, 2000; van der Hart, Nijenhuis, & Steele, 2006; van der Kolk, McFarlane, & Weisaeth, 1996). If what we are experiencing feels more like an enactment, I work within contemporary psychoanalytic theory (Bromberg, 2006; Davies, 1997; Stern, 2010). When the experience feels more like a game, I work within transactional analysis game theory (Berne, 1964; English, 1977; Woods, 2002). Often my shift into one of these three ways of working is not consciously motivated. At times, I find myself naturally moving into one or the other motivated by a change in a session that I have not yet consciously recognized. For example, the client may have experienced something in the session as a trauma trigger and move into a reenactment. My shift to a more intrapsychic approach may be in response to that movement.

Differentiating what is an enactment may also provide useful clinical information about therapeutic progress. For example, an enactment might indicate that the traumatized parts of the client are now able to relate to the therapist in the present rather than as a past object. Although the therapeutic relationship will likely continue to evoke past memories and feelings, the client is more aware that these are rooted in his or her past trauma.

To further clarify the clinical distinctions between these three constructs, the following section provides examples of working with a game, an enactment, and a reenactment along with some comments about the ways I thought about each construct clinically.

176 Edward T. Novak

Clinical vignettes

A game, not an enactment

Mary began the session in a way that was unusual for her. Rather than getting right down to business, because "this is costing me money," she talked about a weekend sporting event. She was upset that her team had lost. Feeling a sense of connection around this event, I noticed myself relaxing, something that tended not to happen in sessions with her. I began to talk with her about the sporting event, offering my own opinion as to why her team had lost. Suddenly, Mary cut me off in midsentence and blurted out, "I don't want to talk about this, it's a waste of my time!" She then began to talk about her week.

I felt stunned and attempted to regain my bearings. I rationalized that this was, in fact, her session, and she could make use of it in whatever way she wanted. However, I knew this was my attempt to avoid something that now needed to be addressed. Being short with family and friends was a repeated pattern for Mary. She had described several incidences that were similar to what had just occurred in our session. I spoke about how I thought what sometimes happened with family and friends might have just occurred between us. As had been the case with other people, Mary had no idea of her impact on me and then felt bad, saying, "This is what I do to people."

From my perspective, this experience was not an enactment primarily because there was nothing new in the experience. That is, it did not involve the discovery of a previously unformulated experience but, rather, a familiar and recognizable pattern that was now part of our experience of working together. In addition, the familiar pattern was explored more within a one- or one-and-a-half-person mode of therapy in that my experience was not discussed. Instead, we focused on helping Mary understand her experiences before, during, and after those types of situations.

An enactment misidentified as a game

Brian had been attending weekly sessions when his feelings of anxiety, which had started to subside, returned. He became less interested in exploring what was going on for him, instead wanting me to provide concrete answers about why he was feeling so anxious. I reminded him of his childhood traumas, which included a history of abandonment, lack of support, and being terrorized, my thought being that his anxiety was connected to those experiences. Brian would agree but then in his next session appear to have forgotten our discussion in the previous session. He was a bright man, so I found his chronic forgetting strange if not irritating.

Several months later, the anxiety seemed to deepen into panic attacks and somatic symptoms that had Brian going to emergency rooms and doctors' offices in the hope that they could discover something medically wrong with him. However, he was healthy, and nothing was found. My irritation and impatience grew as Brian continued to ask me what he should do even while appearing uninterested in reflecting on his symptoms. All he would say was, "I don't know."

At that point, I was thinking and working within game theory. I thought Brian was attempting to make me helpless and ineffective just like all the physicians who could not provide a diagnosis. I guarded against playing an "I'm Only Trying to Help" (Berne, 1964) game as best I could.

Then, following another week of medical testing, Brian spoke of a childhood experience in which his mother and father had been dishonest with him. For some reason, that new material allowed him to become less protective of his parents and to acknowledge their lack of support for him. That weekend I received a text from Brian asking me to clarify something I had said in the session. My initial thought was, "More game." It seemed like I was being set up to provide additional information that would be rejected. However, as I reflected further on his question and our work together, I thought of the last sentence in his text, "This is making sense." I now understood that Brian had not been asking me for answers as much as he was looking for reassurance that everything was going to be OK. That was one of many important needs that had been unfulfilled in his childhood: someone to tell him everything was going to be OK. I could then see what was going on between us not as a game but as an enactment.

Brian was looking for reassurance that neither our work nor I was providing. So, in the next session I merely stated what I had believed to be obvious. I said something like, "Brian, I think we have a very good idea of what is going on and where to go with it. We can do this work, and everything is going to be OK." Brian was silent and then began to cry. My eyes became moist as well. Our enactment revealed that within this strong man there was a split-off need to feel safe, protected, and reassured.

We were beginning to experience a joint reliving of Brian's feelings around his original experience of traumatizing isolation. This joint reliving deepened and intensified in future sessions. Through this work, I began to see his response of "I don't know" to mean "I don't remember." As dissociated experiences from Brian's childhood became available, they seemed to connect with Brian's feelings of anxiety and somatic sensations.

Reenactment: a one-sided reliving of trauma

For many months Jody experienced in her weekly sessions what I would define as reenactments. In her preteen years, a powerful member of the family sexually abused her. As an adult, she was a successful businesswoman who lived life as if everything were great. However, internally, she silently suffered feelings of shame, disgust, and panic.

Jody began each session talking about the week's events only to become increasingly silent as the hour progressed. During the silence, she experienced body sensations that she said were like those she felt during and after her sexual abuse. Sometimes I asked her to describe what was going on; at other times I just sat quietly with her. If this had been an enactment, I would have been contributing in some way to Jody's feelings. For example, perhaps my questions would have felt

178 Edward T. Novak

invasive, or I might have pushed too hard for her to talk about her abuse. My silence might have made her feel that I was ignoring the abuse just as her parents had done when she was a child.

However, it seemed to both of us that merely being in the presence of another person who knew what she kept hidden was evoking her feelings. Neither of us thought they were being evoked by a co-created experience. Her comment that "I always feel this way when I'm alone with a man" seemed to indicate she was in the terrain of a trauma trigger and a more one-sided reliving of her trauma. Thus, what she felt in sessions was processed more as an intrapsychic experience, and over time Jody was able to change her internal experience of me and eventually other men so that it was different from the internal experience associated with her abuser.

Conclusion

Transactional analysis practitioners remain open to examining and, when appropriate, incorporating contemporary research and theory from other disciplines into TA theory and practice. They also sometimes make use of emerging theories and ideas while keeping them separate from transactional analysis. I believe enactments and reenactments are constructs that merit inclusion in transactional analysis theory. However, I also believe that games, enactments, and reenactments should remain distinct from one another based on theoretical and clinical differences between them.

The construct of enactments has theoretical origins in psychoanalysis, and its main clinical usefulness has been to enhance the therapist's ability to work in a two-person relational mode when unconscious experiences are a primary issue. The idea of reenactments is helpful in expanding ways of framing and working with intrapsychic processes within the client, especially those related to trauma memories and dissociation. The concept of games offers a broader way to explore a client's interactions with people in many situations, including at work and in groups and families as well as in the therapeutic relationship. This expansive use of game theory lends itself to remaining independent from enactments and reenactments.

I do not view any of these constructs as privileged. Keeping them separate helps us as practitioners to avoid unhelpful generalizations that may occur if the three are conflated. Thus, each construct retains some uniqueness in theory and clinical function, and each can be used at different times in treatment to understand specific experiences.

References

Aron, L. (2003). The paradoxical place of enactment in psychoanalysis: Introduction. *Psychoanalytic Dialogues, 13*, 623–631.

Bacal, H. (2011). Specificity theory: The evolution of a process theory of psychoanalytic treatment. *American Imago, 68*, 267–285.

Bass, A. (2003). "E" enactments in psychoanalysis: Another medium, another message. *Psychoanalytic Dialogues, 13*, 657–675.

Berne, E. (1964). *Games people play: The psychology of human relationships*. New York, NY: Grove Press.

Berne, E. (1970). *Sex in human loving*. New York, NY: Simon & Schuster.

Bromberg, P. (2000). Bringing in the dreamer: Some reflections on dreamwork, surprise, and analytic process. *Contemporary Psychoanalysis, 36*, 685–705.

Bromberg, P. (2006). *Awakening the dreamer: Clinical journeys*. Mahwah, NJ: Analytic Press.

Caizzi, C. (2012). Embodied trauma: Using the subsymbolic mode to access and change script protocol in traumatized adults. *Transactional Analysis Journal, 42*, 165–175.

Chused, J. F. (2003). The role of enactments. *Psychoanalytic Dialogues, 13*, 677–687.

Chused, J. F., Ellman, S. J., Renik, O., & Rothstein, A. (1999). Four aspects of the enactment concept: Definitions, therapeutic effects, dangers, history. *Journal of Clinical Psychoanalysis, 8*, 9–61.

Cornell, W. F. (2008). What do you say if you don't say "unconscious"? Dilemmas created for transactional analysts by Berne's shift away from the language of unconscious experience. *Transactional Analysis Journal, 38*, 93–100.

Cornell, W. F., & Olio, K. A. (1992). Consequences of childhood bodily abuse: A clinical model for affective interventions. *Transactional Analysis Journal, 22*, 131–143.

Davies, J. (1997). Dissociation, therapeutic enactment, and transference–countertransference processes: A discussion of papers on childhood sexual abuse by S. Grand and J. Sarnat. *Gender and Psychoanalysis, 2*, 241–257.

Eigen, M. (1993). *The psychotic core*. Northvale, NJ: Jason Aronson.

English, F. (1977). Let's not claim it's script when it ain't. *Transactional Analysis Journal, 7*, 130–138.

Erskine, R. G. (1993). Inquiry, attunement, and involvement in the psychotherapy of dissociation. *Transactional Analysis Journal, 23*, 184–190.

Fosshage, J. (2011). How do we "know" what we "know?" And change what we "know?" *Psychoanalytic Dialogues, 21*(1), 55–74.

Greenberg, J., & Mitchell, S. (1983). *Object relations in psychoanalytic theory*. Cambridge, MA: Harvard University Press.

Hargaden, H., & Sills, C. (2002). *Transactional analysis: A relational approach*. London, UK: Brunner-Routledge.

Jacobs, T. (1986). On countertransference and enactments. *Journal of the American Psychoanalytic Association, 34*, 289–302.

Joines, V. (1982). Similarities and differences in rackets and games. *Transactional Analysis Journal, 12*, 280–283.

Karpman, S. B. (2009). Sex games people play: Intimacy blocks, games, and scripts. *Transactional Analysis Journal, 39*, 103–116.

LeDoux, J. (1996). *The emotional brain*. New York, NY: Touchstone Books.

Little, R. (2006). Ego state relational units and resistance to change. *Transactional Analysis Journal, 36*, 7–19.

Massey, R. (1990). The structural bases of games. *Transactional Analysis Journal, 20*, 20–27.

McLaughlin, J. T. (2005). *The healer's bent: Solitude and dialogue in the clinical encounter* (W. F. Cornell, Ed.). Hillsdale, NJ: Analytic Press.

Miller, A. (1984). *Thou shalt not be aware: Society's betrayal of the child*. New York, NY: Farrar, Straus & Giroux.

Minuchin, S. (1974). *Families and family therapy*. Cambridge, MA: Harvard University Press.

Novak, E. (2013). Combining traditional ego state theory and relational approaches to transactional analysis in working with trauma and dissociation. *Transactional Analysis Journal, 43*, 186–196.

Oates, S. (2012). Who decides and what can be changed? *Transactional Analysis Journal, 42,* 176–182.

Schwartz, H. L. (2000). *Dialogues with forgotten voices: Relational perspectives on child abuse trauma and treatment of dissociative disorders.* New York, NY: Basic Books.

Soth, M. (2013). We are all relational, but are some more relational than others? Completing the paradigm shift toward relationality. *Transactional Analysis Journal, 43,* 122–137.

Stark, M. (1999). *Modes of therapeutic interaction: Enhancement of knowledge, provision of experience, and engagement in relationship.* North Bergen, NJ: Book-mart Press.

Stern, D. B. (2003). *Unformulated experience: From dissociation to imagination in psychoanalysis.* New York, NY: Routledge.

Stern, D. B. (2010). *Partners in thought: Working with unformulated experience, dissociation, and enactment.* New York, NY: Routledge.

Stuthridge, J. (2006). Inside out: A transactional analysis model of trauma. *Transactional Analysis Journal, 36,* 270–283.

Stuthridge, J. (2012). Traversing the fault lines: Trauma and enactment. *Transactional Analysis Journal, 42,* 238–251.

Summerton, O. (1993). Games in organizations. *Transactional Analysis Journal, 23,* 87–103.

van der Hart, O., Nijenhuis, E., & Steele, K. (2006). *The haunted self: Structural dissociation and the treatment of chronic traumatization.* New York, NY: Norton.

van der Kolk, B. A., McFarlane, A., & Weisaeth, L. (Eds.). (1996). *Traumatic stress: The effects of overwhelming experience on mind, body, and society.* New York, NY: Guilford Press.

van der Kolk, B. A., van der Hart, O., & Marmar, C. (1996). Dissociation and information processing in posttraumatic stress disorder. In B. A. van der Kolk, A. McFarlane, & L. Weisaeth (Eds.), *Traumatic stress: The effects of overwhelming experience on mind, body, and society* (pp. 303–327). New York, NY: Guilford Press.

Woods, K. (2002). Primary and secondary gains from games. *Transactional Analysis Journal, 32,* 190–192.

Zalcman, M. (1990). Game analysis and racket analysis: Overview, critique, and future developments. *Transactional Analysis Journal, 20,* 4–19.

14

THE ROLE OF IMAGINATION IN AN ANALYSIS OF UNCONSCIOUS RELATEDNESS

Helena Hargaden

> How can we know the dancer from the dance?
>
> *W. B. Yeats*

The impetus for writing this article was my passion for discovering the multilayered meanings inherent in the clinical encounter. In the following case study, divided into two parts, I explore how the use of the imagination, reflection, and therapeutic congruence offer serious methods of analysis enabling us to understand our work more creatively. The following theoretical perspectives are discussed as a way of illuminating these processes: the theory of enactments (Bromberg, 2006; Stuthridge, 2012), Bion's (1959) theory of reverie, the theory of the third (Benjamin, 2004; Gerson, 2004), Jung's (1991) theory of archetypes, and scientific paradigms of the mind (Damasio, 1999; Schore, 2012). This article expands on the relational understanding of projective identification described in the domains of transference, with particular focus on the transformational transference (Hargaden & Sills, 2002).

Part one: Marianne—in the beginning

When Marianne came into therapy she was 34. She was a tall, slender woman, stylishly dressed, and a highly achieving professional in the field of science. Initially, we talked about her current situation as a single parent with an unsupportive male ex-partner whom she experienced as vindictive and unable to parent their young daughter with any consistency. Early in the therapy, Marianne made some decisions to help her disentangle herself from him and achieve economic security for herself and her daughter. Feeling safer and more assured, she began to talk about her childhood. Her background is complex, and her relationship with her mother and siblings would make an interesting study. However, here I will concentrate on Marianne's experience with her father as this is related to the two parts of this article.

When Marianne first described her father's brutal treatment of her (which was both physical and mental), I would become indignant, expressing a type of furious empathy with her childhood experience. Instead of feeling understood, Marianne had felt under threat, which initially puzzled me. At such times, I felt as if I were mentally wrestling with her internalized subjugating father, trying to free the Child from his malevolent influence on her. The most striking consequence of his hold on her manifest self was evident in her excoriating self-criticism. "Sorry" was a frequently used word that was most confusing because it was unclear what Marianne was apologizing for. I learned that the word *sorry* seemed to mean: "Sorry I exist. Sorry that I have an opinion. Sorry that I might be hurting someone with my very presence. Sorry that you might find me difficult."

However, there was also a defiant quality to the way Marianne said "sorry," as though she was angry that she had to apologize. I found myself being very direct and blunt, matching her negative view of herself with a type of maternal ferocity. I tried to show empathy with the vulnerable child who had been under continuous malicious threats from her father. But Marianne could not tolerate thinking about her vulnerability, and so our interactions tumbled over each other, as though competing for space. Both of us lacked genuine confidence in ourselves and each other. It was as if we needed to make our points, make ourselves heard, while both failing to hear the other. We were embroiled in an enactment.

There is clearly a link with games theory to be made here, and for those wishing for a more definitive discussion of the similarities and differences between games and enactments, I recommend Novak's (2015) excellent article on the subject. Here I will concentrate only on the theory of enactments.

An enactment

An enactment is the acting out, in the interpersonal field between therapist and client, of dissociated aspects of their psyches. Bromberg (2006) described an enactment as a rupture in the therapeutic relationship that allows dissociated material to emerge between therapist and client. Stuthridge (2012) viewed enactments in therapy as an opportunity "to discover the lost parts of oneself for both client and therapist" (p. 12). Enactments are, therefore, a means by which unconscious material can emerge in the therapy.

In the enactment with Marianne, I felt that I was up against an implacable force that had entered the space between us, one that left no room for reflection, feeling, or empathy. After such sessions I felt winded. What had happened? I struggled to find my mind. Although I was able to think theoretically about Marianne's need for defense systems, I was emotionally blank and disconnected from any more meaningful reflections. My phenomenological experience during these sessions manifested itself in an odd bodily reaction in which I felt as though air was being pumped into me followed by a sensation of bursting open. I was unable to hold the process. There was no container, nothing but a sense of flying rubbish in which

The role of imagination in an analysis **183**

thoughts, feelings, and ideas were detonated and destroyed. I criticized myself for arguing with her, for not finding more nuanced ways to get at the points I thought should be made, the interpretations I knew had to be offered, the explanations I insisted on.

When I began to recognize that we were in an enactment, I was able to ask myself some questions: Why were my interventions so insistent and forceful? Why did I persist? Insist? Try harder? Viewing my countertransference through a personal lens, I could see I might still be trying to heal my mother. There seemed to be something seductive about Marianne's suffering that resonated with a desperate Child state in me from the past, who, if she had had the words, would have screamed, "No need to carry on being a Victim."

As Stuthridge (2012) pointed out, the dissociation occurs in both therapist and client; it is a form of unconscious relatedness. The dissociated part of me was linked to the unconscious projection of my mother onto Marianne. My mother had had a brutal father. Although I had not consciously understood that as a child, I had tried to compensate for her suffering at the same time that I felt frustrated that all my efforts were wasted because she always sank back into her Victimhood. This was also an example of how transgenerational trauma (Hargaden, 2013b; Wallfisch, 2013) moves unconsciously from one generation to another. My grandfather's war traumas had transmitted themselves through a violent brutality he showed toward my mother, whom I have come to believe he also envied because of her love of books and introverted temperament. In the following discussion, it will become clear how her dissociated transgenerational trauma affected Marianne and also shaped our enacted dialogue. In part two, the dissociated trauma emerges as a visceral experience in the room between us.

When I eventually moved out of the enactment by developing a cognitive understanding of the process I was in with Marianne, I was able to contain my reactions more carefully. However, it was only when I fell into a reverie that the emotional way out of our impasse and the meaning of the enactment became clearer.

Using the third as a way out of the impasse

For those not familiar with the theory of *the third*, it has its roots in Freud's (1953) theory of the Oedipus complex. The theory of the third is a modern and more expanded way of thinking about the function of the father, which is to interrupt the symbiosis between mother and child as part of the healthy development of the self. The third refers to this symbolic father, now translated into a theory of thirds that describes a process by which the therapeutic dyad is interrupted and altered by a third force. Gerson (2004) referred to the creation of a triangular symbolic space that can emerge from a collision of polarities in which a third way is formed. What he meant is that the therapist needs to find a part of her that both participates in the polarity but at the same time is able to find a corner of her mind to reflect on what is going on. It is this corner of the therapist's mind that is called the third. It is as if a third person is introduced into the therapeutic dyad. In this way, the third functions as a symbol for finding a way out of the binary of the therapeutic relationship.

Once you begin considering thirds in this way, you can have as many thirds as you can think of. For instance, Gerson (2004) suggested three categories of potential thirds: developmental, cultural, and relational. The clinical benefits of thinking about thirds are many, one of which is to enable the members of a therapeutic couple to find their way out of binary processes using the third as a symbol (in whatever category).

The emergence of the third in the therapy with Marianne

The third emerged with Marianne in the middle of yet another heated interpersonal dynamic one day. I became aware of a light bouncing off the white shutters in front of the window. It felt almost sunny, although the day was grey. With the light, a feeling of softness came into the room. I rubbed my hands over the wool of my jumper, an action that I found soothing and that helped me to fall quiet. It became possible to feel some emotional warmth and to take time to reflect.

My reflections on the making of a subjugating father

In that session with Marianne, I found myself musing on my work with two male clients with whom I have been working, both over a period of 18 years. These men had been to high-ranking boarding schools. I had learned not only concrete knowledge of how these institutions worked but had witnessed, and at times absorbed, the traumatic experience each had suffered in the British boarding school system (both came to me three times a week for many years). The material conditions were akin to a type of penal servitude. Heating, food, and beds were normally kept to minimal standards. Any expression of vulnerability occasioned severe humiliation, disgust, and punishment (Schaverin, 2015). The reasoning behind such institutionalized torture was apparently to make men who would fight for, and defend, the British Empire. This was how the British stiff upper lip was created. In thinking about my male clients, and the depth of suffering they had endured (one had been sent to school at the age of four), I began to reflect on Marianne's father, who had also gone to boarding school. I used my reflections to open up a conversation with Marianne about what she knew of her father's background.

The destruction of the maternal

Listening to Marianne, it became clear that her father had been raised in conditions of severe maternal deprivation. He had been separated from his mother at an early age and thrown into the boarding school environment where empathy and maternal warmth were denigrated, derided, and destroyed.

I began to understand why my every effort to develop a maternal containing presence had been attacked. My phenomenological experience of mindlessness, of bursting open, of feeling unable to contain, had mirrored how the maternal container had cracked in her father's original experience, separated from his mother at an early age. As I shared my reflections about the nature of boarding schools and their effects on young boys, both Marianne and I began to see her father differently. She had internalized an experience of her father as a demonic monster who ruled his family with brutal authoritarianism, but as we reflected on the meanings inherent in her father's experience, her view of him began to change. Her father emerged in our conversation as a rather tragic figure, a sad person who had been weakened rather than strengthened by his experiences of maternal deprivation. In viewing her father this way, we began to reflect together that his abuse of Marianne was more mindless than personal, that it revealed much more about him than her.

However, there is a tipping point over which you do not go as a therapist, where sympathy for the parent starts to outweigh the damage they have inflicted. Together Marianne and I began to understand the extent of her father's traumatic legacy and how it had shaped her internal world and, indeed, our dialogue and therapeutic interactions. Despite his mindless brutality, she had stood up to her father, and, although terrified, she had fought him on the battlefront of ideas. Paradoxically, she also sought to protect him, intuitively sensing his vulnerability. Thinking together about these dynamics, we began to recognize that his expressed hatred of her was, at times, probably an expression of envy for her spirit of defiance against subjugation, for showing a type of courage and strength that had long since been knocked out of him. Also, we thought, he had envied her natural inclination to try to nurture him, something he both wanted but despised. It was through these conversations that Marianne began to take back the power she had vested in him, to see him for what he was, and to begin a journey toward owning her own agency.

From this perspective, we both began to understand why the emergence of trust and love in the therapy, signified by my ferocious empathy, was so threatening. She was enabled to feel the extent of her desolation and despair and to be more open to the vulnerable self that emerged between the two of us. She moved out of the Victim position (Karpman, 1968) and began to see cause for a legitimate sorrow for the child who had been wounded by a traumatizing narcissistic father (Shaw, 2014).

The cumulative effect of these sessions paved the way for a nonlinear therapeutic process that I will describe in part two of this article. As Marianne became more trusting of me and more open to her feeling world, I was able to feel the strength of being secure in not knowing (Bachelard, 1994) and more able to listen to the unconscious.

To get to this point in the therapy, it was crucial to recognize the enactment, to take time to reflect on my feelings and be open to my introspection. This was the method by which a third way emerged that deepened the therapeutic conversation in the ways I will now describe.

186 Helena Hargaden

Part two: Marianne on the couch

Capturing the nuances and many metaphorical meanings of a clinical encounter is quite a challenge. According to Naiburg (2015), "One of your challenges as a clinical writer is to translate analytic and qualitative experience and the poetry of what we do (and feel and intuit …) with our patients into prose, knowing how inadequate any translation might be" (p. 10). Naiburg's notion chimes with Ogden (2004), who wrote, "An analytic experience—like all other experiences, does not come to us in words. An analytic experience cannot be told or written; an experience is what it is" (p. 16).

Naiburg's and Ogden's ideas are also reflected in the work of Daniel Stern (1985) when he described our first sense of self as the emergent sense of self, the seat of our creativity, which is nonverbal. In Stern's domains of the self, he suggested that the verbal self often alienates us from the emergent self. The philosopher and psychoanalyst Julia Kristeva (1980) described this earliest sense of self as the *semiotic*. She referred to Lacan's theory that the use of language signifies "the father," who interrupts the symbiosis between mother and child. Kristeva argued that it is through the language of the father that we learn to be ashamed, not only of our bodies (associated as they are with the maternal function) but of our fundamental core relational experience, needs, and sense of this semiotic self.

How then to think about, understand, and write about clinical experiences that involve the semiotic, the nonverbal? We need to find a different language because the language of logic, the language of the father, cannot adequately describe the language of the unconscious mind and the multifaceted experience of psychotherapy.

Naiburg and Ogden spoke to the essence of the challenge to put the intensity of multifaceted experience into language. This is of central importance for psychotherapy because the nature of trauma means it has not been metabolized or mentalized (Fonagy & Target, 1998) but is often somatized. The scientific basis for thinking about different types of thinking and language is supported by neuroscience (Damasio, 1999; Schore, 2012). Thus, trauma cannot be dealt with through cognitive means.

In the case study described here, reverie was used as a channel through which to retrieve traumatic experience. Bion (1959) thought that reverie was a crucial variable in the creation of an analytic process that promotes therapeutic action through learning from experience. "An understanding mother is able to experience the feeling of dread, that this baby was striving to deal with by projective identification, and yet retain a balanced outlook" (p. 296). Bion called this ability the *alpha function* in the mother, that is, she is someone who can pick up the projective identification and make emotional meaning out of it. He thought that the therapist's alpha function capacity provided a necessary stimulus for the patient, encouraging a process of transformation that makes it possible to experience that which could not be tolerated or approached before. In other words, therapists must allow themselves to delve into the area of the unknown, to go with the flow of the unconscious, to use their imaginations and listen to themselves. These self-states are necessary to allow for the unspeakable to emerge and then to find different words in which to speak about it. In the following account, reverie becomes a significant method by which that is achieved.

A paradigm of the mind

Neurological research (Damasio, 1999; Schore, 2012) has shown that the brain is capable of two kinds of thinking: One is linear and logical, the other is nonlinear. The left hemisphere of the brain is associated with syntactical speech, and the right hemisphere is associated with emotional and musical expression. Trauma, which exists in the unconscious and/or is usually experienced primarily nonverbally, cannot be dealt with through cognitive means. The language of logic cannot describe the language of the nonlinear unconscious mind.

From a metaphorical perspective, Jung (1991) referred to the linear and logical part of the psyche as the *masculine archetype*. He described the poetic, nonlinear part of the psyche as the *feminine archetype*. Jung's terms have proved controversial over the years because they have sometimes been thought to be stereotyping of gender.

However, I think such criticism misinterprets what Jung meant. I use the terms *feminine* and *masculine* for two reasons. One is that Jung (1991) greatly valued the feminine, by which he did not mean gender but an archetypal, primitive mental image inherent in the collective unconscious. The feminine archetype refers to a quality of receptivity, of spirit, of an energy that he thought formed the core of the unconscious process. The second reason I find Jung's paradigm helpful is because, in his view, the goal of psychotherapy is consciousness, which involves the bringing together of the opposites of masculine and feminine within us. In my view, it enhances our work to be informed by both a scientific and a metaphorical perspective. Logical theoretical clarity gives confidence to the therapist as she or he delves into the mystery and paradox created by metaphor, thus allowing for play, symbol, the tangential, and the unknown: for the discovery of nonlinear unconscious material. Based on these paradigms of the mind, the challenge for the therapist is to recognize the emergence of nonlinear dynamics or the feminine archetype and to use it as a gateway to finding the elusive language of the unconscious. The difficulty for poets in translating their poetry into prose becomes the same problem for psychotherapists when describing their clinical encounters: how to describe and to find language that does not destroy, spoil, or reduce the layers of metaphorical meaning entwined in experience.

Numinous moments

The morning light filters through the shutters as, taking off her stylish suede boots and putting her bag neatly next to them, Marianne segues onto the couch where she lies down. The couch is next to a large window that looks out onto the sea at the end of the road. It is windy today. We fall into a silent immersion. I wait. I feel her quietness. It seems to allow for a quietness in me. This way of being together

188 Helena Hargaden

works well for Marianne. When lying on the couch, she is released from feeling scrutinized and judged. This allows her to enter into a different psychological space, a place that allows for the discovery of other selves. I too feel released from an experience often evoked by her of having to make sense of things. Instead, I have a feeling best described as a release from causality. It is as if I move from watching a river to being in the flow of the river.

In this atmosphere, nonlinear dynamics can emerge and do so in the following way. I fall into a reverie. The description of the following reverie seems quite long, but in real time it was very brief. On the wall in front of me is a picture of Lough Allen in Sligo, the Republic of Ireland, home of my ancestors. Today I am drawn to meditating on it for some reason. The lough suggests depth. I imagine a slight wind ruffling the surface of the lough and find myself musing about how my ancestors taught in the hedge schools. This was the name used by small bands of teachers who taught the Irish language illegally because it had been banned by the British. For no conscious reason, I begin to imagine hiding in the reeds around the lake, feeling the wind blowing through the grass. I feel some anxiety: Will we be safe from the marauding force of the colonizing army? I am steeped in this imaginative space, although, as I say, only for a few seconds in real time, when I hear Marianne speaking, as though she is in my mind, as if she is part of my reverie. "It is windy today." It is as if we are both in the picture, but her low murmur also draws my attention to some inner feeling state she does not often have time to inhabit in her busy life. Marianne continues speaking from this inner state: "I remember my grandmother's house, it was warm and safe. She lived in the country, in the winter it was cold, windy outside …" She trails off. This was where she used to hide from her father. We are in a conversation that is emerging from unconscious self-states— something is opening up and revealing itself to her, to me, to us. I see an image of a hearth and am reminded of Hestia, goddess of the fireside, the "introverted, inwardly focused archetype" (Shinoda-Bolen, 1984, p. 117).

Hestia represents the homemaker, someone who ushers in domestic order. There is a feeling of home, of warmth in the room together with Marianne. The reference to her grandmother also constellates the archetype of the wise old woman. I feel the sense in Marianne of that longing, the need to feel safe and protected from malign forces. Our conversation continues: "My father once attacked me, forcing me against a wall, hitting me. He was furious with me because I had answered him back, had disagreed with him. He told me he would cut my tongue out." My ancestors were hiding from colonial forces, she was hiding in her grandmother's house from a brutal father. We are together, in hiding, safe, immersed in the amniotic sac of the womb. I think of Winnicott's (1953) maternal immersion. Marianne murmurs her feelings. There is trust in me, in us, and I feel that trust. It feels important to be in this moment, not to dissect it with explanation, to deconstruct with interpretation, to penetrate with inquiries. I ponder why I feel like this, as we sit, lie, quietly together. Should I say something of my thinking? Or allow the feeling moments to be? A negative timbre creeps into my thoughts. What am I doing? Is this therapeutic? Should I be doing something, pointing something out, making an interpretation,

The role of imagination in an analysis **189**

introducing some theory? Again, I fall into a reverie that took place over a few seconds, although it sounds much longer.

Feminization

My mind wanders to a conference I had recently attended that involved a gathering of people from differing modalities who were interested in relational ideas. At the end of the day, about 40 of us gathered in a circle. As usual in these situations, the majority of those attending were women. One of my much loved and esteemed colleagues began to talk of his disquiet at "the feminization" of the profession. To feminize means "to make or become feminine; to develop female characteristics" (*Chambers Dictionary*, 2014, p. 566). Because no one had a dictionary at hand, and because language is often as confusing as it is clarifying, his meaning was not entirely clear.

Previously, I had heard him critique the maternal in psychotherapy practice. His view was that psychotherapy seemed dominated by an excessively maternal attitude that manifests itself in controlling behaviors disguised as nurture. He thought this attitude was an obstacle to navigating through what, in reality, are the psychological shark-infested waters of depth psychotherapy. I had some sympathy with this view and think that nurture can be used to sidestep the pain involved in meeting our demons, in becoming conscious and in more truthfully and honestly finding ourselves. I even wrote an article in which I offered a critique of empathy used in this way (Hargaden, 2013a). However, on this day of the conference, for some mysterious reasons, the impact of his thoughts were received rather negatively by his colleagues. His comments were experienced as gender stereotyping, biased, with the inference that women are annoying and stupid. Judging from the passionate and disapproving response by female colleagues in the room, I reflected that he had unwittingly invoked the inner critic that so many women carry within themselves, one that tells them they are unlovable, worthless, and stupid.

The internalized subjugating father

Why, though, was I thinking of this event and my colleague's attitude as I sat with Marianne? Why did this man emerge in my imagination as an introjected archetypal subjugating father, the judge who lays down the laws, a type of Godlike figure who defines what is acceptable and appropriate—in this case, what is proper psychotherapy? This imaginary critic was someone who had the attitude of a tyrant, someone who demanded certainty. I hasten to add that my colleague is nothing like that and, in fact, would be terribly offended if he thought that this was how he was perceived. Indeed, he has a powerful capacity to immerse himself in nonlinear dynamics. However, it was the archetype that had been constellated at the conference that now formed in my mind. It was not my colleague who was the tyrant: It was a part of me! As my client and I sat/lay there together, immersed in the feeling of things, I reflected that the part of me that was self-critical of my introspective, more feminine side, might also be a projective identification. That was probably how Marianne felt about herself, about her vulnerability and her femininity. There was certainly plenty in her history with her father to support that view.

At this point I think it will be clear to you, since I was having these reveries, that I was quiet and contemplative. Such reflections happened quickly, and as I pondered, I heard Marianne's voice, as though out of nowhere, as if in conversation with my unspoken reflections, recalling childhood memories of being viciously attacked both physically and mentally. Nothing would appease her father, it seemed, until she was made a prisoner of his beliefs and ideas and was willing to forgo and sacrifice her subjectivity on the altar of his fatherhood and his need to possess and control her. Marianne was a slender person and had a sensitive, almost fragile sensibility, but she was tough. She had fought her father at every turn, never succumbing entirely to his need to completely possess her mind.

Although I had heard these stories many times before, that day there was a different tone to her recollections. She was more in the experience of what it had felt like. The dissociated self-states of the trauma were making themselves known. Previously, when she had recounted catastrophic events, I had felt angry with her father, which had the effect of making Marianne react defensively. Now, as I listened, I was more in a state of shock, experiencing a strong somatic countertransference in which I felt an almost intolerable sense of my own fragility. In such an imaginative state, linking back to my reverie on the picture, I found myself wondering how easily I might be broken by an invading army, told to succumb to the superior doctrine, forced to forgo my language and religion, that is, be occupied. In the case of the Irish, they had not succumbed. They had been deeply wounded, of course, then went underground, had been divided, shamed, made inferior, and pitied, but many had also grown defiant, quarrelsome, and even violent, as we know.

Similarly, Marianne had fought strenuously against her father, defied his rule, but that meant she had grown strong in a way that was lopsided. She had not been broken, but she was deeply wounded. The violence invoked in her, which is often the case with women, was turned inward against herself through excoriating self-criticism. She had a sharp and argumentative mind; she could hold her ground on any subject. Deep within her, however, was the wound of her vulnerability, her femininity. It was in this way that we both shared a traumatized mind, one hidden in my unconscious that came to the surface stimulated by the picture on the wall. It was a state that mirrored Marianne's experience of male brutality against her body and mind.

How to analyze this process? How to write about this without deconstructing the layers of metaphorical meaning and thereby destroy it by stamping all over the Holy Ground with large theoretical boots? One method of analysis that emerged when writing this article was the use of metaphor to illuminate the experience we had.

Pneuma

I have since discovered a Greek word: *pneuma*. Its earliest meaning, in ancient Greek, was "air in motion, breath, wind" ("Pneuma," 2016, §1.1). A quotation from Anaximenes, an ancient Greek philosopher, says that "just as our soul (*psyche*), being air (*aer*), holds us together, so do breath (*pneuma*) and air (*aer*) encompass the whole world" (§1.1). Viewed in this way, Marianne's reference to the wind was a powerful expression. Her sotto voce murmuring of "It is windy today" was pregnant with meaning. Her voice, like a whisper, seemed to usher in a different type of energy. The reference to the wind, already in my subliminal imaginative experience stimulated by the picture on the wall, suggested a powerful energy, one that was out of my conscious awareness. Maybe it was this energy that caused me to reflect before speaking, an energy that held me back so I did not invade her with interpretations and explanations. By not doing that, I was implicitly challenging that the only power was in the language of certainty. Power was no longer located only in the conscious mind, in logos: Power was now located in the listening for the meanings that were elusive. Power was in allowing for the experience to speak to us. Power was in Bion's alpha function. Power was in the feminine.

I intuitively knew that if I drew Marianne's attention to any dimension of her experiencing she would too quickly and easily move into her head space, trying to sort it out, understand it, reduce it to the language of logos, a language with which she was articulate and that, to a certain extent, she had used to control her life as a way of coping with her cut-off traumatic experiences. I knew, too, that to draw attention to her evolving emotional dependency on me at that moment would make her withdraw. She would feel too conscious of a sense of weakness that would feel overwhelmingly shameful: She would pull up the drawbridge. The maternal container that had been so lacking in the first part of Marianne's therapy was now emerging in me and between us. Catastrophic experience could now be felt, terror and horror could emerge into a container that was strong enough to keep her/us safe.

As this trauma emerged into the room, the story of the trauma made itself felt in her body and mine, in my reflections, and in the search for language and meaning. In part, perhaps the trauma we experienced was a shared collective trauma related to the denigration of the feminine, the trauma of powerlessness and social repression, and a contempt for the vulnerable, the poetic, the uncertainty of things. I believe that I was both a participant as well as a witness to Marianne's trauma and the denigration of her as a person and maybe as a woman.

The thirds

To illuminate these numinous moments, it is useful to also point out some of the thirds that emerged. I think it is Benjamin's (2004) definition of the relational third that most captures the process between Marianne and me: "A quality or experience of intersubjective relatedness that has as its correlate a certain kind of mental space"

192 Helena Hargaden

(p. 7). This relational third refers to an innate sense of self with other that we bring to every meeting; it is the process by which we share experience with each other both consciously and unconsciously. It is within this co-created space that one can directly access the other's emotional experience (Hargaden & Fenton, 2005). Although the relational third is the main context for the numinous moments described here, it will deepen appreciation of the depth of this encounter by recognizing other thirds, in particular, reflections on the cultural archetypal thirds evoked by the picture on the wall, the image of Hestia, the reveries on feminization connecting me with the internalizing subjugating father, the wind, and the wise old woman. All of these help us to capture something of the multiple metaphorical experiences of the clinical encounter.

Conclusion

Hestia was the most influential and widely revered of the Greek goddesses. Her name means *the essence*, that is, the true nature of things. It was through such transformative moments that Marianne began a journey towards finding her true nature.

I realize that in the work I have described in this article I departed almost totally from what would be recognized as classical transactional analysis. Yet the influence of my training in TA and the sense of classical transactional analysis as part of how I think, intuit, and assess is an integrated part of how I work. I value measurable outcomes, for instance, and hence the significance of measuring Marianne's change. It is important that there is a contract so that therapist and client know why and what they think they are doing in the room together, and Marianne and I continuously negotiated what we were doing and why. In many of my shared reflections with her I used terms such as *Child ego state, script, games*, and other transactional analysis terms. Over the years, though, my relational perspective has taken me beyond classical TA thinking toward incorporating the imaginative realm in the clinical encounter.

References

Bachelard, G. (1994). *The poetics of space*. Boston, MA: Beacon Press. (Original work published 1958.)

Benjamin, J. (2004). Beyond doer and done to: An intersubjective view of thirdness. *Psychoanalytic Quarterly, 73*, 5–46.

Bion, W. R. (1959). Attacks on linking. *International Journal of Psycho-Analysis, 40*, 285–300.

Bromberg, P. M. (2006). *Awakening the dreamer: Clinical journeys*. Mahwah, NJ: Analytic Press.

Chambers dictionary (13th ed.). (2014). London, UK: Chambers Harrap.

Damasio, A. (1999). *The feeling of what happens: Body and emotion in the making of consciousness*. London, UK: Heinemann.

Fonagy, P., & Target, M. (1998). Mentalisation and the changing aims of child psychoanalysis. *Psychoanalytic Dialogues, 8*, 87–114.

Freud, S. (1953). The interpretation of dreams. In J. Strachey (Ed. & Trans.), *The standard edition of the complete psychological works of Sigmund Freud* (Vols. 4–5). London: Hogarth Press. (Original work published 1899.)

Gerson, S. (2004). The relational unconscious: A core element of intersubjectivity, thirdness, and clinical process. *Psychoanalytic Quarterly, 73*, 63–98.

Hargaden, H. (2013a). Building resilience: The role of firm boundaries and the third in relational group therapy. *Transactional Analysis Journal, 43*, 284–290. doi: 10.1177/0362153713515178.

Hargaden, H. (2013b, 16 December). Response to Jacobs-Wallfisch's "Wounds of History". Paper presented to Confer at conference entitled "Intergenerational Trauma," Tavistock Centre, London, UK.

Hargaden, H., & Fenton, B. (2005). An analysis of nonverbal transactions drawing on theories of intersubjectivity. *Transactional Analysis Journal, 35*, 173–186.

Hargaden, H., & Sills, C. (2002). *Transactional analysis: A relational perspective*. Hove, UK: Brunner-Routledge.

Jung, C. G. (1991). *The archetypes and the collective unconscious* (2nd ed.). London, UK: Routledge.

Karpman, S. (1968). Fairy tales and script drama analysis. *Transactional Analysis Bulletin, 7*(26), 39–43.

Kristeva, J. (1980). *Desire in language: A semiotic approach to literature and art*. Oxford, UK: Blackwell. (Original work published 1969 in French.)

Naiburg, S. (2015). *Structure and spontaneity in clinical prose*. New York, NY: Routledge.

Novak, E. T. (2015). Are games, enactments, and reenactments similar? No, yes, it depends. *Transactional Analysis Journal, 45*, 117–127.

Ogden, T. (2004). On psychoanalytic writing. *International Journal of Psychoanalysis, 66*, 15–29.

"Pneuma." (2016). In *Wikipedia*. Retrieved from https://en.wikipedia.org/wiki/Pneuma

Schaverin, J. (2015). *Boarding school syndrome: The psychological trauma of the "privileged" child*. London, UK: Routledge.

Shinoda-Bolen, J. (1984). *Goddesses in everywoman*. New York, NY: Harper & Row.

Schore, A. N. (2012). *Affect regulation and the repair of the self*. London, UK: Norton. (Original work published 2003.)

Shaw, D. (2014). *Traumatic narcissism: Relational systems of subjugation*. New York, NY: Routledge.

Stern, D. N. (1985). *The interpersonal world of the infant: A view from psychoanalysis and developmental psychology*. New York, NY: Basic Books.

Stuthridge, J. (2012). Traversing the fault lines: Trauma and enactment. *Transactional Analysis Journal, 42*, 238–251.

Wallfisch, M. (2013, 16 December). Wounds of history. Paper presented to Confer at conference entitled "Intergenerational Trauma," Tavistock Centre, London, UK.

Winnicott, D. W. (1953). Transitional objects and transitional phenomena. *International Journal of Psycho-Analysis, 34*, 89–97.

INDEX

abuse 101, 147, 149–150, 152, 156, 171, 172; *see also* trauma
Adult–Adult therapy 105, 106–107, 109
Adult ego state: Berne's model 3, 59–60, 130; countertransference 44; couples work 81; 'insanity' 125; intrapsychic tension 30; script 144, 151, 156; transference 39–40
aggression 64–65, 114
alpha function 186
Anna Freud Centre 19
Aron, Lew 9, 170
attachment theory 61, 63, 95–96, 98, 105, 126
attunement 18, 66, 99–100

Bacal, Howard 175
Bass, Anthony 14, 170
Berne, Eric: critique of 3–4, 52, 61; game analysis 23, 31; legacy 14, 52–53; theoretical foundations 1–5, 50–53, 75, 125–126; therapeutic interventions 59–60, 71; training 7
bidirectionality, of the relational unconscious 13, 17, 169
Bleuler, Eugen 14–15
Bollas, Christopher 7, 9–11, 17, 67–68, 69, 114, 120–121
Bowlby, John 62–65, 71, 98, 105, 126
Bromberg, Philip 142, 143, 144, 146, 154, 156, 162, 182
Buber, Martin 15

Child ego state: Berne's model 3; complementary transference 40;

concordant transference 41; couples work 81; enactment 182, 183; game theory 168; intrapsychic tension 30; script 144; therapeutic interventions 60, 77–78; trauma 152
Chused, J. E. 169
Clarkson, Petrūska 12–13, 127
complementary countertransference 44, 45, 47
complementary transference 40
con 25–27, 133, 137–138; *see also* game theory
concordant countertransference 44, 45, 47
concordant transference 41
confrontation ruptures 132
contact (game analysis) 31–32
continuity 97, 143, 145, 149, 156
Cornell, William 5–12, 132–133, 136, 143–144, 168
countertransference: Berne's model 3–4; *contra* bidirectionality 17; definition and types 43–48; and enactment 169–170; erotic 88–89, 92, 116–117; and relational needs 99
couples therapy 81
creativity 69–70
crossed transactions 27, 133, 155
crossup (game analysis) 28, 133, 137

Davies, Jody Messler 117, 150, 170, 172, 173
deconstruction 69
destiny drive 10
destructive countertransference 44, 45–46, 47
destructive transference 41
developmental deprivation/deficit 68, 106

developmental trauma 142
dialectics of difference 9–10
disavowal 146, 147, 162, 163
discontinuity 145, 146–147
discount matrix 81
discounts/discount analysis 24, 130
dissociation: and enactment 150–152, 154, 155, 160–161, 172, 174, 182, 183; and erotic transference 117; and trauma 141–147, 149, 161–165
distancing (game analysis) 31–32
disturbance 69–70
Drama Triangle 24, 25, 81

ego/ego states 1, 24, 30, 51, 52, 58–60, 65, 143; *see also* Adult ego state; Child ego state; Parent ego state
Eigen, Michael 164
elaboration 69
empathy 18, 65–69
enactment 98, 141–156, 167–178, 182–183
Erikson, Erik 75
Erikson, Milton 127
erotic contagion/avoidance 117–118
erotic transference 85–93, 116–121
Erskine, R. G. 24, 66
ethical principles 124–128
evocative objects 10

facilitative countertransference 45, 46, 48
facilitative transference 41
failure and rupture 124–139
fantasy 30, 38, 40, 97; *see also* obsessions
fathers 20, 183, 186, 189–190
feminism 13
Fonagy, Peter 19, 144, 145, 146
Formula G 23, 25–28, 133, 137
frame of reference (game analysis) 32–34
Freud, Sigmund 4, 10, 38–39, 57, 71, 147
Fromm, Erich 3

game theory 23–35; hysteria 116–117; obsessions 107–108; projective transference 16; psychodynamic approaches 55; (re)enactment 3–4, 167–178; rupture and failure 133
Ghent, Emmanuel 2, 5–6, 18
gimmick 24, 25–27, 32, 133, 137–138; *see also* game theory
Goulding, M. M. & R. L. 51–52, 106
Green, André 61, 115

Hargaden, Helena 5, 12–20, 85, 105, 106, 131
holding 64–65
homosexuality 119

humanistic approaches 2–3, 15, 17, 53
hysteria 113–122

IARPP (International Association of Relational Psychoanalysis and Psychotherapy) 14
IARTA (International Association for Relational Transactional Analysis) 15–16
id 10
idealization 100, 104–111
identity, and obsession 96–97
imagination 181–192
impasse 8, 132–133, 134, 147, 163, 183–184
inquiry 66, 69–70
'insanity' 125
integrative transactional analysis 130
interpersonal, definition of 17
intersubjectivity 155
intrapsychic tension/conflict 30–31, 60, 68, 145, 156
introjective domain 19
introjective transference 16, 105–106, 116
involvement 66
"I-Thou" theory 15

Jacobs, Theodore 7, 8, 170
Jung, Carl 187

Kohut, H. 16, 63, 65–66, 99, 101, 105
Kristeva, Julia 186

Landaiche, N. M. 132–133
Lewin, K. 39
Lichtenberg, J. D. 62
life position 31
love 114

Mann, David 85, 88, 89, 107, 116
Margulies, A. 70
the maternal 189
McLaughlin, James 7–9, 169–170, 173
mentalization 19, 134, 144, 145, 146, 147, 151, 157
Moiso, C. 12, 151
Moses, I. 65–66, 67
mother–infant relationship 61–62, 100, 120–121
motivational systems 62
moving self 144, 160
multiple self-state theory 143–145
mutual enactment 163
mutuality 13, 15, 17, 128, 163

narcissism 99
Nathanson-Elkind, S. 133
Not-OK dynamic 23, 24, 28

196 Index

object relations theory 64, 68, 76
object usage 9–11
obsessions 94–102, 107, 115–116
oedipal period/Oedipus complex 20, 114–115
Ogden, Thomas 143, 186
one-and-a-half person psychology 131, 172
one-person psychology 3, 5, 59, 131, 132, 171, 172

Parent ego state 58–60, 78, 81, 100, 144, 152
payoff 24, 25–26, 28, 32, 108, 137, 168, 169; *see also* game theory
pneuma 191
Poland, Warren 7, 8, 9
predictability, and obsession 96
pro-active countertransference 45–46
projective domain 19
projective identification 17, 151–152
projective transference 16, 18, 19, 106, 108–109, 116
puer aeternus 110, 114

Racker, H. 38, 39
racketeering 168
racket system analysis 24, 32
Rath, I. 53
reactive patient countertransference 46–48
recognition 145, 150, 154–156
Redefining Hexagon 24
reenactment 171–175, 177–178
regression 77–78, 97
Reichian approaches 113–114
relational approaches 17–18, 75–77
Renick, O. 69
reparative model 6–7
reparenting model 6–7
repression 163
responsibility 8, 127–128
reverie 69, 186–187, 188–189
role analysis (game theory) 24
rupture *see* failure and rupture
Rycroft, C. 38, 43

safe surprises 168
Samuels, Andrew 15–16
Schiff, J. 24, 31, 51, 107
Schore, A. N. 105, 145, 154
Schwartz, H. L. 172
script milestone (game theory) 31–32
script/script analysis 3–4, 55, 75, 142, 144–145, 156
security 100
self-analysis 8, 9
self-determination 126–127
self-disclosure 8, 9–10, 135–136

selfobject 95, 105
self psychology 76
sexuality 7, 113–122, 164; *see also* erotic transference
short-term therapy 81
silence 69
Sills, Charlotte 5, 12–13, 17, 85, 105, 106, 114, 131, 133
social control 3
solution-focused therapy 81
somatization 186
specificity theory 175
splitting 16, 106, 114, 146, 147, 163
stability, and obsession 97–98
Stark, M. 13, 68–69
Stern, Daniel 67, 69–70, 100, 105, 106, 136–137, 146, 150, 155, 156, 162, 169, 186
Stolorow, R. 143, 146
stress 31
strokes 30, 126, 153, 168; *see also* game theory
structural dissociation 161
Stuthridge, J. 171, 182, 183
Sullivan, Harry Stack 3, 69–70, 162, 163
supervision 95
switch mechanism (game theory) 27–28, 30–31

therapeutic relationship: Berne's formulation 1; centrality of 1–2; key principles 6–7; paradigm shifts 1–2, 5–6; self-critique in 11–12; truth and love 57–71
the third 19–20, 134, 183–184, 191–192
Thompson, Clara 3
trance 40
transactional analysis (TA): Berne's work and legacy 1–2, 51–53; cross-cultural and social applications 81–82; ethical principles 124–128; failure and rupture in 124–139; future needs 82–84; limitations 79–81; organizational applications 82; perceptions and status of 50, 74–75; psychodynamic school 50–55
transference 3–4, 16–17, 37–48, 76, 98–102; *see also* countertransference; erotic transference; transformational transference
transformational domain 19
transformational transference 17, 106, 181–192
trauma 81–82, 141–156, 172, 177–178, 183, 186, 187
Trautmann, R.L. 66

truth 57–71
two-person psychology 5, 9, 13, 131, 132, 172, 178

unconscious, the: accessing 17, 186, 187; Berne's formulation 2, 4; enactment 173, 182; game theory 168; impact of culture 129; in infancy 63; limitations of TA 79–80; object usage 10–11; in relational TA 5–7, 13, 15, 171; script 144; self-reflection 5, 80; transference 17, 98, 106, 131

validation 100–101
Victim–Rescuer transference 152, 153
vital base 11

Winnicott, Donald 7, 10, 43, 62–65, 71, 126
withdrawal ruptures 132

Zalcman, Marilyn 23, 24, 35, 168

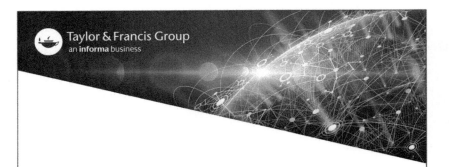